Caught
in the Middle

Caught in the Middle

Contradictions in the Lives
of Sociologists from
Working-Class Backgrounds

Michael D. Grimes
and Joan M. Morris

Westport, Connecticut
London

Library of Congress Cataloging-in-Publication Data

Grimes, Michael D.
    Caught in the middle : contradictions in the lives of sociologists
from working-class backgrounds / Michael D. Grimes and Joan M.
Morris.
      p.   cm.
    Includes bibliographical references and index.
    ISBN 0–275–95711–X (alk. paper)
    1. Sociologists—United States—Attitudes. 2. Sociologists—
Education—United States. 3. Sociologists—United States—Economic
conditions. 4. Working class—United States. 5. Social mobility—
United States. I. Morris, Joan M. (Joan Marie), 1951–
II. Title.
HM22.U5G76   1997
301'.092'2—dc21   97–5586

British Library Cataloguing in Publication Data is available.

Library of Congress Catalog Card Number: 97–5586
ISBN: 0–275–95711–X

First published in 1997

Praeger Publishers, 88 Post Road West, Westport, CT 06881
An imprint of Greenwood Publishing Group, Inc.

Printed in the United States of America

The paper used in this book complies with the
Permanent Paper Standard issued by the National
Information Standards Organization (Z39.48–1984).

10 9 8 7 6 5 4 3 2 1

This book is dedicated to the participants in our study
and, more generally, to all academics from
working-class backgrounds

Contents

Preface

This book is about a unique, and perhaps even a rare, group of individuals—sociologists who come from working-class backgrounds. Our interest in their professional and private lives and in the intersection between the two is not purely academic since we too are from working-class backgrounds and, thus, share with our participants many of the attitudes, beliefs, values, and behaviors that they reveal in this study. Three earlier books on the subject—Ryan and Sackrey's *Strangers in Paradise* (1984), Tokarczyk and Fay's *Working-Class Women in the Academy* (1993), and Dews and Law's *This Fine Place So Far from Home* (1995)—while providing a great deal of descriptive information about the subject of academics from working-class backgrounds, are limited in several ways by their approaches to the subject matter. Each of these sets of authors asked respondents to write more or less unstructured autobiographical essays about their experiences as academics from working-class backgrounds; they compiled these into edited volumes with interpretative materials scattered here and there in the form of introductory essays, section headings, conclusions, and so on. Although we find these studies to be informative and insightful glances into the lives of academics from working-class backgrounds, we also find them lacking in several respects. For one thing, these studies provided few, if any, guidelines to their essayists, and the absence of such guidelines makes it difficult to organize, summarize, and compare their findings since all the essayists were free to construct their contributions as they wished. For another, each of the these studies incorporated into its sample respondents from a number of different disciplines, which makes examining the relationship between a respondent's discipline and her or his responses difficult, if not impossible. Our study corrects these shortcomings, first, by providing our respondents with a structured set of fifty-nine open-ended questions that address key issues that we distilled from the findings of these earlier studies and by asking them to respond to each question; and second, by limiting our sample to the members of a single discipline—in this case sociologists from working-class backgrounds. By these means, we see our study as moving beyond earlier works on the subject, even to the point of subjecting some of their findings and interpretations to a more rigorous examination than their approaches allowed. In this way, we see this study, as we did each of their studies, as paving the way for even more sophisticated research on the subject.

There are a number of persons without whose help this study would not have materialized. First, we wish to thank those of our respondents who have given us permission to identify them as members of our sample. These include Ronald Akers, Thomas Baker, Vern Baxter, Jean Belkhir, James Cassell, Levon Chorbajian, William Cross, David Croteau, Robert Dotzler, Craig Eckert, Coralie Farlee, Pauline Foster, Rita Harmata, Andrew Howard, Elmer Johnson, Bennett Judkins, Shirley Laska, Rhonda Levine, Linda Lobao, Arlene McCormack, Cynthia Negrey, Michael Nusbaumer, Larry Ouelet, Brenda Phillips, Charles Post, Joe Quartullo, Jasper Register, Vinnie Roscigno, Vincent Serravallo, Ree Simpkins, Barbara Tomaskovic-Devey, Debra VanAusdale, Brian Vargus, Katherine Williams, and Brunetta Wolfman. Without the cooperation of these individuals and other members of our sample who chose to remain anonymous, this study would not have been possible. Second, a number of others have read and reacted to our essay guide, questionnaire, and the manuscript. These include Pam Jenkins, Susan Mann, Joachim Singelmann, and Charles Tolbert. Although we did not always follow their advice, we did so much of the time. Third, we would like to thank several graduate students whose help with data management and coding was important. These include Craig and Rebecca Carter, Becky McClanahan, Cara Mathies, and Rebel Reavis. Fourth, we would like to thank the Department of Sociology at Louisiana State University for its assistance in providing logistical support for the study; two members of the staff of the department, Wanda Ashley and Coleen Mitcham, proved especially helpful. Fifth, we would also like to thank our production editor, Meg Fergusson, for her diligence, patience, and support during the editing process. Finally, the senior author also wishes to thank his partner, Susan Mann, for her insights, encouragement, and support throughout the study's duration. Despite the roles that those mentioned above have played in the study, however, we accept full responsibility for any errors, omissions, misinterpretations, and so on that the study may contain. In the paragraphs that follow, we provide a brief overview of the contents of the book.

The book is divided into seven chapters. The first provides an overview of the theoretical perspective we employ in the study. We begin there with a discussion of why we became interested studying sociologists from working-class backgrounds and the important role that Ryan and Sackrey's book *Strangers in Paradise: Academics from the Working Class* (1984) played in this process. We then defend the continued relevance of class in late-twentieth-century

American society, we review the major perspectives on class that have been employed by American sociologists, and we provide the definition of the working class that we employ in the study. We also describe the process through which individuals are located within the class structure of society, stressing the important role that family resources (economic, cultural, and social) continue to play in this process. We then argue that gender intersects with class background in such ways as to produce different effects for men and women. We end the chapter with a presentation of the conceptual model that guides the study.

Chapter 2 describes our research design. There we provide an overview and critique of the approach(es) taken by earlier researchers on the subject, and we identify our study as a "second-generation" exploratory study that builds and improves on the work of its predecessors. We then identify the three major means for gathering data that we employ in the study: a set of fifty-nine open-ended questions that request information concerning respondents' perceptions of the impact of their working-class backgrounds on their lives and careers; a questionnaire that asks more focused questions about personal characteristics, preprofessional and professional work experiences, and the educational and work experiences of parents and/or other significant adult householders and siblings; and a curriculum vita. We report there that we recruited potential participants for the study through advertisements in both national and regional sociological newsletters, that we mailed materials to over eighty potential participants, and that the study is based on the materials returned to us by forty-five respondents. We also compare the demographic and personal characteristics of our sample with those of the general membership of the American Sociological Association (ASA). We conclude the chapter with details about how the study's data were organized, processed, and coded for analysis.

The findings of the study are presented in four chapters, one each for a period in or facet of the life cycles of our respondents. In Chapter 3 we present findings concerning respondents' perceptions about the impact(s) of class background on their childhood and early educational experiences. Here, we first describe the occupation(s) and education(s) of their parents, their awareness of class, and their sense of the importance of their location within the class structure of society. We also examine the roles of parents and siblings in encouraging (or discouraging) our respondents' efforts to acquire formal education. We also review materials on the class composition(s) of both the neighborhoods within which our respondents lived and the schools they attended. Finally, we present data on aspects of our respondents' early educational careers—most particularly the role(s) that teachers played in encouraging their early educational efforts. We also examine gender differences for each of these subjects.

In Chapter 4 we examine the college and graduate educational experiences of our respondents. Here we explore respondents' perceptions of the influence(s) of their class background on a number of different issues including their choice of college or university (for both baccalaureate and graduate training); how they were supported materially; their involvement in extracurricular activities, particularly employment; whether their educational career was continuous or interrupted; their recollections about feeling similar to, or different from, other students; when and how they made the decision to pursue a career in the academy; and any role(s) that mentors might have played in encouraging or facilitating their choices and achievements. For each of these subjects, we also examine the impact of gender on responses.

Chapter 5 analyzes respondents' perceptions about the intersection between their class backgrounds and their professional careers. Some of the issues we address in this chapter include the career paths of our respondents; how these career paths compare with those of sociologists from different class backgrounds; respondent opinions about the relative weights that the various roles (i.e., teaching, research, service) should have in an academic career; the nature of our respondents' relations with fellow faculty members, students, and with the college/university hierarchy; our respondents' area(s) of specialization and theoretical perspectives; our respondents' perceptions about the roles that politics and social activism should play in the lives of professional academics; and their overall satisfaction with the academy as a career option. Once again, we also examine the impact(s) of gender on responses to each of these issues.

Chapter 6 examines aspects of the personal lives of our subjects. Here we discuss the impact(s) of our respondents' class background on their choices of intimate partners, personal friends, and communities of residence. We then explore aspects of the respondents' current relationships with members of their families of origin and childhood friends. Our goal here is to examine the extent of overlap between these two very different class "worlds" and some of the consequences of being caught between them for our respondents.

In the final chapter we first summarize and interpret the findings of the study using our conceptual model as a guide. We then identify and discuss some of the study's limitations and offer some suggestions for future research on sociologists and other academics from working-class backgrounds. We conclude the chapter with a discussion of some of the broader implications of the study's findings.

M.D.G.

J.M.M.

1

Theoretical Issues

This book is based on a simple, yet controversial, premise—that class continues to be an important structural variable affecting the material, social, ideological, and psychological life circumstances of Americans, even in late capitalist society.[1] As we will demonstrate below controversies over the term's meaning, its impacts on the day-to-day lives of the members of society, and its intergenerational transmission—not to mention its potential role as an agent for social transformation—continue unabated. In fact, if there has been one issue in the history of sociology that has dominated debate, it has been class (Edgell 1993:viii).

This study examines just one of the potential consequences of class location—the continued impact(s) of class background on the lives of a group of upwardly mobile sons and daughters of working-class parents who have become members of what one scholar has called "the new class" (Gouldner 1979)—a highly privileged, intellectual, segment of society. The thesis of the study is that these individuals are, in many significant ways, "caught in the middle" between their backgrounds as children from the working class and their current positions as members of a relatively privileged elite within contemporary American society—two class locations with markedly different material, social, ideological, and psychological circumstances.[2] This study identifies and explores "contradictions" in the lives of these members of the new class that result from the contrast(s) between their current life situations as members of this privileged, new class and their earlier lives as children and young adults from the working class.

In this chapter we begin with a discussion of the origins of our interest in the subject matter of the study. Next, we provide a brief overview of the ideologically charged debate surrounding both the meaning and importance of class in twentieth-century American society. Following this, we examine the process through which individuals are placed within the class structure of society and highlight the important role that family background continues to play in the intergenerational "reproduction" of class. We then provide an overview of research on the working class and highlight some of the structural, social, interpersonal, and psychological impacts of class background on the lives of upwardly mobile sons and daughters of working-class families. We conclude the chapter with the conceptual framework that guides the study.

THE ORIGINS OF OUR INTEREST IN THE STUDY

Our general interest in the impacts of class location on the life circumstances of the members of contemporary societies has its origins in our own biographies. We are ourselves children of the working class. As a consequence we see our lives as having been heavily influenced by the material, social, cultural, and psychological circumstances that surround that particular class location. Furthermore, we are convinced that the impacts of our class background persist despite the fact that we have earned postgraduate degrees and are now members of a relatively privileged class with very different life circumstances from those we experienced during our childhoods. In fact, we are convinced that our choice of profession (college professor); discipline (sociology); areas of specialization (various forms of social inequality); our subsequent career histories; and our relationships with colleagues, students, intimate partners, and others have all been impacted in various ways by our backgrounds within the working class of postwar American society.[3]

During the course of our study of social inequality, we came across a book by Jake Ryan and Charles Sackrey with a provocative title—*Strangers in Paradise: Academics from the Working Class* (1984). Like us, its authors were drawn to the subject by their own personal experiences as academics from working-class backgrounds. What perplexed them was an apparent contradiction in their lives: Despite their upward mobility from the class of their parents and childhoods and the material, social, and psychological advantages of their new class location, they remained uncomfortable there; in fact, they even went so far as to view themselves as *strangers* in this new class location (Ryan and Sackrey 1984:4–5). Their own explanation for their continued perceptions that they remained outsiders in their new class location and for their inability to fully enjoy their relative achievements is simple, but important: "It became clear to us that to grow up working class, then to take on the full trappings of the life of the college professor, *internalizes the conflicts in the hierarchy of the class system within the individual, upwardly mobile person*" (Ryan and Sackrey 1984:5; emphasis added). In light of their own reactions to their new lives within the academy, they began to wonder if others with their class background shared similar experiences. They assembled a list of fellow academics from working-class backgrounds and contacted each of them requesting an autobiographical essay describing their experiences. They received a number of responses; they selected twenty-four and incorporated them, along with historical and interpretative materials, into their book.

Two things impressed us about this book. The first is how completely the experiences of this sample of academics from working-class backgrounds seemed to overlap with our own experiences. In fact, we often felt that the essayists had somehow peered over our shoulders and described our personal experiences and feelings instead of their own. The second was the depth of feeling portrayed by these essayists through their narratives. Reading them evoked strong, almost visceral, reactions from us. Once again, we felt that the essayists had somehow gotten into touch with our own, most private, thoughts, feelings, and interpretations about our lives as members of the academy. Based on these reactions, we decided that there was a need for additional research that would build on the foundation laid by Ryan and Sackrey and their participants. This study is our response to this decision.

The focus of this study is on the impact(s) of class background on the lives of a group of upwardly mobile daughters and sons of working-class families who are now members of a new, relatively privileged intellectual class. The choice of adult professionals who have achieved rather substantial upward mobility when compared with their parents may seem to be an odd choice for a study that seeks to demonstrate the *continued* relevance of class. After all, the very fact that these sons and daughters of working-class parents have been able to attain far higher class positions than their parents is often used as evidence to support the notion that the influence of class is *declining*, not *increasing*. As we will demonstrate in this study, however, the lives of these professional academics from working-class backgrounds, despite their upward mobility and both the potential and realized material, cultural, social, and psychological benefits of their new, more privileged, location in the class structure, continue to be influenced in a number of significant ways—most of them negative, by their existential roots within the working class. Lillian Rubin (1976:13), herself an expatriate of the working class, explains why this is true: "No matter how far we travel, we can never leave our roots behind."[4]

DOES CLASS STILL MATTER IN LATE CAPITALIST SOCIETY?

Given the volume, intensity, and duration of the debate surrounding class within the discipline, we begin by sketching the development of class as a concept with both ideological and analytical components.[5] The ideology surrounding class in the United States developed during the period of industrial development following the Civil War and accelerated during the first two decades of the twentieth century. Between about 1900 and 1920, the United States experienced a period of rapid economic growth. There was high employment, a rising standard of living, and the assimilation of a huge number of immigrants of European descent. Within this economic and social context, a belief in the primacy of individual effort (that arose from the early days of the colonial frontier) was reinforced and became widespread. The dominant ideology that developed during this period, labeled "evolutionary liberalism" (Pease et al. 1970), stressed faith in the ultimate vitality of the political economy, a belief that material and social inequalities were decreasing, and confidence that all who were willing to work would share in the country's material prosperity.

During the 1940s and the 1950s, perspectives on social class developed by American sociologists were largely consistent with this dominant ideology. The authors of these perspectives saw class in terms of *status*, as a key link between the individual and the larger institutional structure of society (Davis and Moore 1945; Parsons 1940). They viewed individuals' locations within this status hierarchy as reflections of their successful accomplishments of the requirements for attaining these positions. These requirements, based on consensus about the valuation of the relationship between societal needs and individual role performances, were accepted as legitimate (Parsons 1940). The inequalities created within the status hierarchy were defined by them as necessary for motivating individual actions (Davis and Moore 1945). Through their efforts, the dominant ideology was thus reinforced and became institutionalized within mainstream sociology.

During the 1960s, however, a number of events occurred that challenged key assumptions of this ideology. These included the civil rights movement, the discovery of widespread poverty in the world's most affluent country, the violent deaths of important moral and political leaders, urban unrest, student protest against the war in Vietnam (and the growing frustrations of many Americans about our involvement there), and the increasing dissatisfaction of women with their second-class status. One consequence of the contrast between life in the United States during the 1960s and these earlier periods, was a growing sense of disenchantment with the dominant ideology, particularly among intellectuals, and the gradual adoption of an ideological perspective that has been labeled "structural realism," an ideology that was far more critical of the institutional arrangements of society and their role(s) in generating and sustaining economic, social, and political inequalities. This perspective stood in sharp contrast to the tenets of evolutionary liberalism (Pease et al. 1970:128). In many ways the post-1960s debate concerning the saliency of social inequality and class in American sociology can be said to be "framed" by these two contrasting images of the nature of advanced or late capitalist society and the role that class and social inequalities play in such societies.[6] Following is a brief summary of each position.

Evolutionary Liberalism

More conservative scholars suggest a "weakening of class stratification" (Clark and Lipset 1991:408) and point to such factors as the growth of the middle class, the diminution in lifestyle differences between the middle and working classes, and the increased role that education and acquired skills, rather than family background, play in determining the location of individuals in a putatively equal opportunity society. They generally avoid discussing social classes with recognizable boundaries and, tend to view society as comprising numerous locations or strata arranged in a loosely structured hierarchy with fluid boundaries, whose relationships to each other are cooperative at best or competitive at worst and generally positive sum in outcome (that is, the gains of one group do not necessarily come at the expense of another or others).

Structural Realism

Scholars taking a more radical approach direct attention to other "pieces" of the class puzzle such as the persisting inequalities of wealth and income, the interpenetration of material wealth and political power, and the roles that these important societal resources have come to play in the intergenerational transmission of class in late capitalist society. This perspective views social classes as having structural constraints and identifiable social boundaries. Classes are defined in terms of the possession or nonpossession of key resources such as the ownership of productive property, organizational position, and/or credentialed knowledge. This perspective views the class structure of society as comprising a smaller number of hierarchically arranged locations whose relationships with each other are viewed as antagonistic and conflictual and as generally negative sum in outcome (that is, the gains of one class usually are viewed as coming at the expense of the others).

Because these approaches are inherently value laden, a choice between them cannot be ideologically neutral. Our position is that the latter of these two perspectives provides a more theoretically insightful viewpoint—that class does still matter, even in late capitalist society. Two key tenets—Marx's contention that class is a key determinant of material interests, and Weber's observation that class membership affects the life chances of individuals—reiterated in a recent debate on the subject (Hout et al. 1993:261) form the basis of our support of class as an important contemporary analytical tool.[7]

A CONFLICT MODEL OF THE CLASS STRUCTURE OF LATE CAPITALIST SOCIETY

Our conception of class and class structure is based on Wright's (1985) model. He begins with a set of four assumptions about the class structure of advanced capitalist society that differentiate Marxist scholarship from other research on class: (1) classes are positions (and not the individuals occupying these positions), (2) these positions must be understood in their relationship to other positions, (3) there is an intrinsic antagonism between classes, and (4) this antagonism is located within the productive relations of society (Wright

1976:20).

Within this broad frame of reference, Wright (1985) builds an exploitation-based model of the class structure of advanced capitalist societies based on the control of three kinds of productive resources. According to him, the *primary* productive resource that differentiates classes within capitalist society is the ownership of productive property. He also claims that two *secondary* productive resources are necessary to differentiate among the various nonowner classes in late capitalist society, that is, control over these secondary resources results in the exploitation of others who lack control over them. These secondary resources are: control over organizational assets and control over skills and credentials. We share Wright's conclusions that (1) the class structure of advanced capitalist society is organized around the control of key productive resources, (2) classes can be defined in terms of the amount of control over such resources, and (3) those who control these resources are thereby able to exploit those who do not. In this study, working-class background is defined as a situation wherein the parents and/or other significant adult householders were employed in positions that did *not* exercise control over productive, organizational, or skills and credentials resources during a significant portion of the time our respondents lived with them.

HUMAN CAPITAL THEORY AND BEYOND

During the late 1950s and early 1960s, social scientists became increasingly interested in the mechanisms through which individuals are "located" within the class/status structure of society. One of the earliest (and most popular) of the explanations that emerged was labeled "human capital" theory (Becker 1964).

Human capital refers to a worker's "capacity to produce goods and services" (Thurow 1970:15). The theory postulates that individual workers vary in terms of these capacities and that the major sources for this variation include such things as native ability, formal education, vocational education, on-the-job training, and on-the-job experiences (Gordon 1972:31). A given worker's stock of human capital is not viewed by the theory as a fixed commodity, since it can be increased by additional investments in such things as education, training, skill building, and even additional work experience (Gwartney 1976:422). Indeed, one of the major assumptions of the theory is that, since we live in an equal opportunity society, "[all] . . . . individuals have a nearly unlimited range of opportunities in the course of their lifetimes," both to acquire an initial stock of human capital and to add to that stock as conditions warrant (Gordon 1972: 37). Within this context, the theory views individuals as rational; self-interested; in possession of sufficient information about both the opportunity structure and the requisite human capital skill requirements for different occupations within that structure to make an informed choice among them; as capable of making decisions concerning the acquisition of human capital skills in much the same way as they make other decisions—by weighing the costs and the benefits of such investments when compared with alternative uses of their time; and, importantly, as being equally advantaged when compared with others in terms of the resources necessary to acquire these skills and abilities.

The theory also assumes that workers are hired, paid, and promoted based on their "marginal productivity" as measured by their human capital skills (i.e., it assumes that there is an "equal opportunity" labor market in society). In this essentially "meritocratic" system, then, the locations individuals occupy in the economic structure of society reflect their relative marginal productivity when compared with others.

Many of the assumptions of human capital theory overlap with the sociological perspective on social inequality that was popular during this same period in U.S. history—the functionalist perspective. For example, the leading spokesperson for this perspective, Talcott Parsons (1940:841) defined society's system of "social stratification: as the differential ranking of the human individuals who compose a given social system and their treatment as superior and inferior relative to one another in certain socially important ways." Parsons used the term "status" to describe the location of a person (or family) within the stratification system and linked this location to the economic realm as follows: "We determine status very largely on the basis of achievements within an occupational system which is in turn organized primarily in terms of performance and status within functionally specialized fields" (Parsons 1940: 857). Thus, according to the functionalist perspective, an individual's relative success in the economic realm (i.e., based on the acquisition and application of human capital skills to compete for, secure, and keep a job) generates prestige for the individual and thus locates the individual within the stratification system of the larger society.

From our viewpoint this perspective on the process through which individuals are positioned within the social structure of society via their relative stock of human capital skills is flawed because it is based on the assumption that human beings are "socially atomized" actors whose behaviors are affected minimally by their relations with those around them (Granovetter 1985:481). This assumption is challenged because it ignores the interconnections among the individual and the larger social structure—particularly with his or her family and other social groups (such as friends, acquaintances, classes, ethnic communities, and so on)—and the advantages (or disadvantages) that these interconnections provide individuals both in their efforts to acquire human capital skills and in the subsequent application of them to maximum advantage in the labor market.[8] In the words of one critic of the theory, "Economists fail to acknowledge that actions are shaped, redirected, and constrained by the social context and that norms, interpersonal trust, social networks, and social organization are important influences on society and the economy (Coleman 1988:S96).

A leading critic of human capital theory, Pierre Bourdieu (1984,1986), takes the position that these "social organizational" resources are sufficiently important in late capitalist society that they should be viewed as additional, alternative, forms of capital. In such societies, Bourdieu distinguishes among three different "guises" that capital can assume: economic capital (money and property), cultural capital (knowledge and skills), and social capital (a network of relationships with others). He attaches greater importance to these alternative, social organizational, forms of capital than do the perspectives of most human capital (and functionalist) theorists: "It is in fact impossible to account for the structure and functioning of the social world unless one reintroduces capital *in all its forms*" (Bourdieu 1986:242; emphasis added). Contrasting late capitalist with earlier capitalist society, Bourdieu claims that, though economic capital remains the most convertible (and thus most useful) form of capital in both, another major avenue to success in late capitalist society increasingly involves the other two alternative forms of capital—especially cultural (in the form of education and training) but social capital as well.[9] Because of their growing importance, Bourdieu focuses much of his attention on the intersection between these latter two forms of capital—especially on the role(s) they collectively play in the "production" and "reproduction" of the class locations of individuals within the social structure of late capitalist society. With particular regard to the latter of these outcomes, he remarks:

From the very beginning, a definition of human capital, despite its humanistic connotations, does not move beyond economism and ignores, *inter alia*, the fact that the scholastic yield from educational action depends upon the cultural capital previously invested by the family. Moreover the economic and social yield of the educational qualification depends on the social capital, again inherited, which can be used to back it up. (Bourdieu 1986:244)

What Bourdieu is saying here, in sharp contrast to the proponents of human capital theory, is that differences in these alternative (social organizational) resources cannot be ignored as factors in the process by which individuals are located within the economic structure of late capitalist societies.

The Forms of Social Organizational Capital

Bourdieu differentiates between two forms of social organizational capital—cultural and social. Cultural capital refers to a broad range of knowledge about the world within which the individual lives.[10] Included here is a variety of different forms of knowledge, some of which may be "institutionalized" by educational certification; in addition to these more specialized forms of knowledge, cultural capital also refers to knowledge about such things as language, decorum, and fashion and knowledge about the arts, music, literature, etc.[11] To Bourdieu, these various cultural competencies have utility because they can be "converted" into the other forms of capital (i.e., economic and social). And, since they are not equally possessed by all the members of a society, their relative scarcity generates advantage (power) and distinction for those who possess them.[12]

Social capital, in contrast, "inheres in the structure of relations between actors and among actors" (Coleman 1988:S98). It takes the form of "obligations, expectations, and trustworthiness of structures," "information channels," and "norms and effective sanctions" (Coleman 1988:S102-S104). Each of these can be employed to advantage, first in the acquisition of human capital skills and then later in the labor market itself. For example, the social capital of the family consists of the relations between parents and children. Within the larger community, social capital consists of the relations among parents and the relations between parents and the institutions of the community. In this context, the better "connected" a family is to other families, groups, and institutions, the more social resources it has available for its members' subsequent appropriation.

Capital and the Class Structure of Society

Bourdieu uses the distribution and reproduction of these three different forms of capital as the defining feature of his model of the class structure of late capitalist society. In his words: "The primary differences, those which distinguish the major classes of conditions of existence, derive from the overall volume of capital, understood as a set of actually usable resources and powers—economic capital, cultural capital, and also social capital" (Bourdieu 1984:114). As this statement suggests, Bourdieu takes a perspective on class that has greater affinity with Weber's notion of status group than it does with Marx's viewpoint on class, since he deliberately eschews Marx's contention that economic capital alone is the resource that differentiates classes in capitalist society. Bourdieu, instead, embraces Weber's emphasis on a greater diversity of resources and the resulting impact(s) of these resources on lifestyle differences as his major means for identifying and differentiating among groups (Gilbert and Kahl 1993:8–12).[13]

Applying Bourdieu's perspective to the present class structure of capitalist societies, individuals and families with monopolistic control over economic capital constitute the upper class. Membership in the remaining classes is determined by the relative amount of economic, cultural, and social capital possessed by the individual/family and how these are used to advantage in the labor market. For Bourdieu, the most important forms of cultural capital, and those that differentiate members of the middle class from those of the working and lower classes, are forms of "institutionalized" cultural capital—formal education[14] and the other forms of "cultural" capital that normally accompany its "reproduction" from one generation to the next.

CLASS AND SOCIALIZATION

Sociologists have long had an interest in the issue of the intergenerational transmission of class. Like most debates surrounding class, perspectives on the relative influence of the class of origin on the class of destination of the next generation are imbued with ideology. On one side, conservative social scientists (including human capital theorists and functionalist sociologists) tend to view the class structure of society as more fluid and open. As a consequence they stress the importance of individual "achievements"—particularly the acquisition of formal educational credentials when contrasted with ascriptive attributes such as family background, gender, ethnicity, and race—in the class placement process (Clark and Lipset 1992). On the other side liberal/radical social scientists view the opportunity structure of late capitalist society as more rigid and closed. As a result of this assumption, they place greater emphasis on the roles that ascriptive characteristics such as family background, gender, ethnicity, and race, play in the class placement process (Hout et al. 1993).

Our perspective on the subject falls between these two extremes. On the one hand, the subjects of our research—sociologists from working-class backgrounds—are the upwardly mobile sons and daughters of working-class parents and their mobility is more consistent with the former than with the latter viewpoint on the subject. On the other hand, we believe that the members of this elite group are (even rare) exceptions, rather than the rule, in contemporary American society (though evidence on this issue remains unclear at this point in time) and their relative successes may not have come without certain structural, interpersonal, and psychological costs, outcomes more consistent with the liberal/radical viewpoint on the subject.

Scholars within the liberal/radical tradition insist that *parental class location* is a key influence on the relative success of an individual within late capitalist society. For these scholars, class is either defined by, or reflects differential access to, key societal resources.[15] Thus, families possessing more of these resources are better able to assist their children in enhancing their innate capacities and in applying their diverse talents (both innate and acquired) to advantage in competition with others for better locations within the system.[16] Evidence to support this viewpoint comes from several different sources. A long tradition of research surrounding the work of Melvin Kohn (Kohn 1969; Kohn and Scholler 1983) has established that parents, in the process of socializing their children, tend to stress the very values, behaviors, and orientations for which they are/were rewarded in their own occupational experiences.[17] This research has established that "parents from higher social classes . . . placed greater emphasis on self-directed behavior and thought patterns, whereas lower classes placed greater emphasis on conformity, obedience to external authority, and external appearances" (Spenner 1988:71). This research has also connected these same occupationally linked values and behaviors to orientations toward, and success in acquiring, higher education by the next generation (Gecas 1978).[18]

Others such as Aronowitz and Giroux (1991), Bourdieu (1984,1986), Bowles (1972), and Robinson (1984) tend to take a somewhat broader viewpoint on the intergenerational reproduction of the class structure by stressing the general roles that economic, cultural, and social resources play in the process.

Their emphasis reflects, in part at least, an awareness of the growing technological sophistication of late capitalist economies and the increasing role that formal educational credentials have come to play in differentiating between the middle and the working and lower classes in these societies (Robinson 1984). Thus, the acquisition of formal educational credentials becomes *the* crucial determinant for membership in the middle class, and as a general rule, middle-class families (and those families ranked even higher in the class structure), with their greater material, cultural, and social resources are simply better equipped to support their children's efforts to acquire these skills.[19] In the words of Bourdieu (1984:70–71):

The embodied cultural capital of the previous generations functions as a sort of advance (both a head-start and a credit) which, by providing from the outset the example of culture incarnated in familiar models, enables the newcomer to start acquiring the basic elements of the legitimate culture, from the beginning, that is, in the most unconscious and impalpable way.

In summary, what these liberal/radical scholars are saying is that independent of innate abilities, the children of upper- and middle-class families have at their disposal important (economic, cultural, and social) resources that help to ensure that they will acquire the human capital skills necessary to follow in the class footsteps of their parents.

If these scholars are right, then it stands to reason that the children of working-class families, independent of their innate abilities, are disadvantaged, in a number of ways, when compared with their middle-class and upper-middle-class counterparts. For example, that which comes so naturally to the children of the middle class, who have spent their early lives literally surrounded by the middle-class culture, does not come so easily to the children of the working class, who have spent their early lives in very different material, cultural, and social environments. As one student of the working class notes: "Insofar as knowledge is always biased and shot through with class meaning, the working class student must overcome his [*sic*] inbuilt disadvantage of possessing the wrong class culture and the wrong educational decoders to start with" (Willis 1977:128).

In fact, as Bourdieu (1984:71) argues, the children of the working class, should they be fortunate enough to have the abilities, motivation, and other resources necessary to gain access to higher education, often have to engage in "deculturation," "correction," and "retraining" in order to undo the effects of earlier inappropriate learning within a working-class environment. Such undoing and relearning are never as efficiently acquired as when done unconsciously as a part of growing up in a middle-class home environment. For example, though working-class children are exposed to some types of cultural capital in school, there are many pieces of the cultural mosaic of middle-class life that the school does not effectively transmit to its students—knowledge of the arts, music, literature, and other objects of "high" culture; information about manners, decorum, fashion, and style; vocabulary and language skills, for example—things that contribute to an individual's "presentation of self" and otherwise facilitate successful participation in middle-class life.

Thus, even if working-class children manage to overcome the myriad of obstacles between them and their entrance into the educational establishment, they will still be judged by others (teachers and administrators as well as classmates) not only in terms of their academic performance but also in terms of these other indicators of cultural competence. It is no wonder, then, that so many working-class kids get "cooled out" of the system early and end up in the same (or worse) situation as their parents (Willis 1977). It is also clear that those who do manage to continue forward into higher education will face far greater obstacles to success than their middle-class counterparts. Nor do the difficulties faced by children from the working class end with receipt of the degree or certificate—they continue beyond this point as individuals from working-class backgrounds who must adjust to the larger middle-class and upper-middle-class vocational and social environments. It is in such senses as these, then, that we see our sample of academics from working-class backgrounds as caught in the middle between the class location of their parents and their own, new and very different, class location.

THE WORKING CLASS IN POSTWAR AMERICA

Bourdieu (1984, 1986) and others, who explain the intergenerational "reproduction" of class by means of differential access to the resources necessary to acquire market advantage, base their argument on the notion that the life circumstances of the members of the various classes are sufficiently different from each other in terms of these resources to generate advantages for some and disadvantages for others. It seems necessary at this point to highlight some of the differences between working- and middle-class life that have been demonstrated by previous research. This section of the chapter describes life within the working class of post–World War II American society and characterizes some of the consequences of this lifestyle for its members. We call particular attention to those consequences that impact the resource base that working-class families have at their disposal to assist their children's efforts toward upward mobility.

The American Working Class, 1950s Style

Theorists of the 1950s, including Bell (1960) and Galbraith (1958), writing amidst the general material prosperity of early post–World War II American society, envisioned the gradual melioration of the material (and ideological) differences between the middle and the working class and the emergence of a single, amorphous middle class that would incorporate most of the members of society. Their image of future "postindustrial" society stressed growing prosperity for all Americans and the continuing decline of both workplace and lifestyle differences across class groups. What they did not, and perhaps could not, have anticipated was that these predicted outcomes depended heavily on a level of economic prosperity that was an aberration of the early post–World War II period in world economic history and that it would wane as the economies of the other advanced capitalist economies began to rebuild their industrial bases and to compete successfully with the United States during the late 1960s and the early 1970s (Kennedy 1987).[20]

The Working Class within Late Capitalist America

We contend that there are five interrelated trends that began during the decade of the 1960s that have had significant negative impacts on the American working class: (1) the failure of working-class wages to keep pace with inflation, (2) the "deskilling" of many working-class jobs, (3) the declining role of unions in both the economy and in politics, (4) the growing importance of higher education as a qualification for even minimally adequate jobs in the labor market, and (5) the disappearance of better-paying blue-collar jobs within the manufacturing sector of the economy.[21]

One of the most significant trends within postwar U.S. history has been the declining material circumstances of the working class. The greatest losers in the adjustments within the American economy made necessary by the increasingly competitive global economy were those located toward the bottom of the economic structure—the working class and the poor.[22] Karoly's (1993) study of the U.S. income distribution during the past twenty-five years not only reveals both continued income inequality and a general diminution in the standard of living for all Americans, especially since the early 1970s but also that those toward the bottom of the income distribution have suffered the most.[23] Just one example of the increasing "fragmentation" of the middle class that has been the subject of much recent popular attention is the fact that the average real wages of high school graduates (most members of the working class have no more than a high school education) fell dramatically betweeen 1970 and 1990, while those of college graduates only increased slightly. Increasingly then, as Rubin has observed (1994:31), the families of America's working class, even those with two wage earners,"live on the edge."[24]

A second response to growing competition from other advanced capitalist economies was automation (Analytica 1986).[25] Perhaps the best example of the effects of automation on the labor market for blue-collar work is from the manufacturing sector, historically the highest-paying, most prestigious, and stable sector of the blue-collar opportunity structure. In the case of automobile manufacturing, for example, the response to increased foreign competition and declining market shares was a substantial program of production automation during the late 1970s—this response not only displaced thousands of workers, it also significantly reduced the scope of control of those who kept their jobs (Analytica 1989; Aronowitz and DiFazio 1995; Bluestone and Harrison 1982).

The later postwar years were also difficult ones for labor unions. Although the United States has always had the smallest portion of its workforce in unions of any advanced industrial society, the decades of the 1930s, 1940s, and 1950s were truly halcyon days for the American labor movement. Despite the traditional antiunionism of America, by the end of the 1950s, over one-third of the American workforce was organized into unions and labor was an active player in local, regional, and national politics.

During the economic downturn of the 1970s and the 1980s, the strength of unions, both in terms of numbers and political influence, declined precipitously. President Reagan's decertification of the Professional Air Traffic Controller's Organization during his first term in office is symptomatic of the widespread antiunion sentiment within American society during the 1980s. Today, the percentage of the American workforce in unions has fallen into the low teens, and the influence of unions has diminished in American political life (Bowles and Edwards 1993).[26]

The continued automation of the economy of late capitalist society and the growth in the proportion of the workforce that is managerial and technical has also meant that workers without advanced training beyond the high school diploma are either relegated to the least well-paid sectors of the economy or are excluded outright from regular employment. Bowles (1972), Edwards (1979), and Robinson (1984) document the process through which control over the day-to-day operations of capitalist enterprises has passed from owners to managers and technocrats; they also stress the important role that formal educational credentials have come to play in gaining access to these latter positions. Opportunities for those without such credentials are confined to the minimum-waged margins of the economy—an outcome, given the precipitous decline in wages at the bottom of the labor market noted above, far more detrimental to the members of the post–World War II working class than it was to earlier generations of workers.[27]

The last element in the equation explaining the erosion of the position of the working class in late capitalist society is the decline of high-paying manufacturing jobs. Peter Drucker (1993:69) estimates that manufacturing jobs declined during the fifteen-year period ending in 1990 from about one-quarter of the American labor force to less than one-fifth, and he expects it to continue to decline to about 10 or 12 percent during the next decade. Although some of these lost jobs have been or will be replaced, many of the replacement jobs will be low- or even minimum-waged jobs in the service sector. As a result, Harrison and Bluestone (1988) conclude that the employment market in America is becoming increasingly polarized between higher-waged and lower-waged sectors, with very few jobs in the middle.

When the effects of these five trends are combined, the result has been the growing *marginalization* of the working class from the mainstream of American life during the later post–World War II period (Aronowitz and Giroux 1991). The consequences of this process encompasses much, if not all, of their life experiences.

Consequences of Working-Class Marginalization

The growing marginalization of the working class in the economic structure of late capitalist society has been accompanied by a number of profound consequences for its members—consequences that are cultural, institutional, familial, and personal in nature. For example, Aronowitz and Giroux (1991) claim that the culture's image of a group mirrors its relative position within the economic and political structure of society. To demonstrate this point, they analyzed the characterization(s) of the working class by mass media during the past thirty years. Their results show that during the 1950s, when large-scale industry dominated the American economy and the productivity of American blue-collar workers was central to the economy's prosperity, blue-collar work was afforded considerable status in media representations (Aronowitz and Giroux 1991:179). The image(s) of the working class during this period often stressed such positive qualities as devotion to the work ethic, character, craftspersonship, honesty, perseverance, and so on. In sharp contrast, by the 1980s, when the position of the working class had declined along with the "deindustrialization" of the economy, their analysis demonstrates that the culture's image of the working class became more negative and such characteristics as ignorance, bigotry, and violence were more commonly employed in media representations of the group.[28] They also point to another recent trend within the media that supports the continuing marginalization of the working class—the virtual disappearance of any representation of the group whatsoever.

Obviously, the image of a group within the overall culture of society has important consequences for the way(s) the group is regarded and treated by society as a whole, especially within its institutional infrastructure. Our example of how negative cultural stereotypes influence the attitudes and behaviors of institutional actors toward members of the working class is taken from education. A long line of research, beginning with Bowles and Gintis's classic study *Schooling in Capitalist America* (1976), has shown that education in America's public schools, despite its defenders' claims that it is meritocratic, actually helps to reproduce, rather than reduce, class inequalities intergenerationally. This reproduction occurs as a consequence of the way(s) that the daughters and sons of the working class and their parents are treated by the educational institution. Research has demonstrated that school administrators, counselors, and teachers treat working-class students differently from middle-class students.[29] Some examples include expecting less of them than their middle-class counterparts; placing them in vocational, nonacademic tracks based on stereotypes rather than abilities; and even "cooling them out" of the education system altogether (Rubin 1994; Sennett and Cobb 1972; Willis 1977).[30]

Research on parental involvement in the educational process has also shown that class differences between teachers and school administrators and working-class parents (often exacerbated by the parents' perceptions of the social distance between themselves and school officials) frequently discourage their effective participation in their childrens' educations (Lareau 1989). Given the important role that parental support has been shown to play in a child's academic success, reduced working-class parental involvement is bound to inhibit, rather than to enhance, the educational successes of its children (Lareau 1989; Parcel and Menaghan 1994). The home environment of working-class families is affected by such things as the rewards (both material and psychological) of the family's breadwinner(s), the overall culture's assessment(s) of members of the working class, and the assessment and reactions of institutional actors to workers and other members of their families. Our discussion of these impacts below is organized into four general areas: material, cultural, social, and psychological.

Obviously the material circumstances of working-class families are increasingly worse off than those of middle-class families. These diminished material circumstances reflect themselves in a number of ways—in the character of neighborhood and house in which the family lives, in the family's daily standard of living, in the necessities and luxuries of life the family can afford, and in the social and recreational activities the family can enjoy.

The working-class family also faces a number of negative cultural consequences, not just because of the increasingly negative stereotypes that are used to characterize them, but also because the average working-class parent has less formal education than do his or her middle-class counterparts. It is widely understood that the level of formal education of parents contributes not only to the family's relative location within the class hierarchy of society but also to what might be called a family's "cultural support structure." This support structure includes such things as the presence of books and other reference materials within the home; the knowledge necessary to help a child with homework assignments and class projects (not to mention the parents' willingness/ability to monitor the child's academic performance and to intervene, when necessary, in the child's interests); encouraging appreciation of, and even providing lessons in, music, dance, voice, acting, and so on; visits to museums, libraries and concerts; travel; and role modeling in terms of job/career, dress, manners, language skills, and so on.[31]

Working-class families are also disadvantaged in terms of social resources. Previous research has shown that the wider and more diverse a family's relations with other individuals, families, groups, voluntary associations, and institutions, for example, the greater the potential advantages for the family and its members (Coleman 1988). Thus, the family's class position in the community impacts the breadth and depth of these social resources. Research that extends back nearly forty years (Hollingshead 1949) supports the notion that children located within the working class are disadvantaged when compared with their middle-class counterparts in terms of these important linkages to others within the larger community.[32]

Finally, a number of researchers have examined the psychological consequences of the day-to-day realities of performing working-class jobs in late capitalist society. Shostak (1969), for example, has shown how the increasing marginalization of blue-collar work has impacted the subjective identification of blue-collar workers with their jobs. As the status, meaning, and satisfaction they derive from their work and their coworkers declines, workers begin to suffer psychologically. In this context, Rubin (1976:19) states that instead of blaming others (such as the overall society or the global economy) for the transformation(s) in their work and their own diminishing status in society, in the community, and at home, in our putatively equal opportunity society "turning inward with self-blame is common among the men and women I met—a product, in part of the individualist ethic in the American society which fixes responsibility for any failure to achieve the American dream in individual inadequacy." Some of the negative psychological consequences for the incumbents of working-class jobs that have been identified by previous research include a loss of a sense of dignity, lower self-esteem, a growing sense of anxiety about status, alienation, lowered levels of ambition, a deficit of emotional energy, a sense of failure, feelings of lack of control over one's life, and so on.[33] Research has also shown that these psychological stresses that workers experience at work impact their home environments in a number of negative ways (Eitzen and Zinn 1989; Rubin 1976, 1994). In the words of Rubin (1976:165), "the work they do powerfully affects the quality of family life. What happens on the job during the day colors—if it doesn't actually dictate—what happens during the evening."

In light of this evidence, it seems clear to us that the working-class home environment is different from its middle-class counterpart in a number of ways and that many of the differences between the two are disadvantageous for the members of working-class families.[34] It also seems clear that these differences are unavoidably implicated in the intergenerational reproduction of class in late capitalist societies.

Yet, despite all the disadvantages of working-class home environments noted above, some of its children and young adults do manage to achieve upward mobility when compared with their parents and, in many cases, with their siblings and peers as well. It is this group of working-class expatriates that is the focus of our study, and, though we are interested in and will explore their "paths" to success, we are also interested in how their working-class backgrounds influence the ways they "fit into" their new worlds—how they relate to their careers and to their middle-class colleagues; how they manage to construct a new identity for themselves that is very different from those of their parents and siblings; how comfortable they are with this new identity; and how they deal with the sharp contrast(s) between their new lives and those of their parents, their siblings, and childhood friends who have remained within the working class. Next we explore some of the consequences of upward mobility for the members of the working class.

Consequences of Upward Mobility from the Working Class

A number of studies have addressed the negative consequences of upward mobility from the working to the middle class. If there is one finding that consistently emerged from this research, it is that coming from one social world and then attempting to become a part of a second, very different, social world often leaves the individual caught in the middle of the two and feeling like a part of neither. This section of the chapter examines this issue in greater detail, focusing on the relations of upwardly mobile persons with their class of origin and their class of destination and on some of the negative consequences of their complete integration into neither.

Previous research has shown that there are a number of consequences of upward mobility for the individual's relations with his or her class of origin. For example, it is common for the upwardly mobile individual to accept the dominant culture's negative assessment of the working class (Law 1995:7). As a result, working-class expatriates are often ashamed of both their families and their class backgrounds (Dews and Law 1995:3, Rubin 1976:12, Rubin 1994: 162-163; Ryan and Sackrey 1984:75; Sennett and Cobb 1972:133; Tokarczyk and Fay 1993:21). In the words of one upwardly mobile academic from the working class (Peliz 1995:282), working-class students "often feel shame at their origins and internalize the belief that they and their families are lazy or stupid." Yet, despite these feelings, they may also feel a sense of disloyalty to their families and friends and a sense of guilt for their success(es). For example, Ryan and Sackrey (1984:119) have observed that successfully mobile members of the academy from working-class backgrounds "might well believe that they have actually betrayed the people left behind." Rubin (1994:46), herself, admits to: "a terrible sense of disloyalty. . . . to parents who did their best in a world where the cards were stacked against them." These somewhat contradictory feelings are often accompanied by a sense of separation, alienation, or isolation from parents, siblings, and childhood friends who remained within the working class (Dews and Law 1995:1-2,85; Ryan and Sackrey 1984:202; Rubin 1994 150-151; Sennett and Cobb 1972:134; Tokarczyk and Fay 1993:78-80). O'Malley (1984:306) laments, "Yet when I go home, no matter how hard I try, I can not go home." Tokarczyk and Fay (1993:21) state:"Many of us have felt . . . that we can no longer speak to our parents and our families; that we have been irrevocably changed by our doctoral training in a way that shuts down, rather than opens up, communication for us with those who have provided us with nurturance and role models." As these findings suggest, upwardly mobile academics from working-class backgrounds are transformed by their education and training. They are also the victims of the ambivalence that their parents, siblings, and working-class friends begin to feel toward them as members of what is, in many senses to them, an alien class.[35] Thus, in a slightly different sense than intended by Ryan and Sackrey (1984), they unavoidably become "strangers" to their parents, siblings, and other members of their class of origin. Frost (1984:257), for example, regrets that "it is also difficult to relate to working class folks who tend not to trust you since you got to be a Doctor." hooks (1993:101) observes: "It is difficult for me to talk about my parents and their impact on me because they have always felt wary, ambivalent, mistrusting of my intellectual aspirations even as they have been caring and supporting."

At the same time, research has shown that academics from working-class backgrounds often feel a part of neither the academic community nor the larger middle-class within which it is located. With regard to the former, Ryan and Sackrey (1984:75) observe that "academics from the working class have a sense of 'separateness from the academic community' of being a stranger, distanced from an authentic sense of self." Tokarczyk and Fay (1993:3) make the point that women academics from the working class "were frequently uncomfortable with the language they used, afraid that their voices would slip into dialect or working-class patterns." Gardner (1993:51) observes: "Working-class faculty often see themselves as outsiders or as marginal members of the academy." This sense of difference from other members of the academy leads many academics from the working class to feel out of place in their new home and sometimes even to feel undeserving of their newly acquired positions in society (Brandt 1984:72; Brown 1984:137; Callello 1995:130; Gardner 1993:51; Langston 1993:67; O'Malley 1984:311) In the words of Charlip (1995:27), "Despite my accomplishments. . . I still have the sneaking suspicion that someone will shout 'Fraud!' and send me away. A part of me doesn't believe that I can really know as much as they do or that I will ever fit in."

Research has also demonstrated that this discomfort with academia extends to the larger upper-middle-class community within which most academics find themselves after their workday ends as well. Langston (1993:67) comments that "coming from a working-class background guarantees that you will feel uncomfortable in middle- and upper-class settings. . . . Keeping up with a different set of 'manners' and pretentious small talk is an exhausting experience. Charlip (1995:38) offers another interesting example of this sense of distance from her middle-class friends: "the problem isn't knowing the material in class, but knowing the references made over cappuccino."

Academics from working-class backgrounds, then, do seem to be caught in the middle between the working class of their childhoods and early adulthoods and the upper-middle-class status they come to occupy as members of the academy. Callello (1995:130) uses the phrase "borderline state" and defines it as "a sense of being neither here nor there." A number of other academic expatriates from the working class have also documented this sense of marginality that they feel in their new class environment. Tokarczyk (1993:312), for example, feels she is "pulled between two worlds, between my working-class and academic status."

Previous research documents a number of the psychological consequences of this marginalized location between classes that academics and other upwardly mobile members of the working class occupy. Some of these are feelings of low self-esteem and self-worth (Gardner 1993:53; Overall 1995:214; Rubin 1976:55; Shostak 1969:159). For example, Shostak (1969:159) concludes that the blue-collar achiever "may not easily free himself [*sic*] of nagging doubts about . . . self-worth." Other reactions include feelings of inadequacy, inferiority, and insecurity about self (Charlip 1995:39; Ryan and Sackrey 1984:83; Sennett and Cobb 1972:26–27). Overall (1995: 215) admits to "the feeling of not being good enough to succeed in middle-class academia." Other consequences include feelings of social isolation, of rootlessness, loneliness, self-estrangement, marginality, and exile (Frost 1984:257; Gardner 1993:49; Langston 1994:69; Puck 1984:181; Shostak 1969:157–158; Tokarczyk 1993:312). Tokarczyk (1993:312) captures these feelings in the following statement: "The one pervasive metaphor. . . . that comes to me is the metaphor of exile, homelessness. It is a sense of being uprooted, of being wretched from the world of one's parents and siblings, with only a tenuous possibility of putting down new roots." Another reaction is a sense of "internalized conflict" generated by the fact that "the old and the new [cultures]. . . . are antagonistic to each other and conflictual" (Gardner 1993: 51; Overall 1995:214; Ryan and Sackrey 1984:107).

From this overview of previous research on the subject, it seems clear that academics from working-class backgrounds face unique problems adjusting to their new location(s) within the class structure of advanced capitalist society and that many of these problems result from the contrasts between their backgrounds as members of the working class and the demands (both on and off the job) of their new location within the upper-middle class. Thus, they characteristically feel that they are not a part of either class. It also seems that this sense of marginalization carries with it a number of negative structural, social, interpersonal, and psychological consequences for these individuals. Before presenting the conceptual model that will guide our research, it is necessary to mention briefly the role that gender plays within the academy and how its impact(s) intersect with those of class.

GENDER, CLASS, AND THE ACADEMIC EXPERIENCE

Accompanying the (re)entry of women into the labor force in larger numbers, which began during the late 1960s, has been a growing awareness that their experiences in the workplace, for a variety of reasons (such as their [culturally reinforced] need to "juggle" career and family responsibilities), were not the same as those of their male counterparts. These differences have given rise to, among other things, the feminist movement and scholarship that has specifically focused its attention on gender (Orlans and Wallace 1994:250). It should come as no surprise, then, that as the number of women in the academy increased, their roles began to receive greater scholarly scrutiny.[36] By now, there is little disagreement among scholars that women who work in the academy must confront daily a *sexist* institution and the numerous negative consequences that accompany this confrontation (Barker 1993, 1995; Orlans and Wallace 1994; Tokarczyk and Fay 1993). As we have argued thus far in this chapter, however, differences in class background constitute another area of confrontation that has not been adequately explored to date. Because we are convinced that the impacts of the two (class and gender) interact with each other, our expectation is that working-class men and women do not experience the academy in the same way(s).[37] As a result of this belief, our study will also examine the impact(s) of gender on respondents' perceptions about academic life.

THE CONCEPTUAL MODEL

This last section of the chapter presents the conceptual model that guides our study. The materials we have reviewed in this chapter lead us to a conceptual model whose major points are:

1. Class remains a major variable influencing the life chances of the citizens of late capitalist society.
2. The life experiences of the members of the middle and the working classes are not converging as some earlier theorists have suggested, but, indeed, remain divergent in many crucial respects—particularly in the relative material, cultural, and social resources that each class has available for expropriation by its members.
3. The opportunities for success afforded children in late capitalist society (stil) depend heavily on the relative resources that their families make available for their appropriation.
4. The relative resource advantage of middle-class families (not to mention those families located even higher in the class structure), all other things being equal, means that more of their children will acquire greater human capital skills than will children from the working class—this difference serves to "reproduce" the class structure of American society intergenerationally.
5. Despite the relative resource disadvantages that working-class children face, some (few?) do, nonetheless, acquire the "institutionalized" human capital skills necessary to move upward in the class structure, some even to upper-middle-class status.
6. Such upward mobility from the working to the middle and upper-middle classes is never complete, however, because it is impossible to completely escape the influence(s) of one's class background.
7. As a result, upward mobility carries with it a number of significant structural, social, interpersonal, and psychological consequences for those members of the working class who do manage to move up in the class structure because of their acquisition of human capital skills.
8. Since gender has also been shown to be an important structural variable affecting the life chances of individuals in late capitalist society, its interaction with class means that the nature of the various consequences of upward mobility will be different for men and women from working-class backgrounds.

22 Caught in the Middle

This study employs extensive data provided by a group of sociologists from working-class backgrounds to examine their perceptions of the various consequences of their upward mobility to membership in the academy and the upper middle class.

NOTES

1. The phrase "late capitalist society" is employed in this study to distinguish modern, monopoly, capitalist society, from its more competitive predecessor.

2. It occurs to us that the phrase "caught in the middle" can have another meaning as well—that of being "trapped in the middle class and, in a number of ways, being unable to return, even temporarily, to the working class. A number of working-class expatriates have voiced feelings of being inalterably separated from their families of origin and from childhood friends and associates. Podhoretz (1967:52) documents his own movement from working to upper-middle class and the fact that, once the move was made, he could no longer feel comfortable with the world from which he had come. This second meaning of the phrase was also cleary present in the responses of our study's participants.

3. It might seem odd that we are claiming that even our choice of profession is an artifact of our working-class backgrounds, since many theorists view upward mobility as occurring, in some senses, despite what some would label a "culturally disadvantaged" working-class background. On the contrary, we view our mobility opportunities as having been enhanced by our working-class backgrounds, by the stigma attached to them (our backgrounds) and to us (as members of the working class), by society as a whole, and by our middle-class peers. In other words, we see our achievements, in part at least, as a form of self-defense that attempts to shore up self-image problems generated by growing up as a member of working-class American society (See Sennett and Cobb [1972] for a similar viewpoint).

4. Tokarczyk and Fay (1993:5) also provide supporting evidence for this claim: "Some people believe that the fact that women from the working class have achieved careers indicates that there is mobility in American society; and, hence, class is not restrictive. We maintain that there is a definitional problem with this, that people do not pass out of one class into another, although their tastes, expectations, and habits may change as class identity shifts. Moreover, people raised in working-class families that have been subtly and consistently demeaned through America's class structure retain the scars of that experience."

5. Much of the material in this section of the chapter is taken from Grimes's (1991) overview of the use of class within American sociology since the turn of the century.

6. A recent exchange in the *International Journal of Sociology* between Clark, Lipset and Rempel (1993) and Hout, Brooks, and Manza (1993) typifies the two ideological extremes that are present in this debate.

7. In contrast to our viewpoint, a recent book by Pakulski and Waters (1996) has the provocative title *The Death of Class*, and attempts to show how class has lost its utility as a sociological concept. And still more recent is a book by Erik O. Wright, titled *Class Counts* (1997) that defends the continued relevance of class.

8. Parsons, himself, after initially minimizing the role of family background in the status attainment process in modern capitalist society (Parsons 1940), later assigned it a greater, but still a far more limited, role than do his critics (cf. Parsons 1953).

9. Bourdieu clearly views the three forms of capital as arranged in a sort of hierarchy, with economic capital at the top, cultural capital in the middle, and social capital at the bottom in terms of the relative influence of each on the other(s). Thus, those with economic capital either have or can gain access to the other two, whereas those with just cultural capital are better off than those with neither economic or cultural capital, but are still worse off than those with economic capital. The acquisition of social capital, on the other hand, is more dependent on the other two forms (Bourdieu 1986:249).

10. Ann Swidler (1986) makes the important point that the notion of culture not only contains "ultimate values" but also contains a "tool kit" of habits, skills, and styles that are useful in pursuing these ends. Her perspective on this subject overlaps with Bourdieu's viewpoint.

11. Bourdieu (1984) notes that cultural capital takes three different forms. The "embodied" form is the most fundamental of the three and refers to all knowledge acquired by the individual; the "objectified" form refers to cultural objects such as paintings, literature, and so on; and the "institutionalized" form refers to academic credentials.

12. In his words, "any given cultural competence (i.e., being able to read in a world of illiterates) derives a scarcity value from its position in the distribution of cultural and yields profits of distinction for its owner" (Bourdieu 1986:245).

13. As noted earlier, Wright (1985) also incorporates "pieces" of Weber into his model of the class structure of advanced capitalist society. In particular, he adds "organizational" and "skills" resources, clearly more Weberian than Marxist resources, to the traditional Marxist notion of the ownership of productive property, in his effort to describe the class structure of late capitalist society.

14. See Robinson (1984) for an informative discussion of the changing relationship betweeen ownership and authority in late capitalist society, the growth of the managerial class in such societies, and the increasing importance of formal educational credentials for membership in this group. Wright's (1985) model of the class structure of late capitalist society also stresses the role(s) that credentials like formal education play in the class placement process.

15. As noted in the text above, these scholars either take a narrower viewpoint that class only reflects differential access to economic resources (the more Marxist position) or a wider viewpoint that class reflects differential access to economic, cultural, and social resources (the more Weberian position, although a number of neo-Marxist scholars such as Wright [1985] have also included such additional variables in their models of the class structure of late capitalist society).

16. These scholars typically make the implicit assumption that the distribution of innate talents among the members of the different classes is similar, if not identical, no matter the class's particular location in the class structure of society.

17. There are several good overviews of this research tradition. See Gecas (1979) and Spenner (1988). See Parcel and Menaghan (1994) for a more recent summary of the findings of this research. See also Haveman and Wolfe (1994) for additional information

on this subject.

18. Lareau (1987, 1989) and Parcel and Menaghan (1994) have extended this line of inquiry by demonstrating that middle-class parents are also better equipped than their working-class counterparts to assist their children in navigating the complex maze of education in late capitalist society. Lareau (1989) also makes the important point that the difference between families is not so much in their desire for their children's success, but in their relative abilities to marshal resources to assist their children's efforts toward that success.

19. Ehrenreich's provocative book *Fear of Falling* (1990) makes the point that middle-class parents are fearful that their children will not acquire sufficient formal education to follow in their footsteps as members of the middle class. She notes that this crucial resource (and its advantages) is about the only inheritance that these parents can hope to provide their children.

20. It should be noted here that other scholars have disagreed with the perspective of these authors and insisted that despite the economic prosperity of the period, the benefits were unevenly shared and that important differences across class groups remained (Rubin 1976; Sennett and Cobb 1972; Shostak 1969). Rubin (1976:204) captures the perspective of these latter scholars when she says "the affluent and happy worker of whom we have heard so much in recent decades seems not to exist."

21. These trends have been linked to the "globalization" of the world economy (Bartlett and Steele 1992; Bluestone and Harrison 1982). See also Thurow (1996).

22. Bluestone and Harrison (1989) document a number of the negative consequences of the economic "restructuring" of the U.S. economy that began during the early 1970s. Bowles and Edwards (1993) also present a macrolevel analysis of the transformation of the U.S. economy in the postwar period. Bartlett and Steele (1992) trace the continuing evolution of the U.S. economy through the 1980s. Danziger and Gottschalk (1993, 1995) discuss income trends in the early 1990s.

23. See Levy and Michel (1991) for a comprehensive overview of trends in family income and wealth in the post–World War II America. Census data also confirm that the workers toward the bottom of the income distribution have also suffered the greatest declines in income (U.S. Bureau of the Census 1990). Updates are available in Danziger and Gottschalk (1995).

24. Harrison and Bluestone (1988:3) agree with Rubin's characterization: "The standard of living of American workers—and a growing number of their families—is in serious trouble."

25. Aronowitz and DiFazio (1994) offer a good summary of the automation of late capitalist economies and the marginalization of workers that results.

26. We should note that labor's actions in the 1996 presidential election stand in rather sharp contrast to their role(s) in the recent past. It is also interesting to note that the reactions of other interest groups, most particularly those from the business sector, to these actions seem somewhat hypocritical given their own massive material donations to politicians and political parties.

27. Danziger and Gottschalk (1995) provide detailed documentation of this trend.

28. Rubin (1994:38) includes media representations in her efforts to examine the impact(s) on working-class children: "their class position makes itself felt in a hundred ways, from parents who are weighed down by their own sense of failure, to television

images that glorify the successful professional and turn working-class men and women into doltish caricatures.

29. Sennett and Cobb (1972:81) note that "teachers act on their expectations of the children in such a way as to *make* the expectations become reality."

30. Rubin's (1976:55) summary of these impacts on children of the working class is insightful: "Children know. They know when their teachers are contemptuous of their family background, of the values they have been taught at home."

31. Scholars such as Bourdieu (1984), Coleman (1988), Lareau (1989), and Rubin (1976, 1994) have documented many of these cultural differences between middle- and working-class families.

32. See Bourdieu (1984); Coleman (1988); Lareau (1989); and Parcel and Menaghan (1994) for more modern evidence supporting this claim.

33. Sources for these include Aronowitz and Giroux (1991), Kohn and Scholler (1969), Lareau (1989), Rubin (1976, 1994), Sennett and Cobb (1972), Shostak (1969).

34. Rubin (1976:85–86) summarizes these differences well: "Parents in professional middle-class families have a sense of their own success, of their ability to control the world, to provide for their children's future, whatever that might be. . . . For working-class parents, however, the future is seen as uncertain, problematic."

35. In this context, hooks (1993:101) observes: "Like many working-class folks, they feared what college education would do to their childrens' minds even as they unenthusiastically acknowledged its importance."

36. For women in academia, two excellent anthologies that contain autobiographical essays have been published: Tokarczyk and Fay, *Working-Class Women in the Academy* (1993), and Orlans and Wallace, *Gender and the Academic Experience* (1994). For working-class women in general, see Ruth Sidel, *Urban Survival* (1978) and Janet Zandy, *Liberating Memory* (1995).

37. Barker (1995:69) sees this relative lack of attention to the intersection between class and gender in the academy as a response to an erroneous stereotype about women in the academy—that they are all from middle-class backgrounds.

2

The Research Design

Like most intellectual work, this study's approach is a response to our assessments of the relative strengths and weaknesses of previous efforts to examine the intersection between class background and membership in the academy. As noted in Chapter 1, our initial interest in the subject was stimulated by Ryan and Sackrey's thought-provoking study of working-class academics titled *Strangers in Paradise* (1984).[1] Motivated by their own experiences as academics from the working class, these authors assembled a group of scholars from similar backgrounds and asked them to participate in their study. The main source of data for their study was an autobiographical essay that participants completed on their perceptions of the impacts of their working-class origins on their lives and careers as members of the academy. Although they provided few other guidelines for the writing of this essay (they did send respondents a sample essay), the authors explicitly asked participants to include responses to four issues/questions: (1) How do you feel about your colleagues and their values? Have you enjoyed a sense of membership in the academy? (2) How has your experience been with students from a higher income family than your own? What has that been like for you? What has it been like to teach students from your own class background? (3) Has your job(s) worked for you? Would you do it again, or would you seek some other kind of work? (4) What has been your experience with academic authority? These essays, with minimal editing, were loosely grouped ex post facto to form the backbone of the book; the authors added materials that both detailed the setting of post–World War II American academic life which provided the opportunities for the upward mobility of these students from working-class backgrounds and offered an interpretive framework for the essays. The authors' own label for their approach is "systematic social commentary and criticism" rather than "systematic data gathering and reporting"[2]; they offer as a defense for this choice the rudimentary state of knowledge about the subject matter of interest.

The approach taken by Ryan and Sackrey (1984) has both strengths and weaknesses. Its major strengths are its flexibility and openness. In situations wherein researchers do not yet have a fund of available knowledge from which to conceptualize a set of issues, allowing respondents free rein to build their own frameworks (or to "define their own realities") is certainly a wise (and often unavoidable) choice. The goal of such research is generally exploration, or "to satisfy the researcher's curiosity and desire for better understanding" (Babbie 1995:84), and certainly occupies a well-deserved place within the social science repertory.[3] In fact, a major contribution of such research is to provide baseline information that subsequent researchers can use to advantage in designing better approaches that will yield even more detailed information about the subject.

A major weakness of exploratory research is that it "seldom provide[s] satisfactory answers to research questions" (Babbie 1995:85). For example, giving respondents free rein to frame their own questions often results in questions (and answers) that may not be ideal for use in social science research. This freedom also makes it difficult to compare responses across different subjects since there is no guarantee that respondents will pose or address the same questions. This problem leads to a dilemma. On the one hand, allowing respondents to pose their own questions maximizes their freedom to reflect on the subject and to select those issues that seem most salient to them (it likewise minimizes the researcher's influence on the questions selected or raised). On the other hand, this process provides no guarantee that the results will be useful to the researcher (either in the sense that questions may be phrased in ways that render them less useful or that different respondents may not include the same issues in their selection of questions). Although there is no simple solution to this dilemma, we believe that it is possible to improve on the approach employed by Ryan and Sackrey and to design a procedure that allows respondent freedom at the same time that it ensures greater comparability across respondents. As will be demonstrated in this chapter, the approach we employ comes somewhat closer to Lindblom and Cohen's (1979) "systematic data gathering and reporting" than did Ryan and Sackrey's study.[4]

THE RESEARCH DESIGN

In this section, we outline what we have chosen to call a "second-generation" exploratory study of sociologists from working-class backgrounds. It, like its predecessors, remains exploratory because we do not believe that there is yet sufficient information known about the subject matter to permit a more methodologically sophisticated approach. Despite its similarity to their approaches, we nonetheless have added the qualifying phrase "second-generation" to our label to acknowledge the fact that in contrast to these earlier studies, whose authors were forced to work from scratch in designing and conducting their study, we had the good fortune of being able to use their work as a bench mark in the design of our study. As we describe our approach, we will make an effort to identify both the similarities and differences between it and its predecessors.

We decided to follow Ryan and Sackrey's (1984) lead and to employ a self-administered survey as the data-gathering strategy for the study. One motivation for this choice seems obvious—the subjects of our research are geographically dispersed over a wide area and it would be expensive, even if it were otherwise possible, to assemble them for the study. Second, our respondents are excellent candidates for a self-administered survey because they are both literate and relatively culturally homogeneous (Dillman 1983). Other motivations for our choice of a self-administered survey include the sensitive nature of the subject matter of our study and the amount of time required to provide the materials (for example, some of the respondents took over twenty hours to complete the materials we requested!), two additional advantages identified for self-administered surveys (Dillman 1983).

The Data-Gathering Instruments

We employ three basic data-gathering instruments in the study: an essay guide, a questionnaire, and a vita. The instrument most central to our study is the essay guide. Recall that Ryan and Sackrey (1984) asked respondents to write autobiographical essays about their perceptions of the impacts of their working-class backgrounds on their lives as members of the academy. In addition to providing a sample essay, Ryan and Sackrey explicitly listed four issues about which they were particularly concerned: relations with and assessments of colleagues, the class background of students, satisfaction with job, and relations with academic authority. In response to these requests—both general and specific—the respondents generated lengthy essays that provided rich and detailed insights into the subject matter. We sought to preserve as much as possible of the unique data provided by their approach; however, we also wanted to take advantage of the insights derived from their work and to assure greater comparability across respondents. Our solution to this dilemma was simple. We first carefully reviewed each of the essays in their book, making a list of the issues it addressed. We then compared the lists derived from all the essays and eliminated duplicates. The result was nearly sixty issues.

Our next task was to organize these issues into a sequence for presentation to our participants. What became apparent almost immediately was that an obvious (and useful) way to sequence the issues was to arrange them to loosely follow the life cycles of our respondents. The result was their organization into four areas of potential impact: childhood and early educational experiences; graduate training; professional career; and relationships with intimate partners, family of procreation, and childhood friends.

Because we remained concerned that our essentially "closed" list of issues, despite the means by which they were derived, might still exclude some issues that were important in the lives of academics from the working class, we also made use of another rather innovative technique that has been employed to gather data on subjects about which little is known in advance—the focus group. "Focus groups are basically group interviews . . . [that rely] . . . on interaction within the group, based on topics that are supplied by the researcher, who typically takes the role of a moderator." (Morgan 1988:9–10). Such group discussions have a variety of different uses, including our purpose for its application—"developing interview schedules and questionnaires" (Morgan 1988:11). We invited three sociologists from working-class backgrounds to meet with us to discuss their impressions of the diverse impacts that coming from a working-class background has had on their careers as academics. As a result of the three-hour discussion that followed, we added issues to our list we had not already included and clarified others. The focus group exercise gave us greater confidence that our approach was inclusive and that the result was a list of issues that adequately reflected the concerns of our participants.

Following this step, we framed questions that reflected the content of each of the issues. As a part of this process, we considered whether we should use open- or closed-ended questions. A review of the literature on question format revealed that there are two important situations wherein open-ended questions are preferred in research: (1) when there is not enough known to organize response categories and (2) when dealing with sensitive subject matter (Converse and Presser 1986:34). Because, in our view, the subject matter of our research satisfies both these criteria, we elected to use open-ended questions in this part of our study. The result of these procedures was an essay guide that our respondents used to structure their responses. This guide consists of fifty-nine questions, organized (as noted above) into four different areas of concern (See Appendix A for a copy of this essay guide).[5]

A second data-gathering instrument, a questionnaire, was also constructed. This instrument consists of a number of closed-ended questions that provided greater detail than participants were likely to provide in response to questions in the essay portion of the exam. In particular, we were interested here in information about participants' employment histories (during both educational and professional careers); information about spouse/significant others,' parents', and siblings' educational and occupational attainments/positions; and demographic information about the respondents (this instrument is presented as Appendix B).

The third source of data for the study consists of the curriculum vita of each of our participants. As is customary, these documents contain information about degrees, professional positions, awards, areas of specialization, and teaching and research activities. Given the common focus of these three instruments, there is some overlap among them.

Information derived from each of these sources constitutes the data for the study. Details concerning how the data were organized for use in the study will be presented later in the chapter.

THE SAMPLE

The problem of sampling "hidden" populations, such as academics from working-class backgrounds, is a difficult one. Professional associations of sociologists that collect data on members such as the American Sociological Association or the Southern Sociological Society do not, as a rule, collect data on such things as the class of origins of members. This fact, combined with our strong suspicion that sociologists from working-class backgrounds probably do not make up a sufficiently large enough minority of the members of such organizations to be captured by any feasible random or systematic sampling of the membership lists of such organizations, means that parametric approaches to sampling them (along with their obvious inferential advantages) were out of the question. Others have solved the problem of sampling groups whose size and/or identifiability makes them difficult to sample by more conventional means in other, necessarily more innovative ways. One of the most useful of these approaches is "snowball" sampling. This technique allows researchers to collect an interactive sample, that is, to sample people who are involved in some way in a common social network (Denzin 1989). Thus, to the extent that members of a target universe know each other and/or are in contact with one another, they can be sampled using this approach. Ryan and Sackrey (1984:6) chose this method for their study. They initially wrote to over 150 academics and invited them both to be a part of the study and to recommend other potential participants. They also advertised the study by word of mouth at professional meetings. In the end, they received materials from about sixty-five respondents, from which they selected the twenty-four that they included in their study. In terms of sociodemographic characteristics, all their participants were from European American origins, most were social scientists, and all but two were male.

Our approach is similar to, yet slightly different from, that of Ryan and Sackrey (1984). It is similar in that we also used a snowball-type procedure for gathering our list of potential participants. It is slightly different in the particular way we contacted and gathered our participants and in that we chose to confine our study to sociologists.[6] We began by publishing announcements in the newsletters of the national and the ten regional sociological associations. In the announcement (see Appendix C) we described the study and invited interested persons to contact us. We sent those who contacted us a more detailed description of the study, including the materials we required of participants. We asked them to write back to us if they thought that they might be interested in being a part of the study (we also asked them to nominate others who might be interested in participating in the study). We also advertised the study on the message boards at two sociological conventions. By these means, we assembled slightly more than eighty potential participants. We then sent each of them a packet containing a cover letter, the essay guide, the questionnaire, and instructions for the use of the materials. We set a ninety-day deadline for the return of the materials to us. Approximately thirty days past that deadline we sent out a reminder to those who had not yet returned the materials encouraging them to get the materials to us as soon as possible. Since a number of those who did return materials failed to include all that we had requested (i.e., responses to the questions in the essay guide [both "hard" and "electronic" copies], a completed questionnaire, and a recent vita), we also sent reminders to those who failed to include these materials. We subsequently received the missing items from most. The data analysis below is based on forty-five participants.[7] Obviously, these forty-five sociologists do not constitute a random sample of sociologists from working-class backgrounds (even less are they in any way a sample of all sociologists!). As we noted earlier in the section, assembling the universe of American sociologists from working-class backgrounds would be a daunting task clearly beyond our temporal and material resources, even if it were possible. Thus our claims for the generalizability of our findings to all sociologists from working-class backgrounds will (and should) be modest. Despite this, however, because socio-demographic and employment information is available on American sociologists from the ASA (American Sociological Association 1992), we compare our respondents to this larger universe of sociologists in the next paragraph. The reader should be cautioned that this comparison has two important limitations. First, as noted above, the ASA does not collect information about the class background of its members, so we could not separate from the general membership of the Association those from working-class backgrounds. Second, not all sociologists belong to the ASA, so even its data should not be assumed to be representative of all American sociologists. Despite these limitations, however, a comparison between our sample and the membership of the ASA is informative.

Table 2.1 displays comparisons between our sample of working-class sociologists and the membership of the ASA on the following attributes: gender, race/ethnicity, age, sector of employment, type of employment, and tenure status. As presented in Table 2.1 A, our sample is similar to, but not identical with, the membership of the ASA in terms of gender; the female/male percentages in our sample are 47/53, whereas those of the ASA are 41/59. In terms of race/ethnicity, our sample also resembles the larger universe in that over 80 percent of both groups are of European American descent (see Table 2.1,B). Data on age (See Table 2.1,C) reveal that our sample of sociologists from working-class backgrounds is slightly younger than the membership of the ASA (for example, 60 percent of our sample is younger than forty-five years of age, whereas only 50 percent of the membership of the ASA is this young). We also had available data on the sector of employment of the membership of the ASA and were able to compare these proportions with those in our sample (see Table 2.1,D). These data show that our respondents are marginally less likely to be employed in universities with graduate sociology programs (44.4 percent

Table 2.1
A Comparison of Our Sample of Sociologists from Working-Class Backgrounds and the Membership of the American Sociological Association

A. Gender

	Our Sample		ASA Membership	
	N	%	N	%
Females	21	46.7	4,513	40.6
Males	24	53.3	7,854	59.4
Totals	45	100.0	12,917	100.0

B. Race/Ethnicity

	Our Sample		ASA Membership	
	N	%	N	%
African American	2	4.4	389	3.9
Asian American	—	—	761	7.5
European American	40	88.4	8,657	85.6
Hispanic American	3	6.7	243	2.4
Native American	—	—	62	.6
Totals	45	100.0	10,112	100.0

C. Age

Age	Our Sample %	ASA Membership %
34 below	13.3	19.9
35–39	24.4	12.7
40–44	22.2	16.9
45–49	15.6	17.9
50–54	8.9	11.3
55 above	15.9	21.3
Total(*n*)	45	10,470

Table 2.1 (cont.)

D. Employment Sector

	Our Sample		ASA Membership	
Employment Sector	N	%	N	%
Universities with Graduate Sociology Degrees	16	44.4	642	47.4
Universities with Bachelor Sociology Degrees	9	25.0	149	11.0
Four-Year Colleges	1	2.8	134	9.9
Community/Junior Colleges	4	11.1	62	4.6
Elementary/Secondary Schools	—	—	16	1.2
Federal Government	2	5.6	41	3.0
State/Local Government	2	5.6	67	4.9
Not-For-Profits	—	—	132	9.7
For-Profits	—	—	74	5.5
Self-Owned Businesses	—	—	15	1.1
Independent Consultants	—	—	22	1.6
Itenerate Instructors	2	5.6	—	—
Totals	36*	100.0	1,354	99.9

*Excludes students

Table 2.1 (cont.)

E. Type of Employment

	Our Sample		ASA Membership	
	N	%	N	%
Type of Employment				
Post-Doc	—	—	22	1.7
Academic-Teaching	29	80.6	778	60.4
Research	4	11.1	274	21.3
Administration	3	8.3	146	11.3
Applied (non-research)	—	—	56	4.3
Writing/Editorial	—	—	12	0.9
Totals	36*	100.0	1,288	99.9

*excludes students.

F. Tenure Status

	Our Sample		ASA Membership	
	N	%	N	%
Tenure Status				
Tenured	18	50.0	377	33.5
Not Tenured/Tenure Track	6	16.7	157	13.9
Not Tenured/Not Tenure Track	6	16.7	181	16.1
Tenure not Applicable	6	16.7	411	36.5
Totals	36*	100.1	1126	100.0

*excludes students

versus 47.4 percent) and that they are slightly *more* likely to be employed in
universities that offer a bachelor's degree in the field than is the ASA
membership (25 percent versus 11 percent for the ASA). If these two categories
are combined, over 69 percent of our sample is employed in one or the other of
these two categories, whereas only 58 percent of the membership of the ASA
is so employed. The next comparison is with type of employment (See Table
2.1,E). Over 80 percent of our sample of sociologists from working-class
backgrounds are employed in academic-teaching roles, whereas only about 60
percent of the ASA membership are employed in such roles. Next, we compared
the tenure status of the members of our sample with the membership of the
ASA. As presented in Table 2.1,F., fully half our sample hold tenured positions
as compared with only about a one-third of the membership of the ASA.
Finally, 20 percent of our sample of sociologists from working-class
backgrounds are students (see Table 2.2), compared with 24.9 percent of the
membership of the ASA (American Sociological Association 1995). To conclude
this comparison, our nonrandom sample of sociologists from working-class
backgrounds, is both similar to, and, in some cases, slightly different from the
membership of the ASA in terms of a number of important socio-demographic
and employment indicators. This fact should be kept in mind when evaluating
our findings.

Table 2.2
The Employment Positions of Our Sample of Sociologists from Working-Class Backgrounds

Position	N	%
Professor	9	20.0
Associate Professor	9	20.0
Assistant Professor	6	13.3
Lecturer/Adjunct Professor	5	11.1
Researcher	5	11.1
Administrator	2	4.4
Student	9	20.0
Totals	45	99.9

ENSURING PARTICIPANT AUTONOMY

In a study that involves life-history materials and potentially candid personal observations about institutions and individuals, it is imperative that the anonymity of participants be protected. Our normal concern about this problem was heightened by the fact that a number of the participants who returned materials early during the data-collection period explicitly expressed concern that the confidentiality of their contribution be afforded maximum protection. This section of the chapter discusses the steps in the procedures by which confidentiality was ensured.

Upon receipt of a participant's materials, the first step was to add the name and address of the participant to a master log sheet and to assign a unique identification number to the participant. Second, electronic and photocopies of the respondent's materials were made, and the original materials were stored under lock and key along with the master log sheet; only the principal investigators have access to these materials. Third, any mention of the participant's name on the photocopies was either removed or made illegible. Following this, a second set of photocopies was made from the first copy. *Only* these two sets of copies were used in the analysis phase of the research.

A second way that participant anonymity was ensured is that any references to individuals in our reporting and interpretation are limited to gender and age. In addition to these precautions, concern about protecting the confidentiality of participants motivated us to take an additional step. Here, all (already disguised) references to individuals were examined in the context of their usage in the narrative of the study as a final check to assure that they cannot be linked to specific individuals.

DATA ORGANIZATION AND CODING

This section of the chapter presents information about how the data are organized and/or coded for analysis. We discuss, in turn, organization and/or coding for each of our sources of data.

Data from the Essay Guide

The essay guide contained fifty-nine questions organized into four groups according to the particular focus of the question. As discussed earlier, since we decided that it would be premature to attempt to construct closed-ended response categories for these questions, we chose to leave the questions open-ended. Although such a choice does maximize respondent freedom (to "frame" their own reality, so to speak), it is not without its costs—the major of which is that this response format presents a much more formidable coding challenge. Our solution to this problem was simple. We first organized the data by question rather than by respondent (i.e., we "grouped" all responses to question 1, question 2, etc.). We then read (and reread) the (sampled) responses, seeking a means by which to summarize and/or organize them. Our success depended on the particular issue in question. For some, we were able to collapse the responses into a small number of discrete categories that did little violence to the data; for others, our efforts were less successful. We also selected (at this stage in the analysis) direct quotes from respondents that "typified" important points with reference to the issue raised in the question. Because we were also concerned with the reliability of our coding of these open-ended questions, we used two coders for each question and made systematic comparisons of their results.[8] We will discuss the particulars for each question in our presentation and analysis of the data in the chapters that follow.

Data from the Questionnaire

The questionnaire contained a number of questions, many of which were closed-ended (see Appendix B for a copy of the questionnaire). The coding procedures for each of these questions are discussed in Appendix D.

Data from the Vita

Data from respondents' vitae were employed as a cross-check for information that was unclear on one or the other of sources. These particular data also provided more detailed insights into the career patterns of our respondents which is the subject of Chapter 5.

DATA ANALYSIS AND PRESENTATION STRATEGY

As noted in the previous section of the chapter, the study is organized around three data-gathering instruments: a set of fifty-nine open-ended questions, a lengthy questionnaire, and the vitae of the respondents. One of our decisions was to organize our materials according to the life cycle of the respondents. As a result, the major data-gathering instrument—the essay guide—is divided into four sections as follows: childhood and early educational experiences, later educational experiences including undergraduate and graduate work, professional and career experiences, and relationships with adult intimate partners and family of procreation. In the materials that follows, a chapter will be devoted to each of these areas of the life cycle of the respondents.

Within each of the chapters, presentation and analysis of data will generally follow the order of the questions in the essay guide for the particular area in question (see Appendix A for the essay guide). For each of the questions in the essay guide, we will first summarize the theoretical rationale for the question. we will then discuss the coding categories that emerged from our analysis of the open-ended responses to the question. We will then summarize the responses of our participants to the question according to these categories by means of percentages (we also report the reliability of our coding for each of the open-ended questions). Since we are also interested in the impact(s) of gender, we will then compare the response patterns of female and male respondents to the question and discuss the results of these comparisons.[9] Finally, we will provide typical and, occasionally, unusual, direct quotes from our participants in an attempt to provide the reader with some of the "flavor" of their responses to the question. Where appropriate, data from participants responses to the questionnaire and from their vitae will also be used to supplement the materials derived from their responses to the open-ended questions.

NOTES

1. Although our study was in the field, we discovered a second book that had just been published on the subject by Tokarczyk and Fay (1993). This book took the same general approach as did Ryan and Sackrey (1984) but confined its attention to women. There is now a third book on the subject by Dews and Law entitled *This Fine Place So Far from Home* (1995). This latest book also takes a similar approach to the subject as the others.

2. They cite Lindblom and Cohen's *Usable Knowledge* (1979) as the source for this label. In this provocative book, the authors argue that "professional social inquiry" (PSI), their label for much "institutionalized" social science research, though useful, is rarely sufficient by itself when addressing many of the problems facing society (and, by implication, the social science community). They argue for a more inclusive approach that combines PSI with other, more "ordinary" forms of inquiry. Ryan and Sackrey clearly view their approach as falling within this, more inclusive, category of research strategies.

3. Babbie (1995:84) lists three purposes of exploratory research: "to satisfy a researcher's curiosity and desire for better understanding . . . to test the feasibility of undertaking a more careful study . . . [and] to develop the methods to be employed in a more careful study."

4. We should make note of the fact that not all would agree with our efforts to improve on the approach(es) of past research. The coauthor of a recent collection of essays on the subject that takes a similar approach to that of Ryan and Sackrey (1984), Carolyn Law (1995:5), makes the point that "only autobiography is a sensitive enough instrument to register the subtle activity of social class in a milieu in which class is supposedly a nonfactor." Although we believe that an autobiographical approach has its merits, we also believe that it is now time for a new and more analytical approach to the subject.

5. As an additional step to ensure that we did not exclude other important issues, we also made it clear in the exit instructions at the end of the essay guide that we welcomed participants to broach and discuss any additional issues they felt important that were not covered by the questions in the guide (parenthetically, few did so).

6. In contrast to Ryan and Sackrey's sample, which largely consisted of social scientists, we decided to limit our attention to sociologists. The major reason for this decision is that we wanted to examine linkages between class background and substantive/theoretical interests and limiting our study to sociologists facilitated this goal.

7. The size of our sample of respondents differs slightly from chapter to chapter and from data source to data source. We did have complete questionnaires from forty-five respondents. The *N's* for the open-ended questions range from forty to forty-two depending on the section of the essay guide in question.

8. One of the greatest liabilities of open-ended questions is the difficulty of coding them. Our approach to this problem was simple. First, we used coders who were either professional sociologists or advanced graduate students. Second, coders read information on coding qualitative data (materials from Strauss, *Qualitative Analysis for Social Scientists*, [1987]) and attended a coder training session during which the goals and the procedures of the task were presented and discussed. Third, each question was coded by two researchers (one of these was always an author of the study). Fourth, the results of the coding for each question were compared, and any disagreements resolved (see Kirk and Miller [1986], for a general discussion of reliability and validity in qualitative research).

9. Recall that Tokarczyk and Fay's book *Working-Class Women in the Academy* (1993) confined its attention to women academics from the working class. Given our sensitivities to gender, we had already decided to use it as the major stratifying variable in our study; their book confirmed the soundness of this decision.

3

Learning to "Make Something" of Ourselves

From the earliest days of our childhoods within working-class households, we were told that we were expected to "make something" of ourselves. This was generalized advice, however, and it was seldom accompanied by more detail about *what* that should be. We were never, for example, presented with pictures of ourselves as doctors or lawyers or scientists. As we grew older, we came to understand that to "make something" of yourself meant things like working hard and being dependable, staying out of trouble, and becoming financially independent of your parents' support as soon as possible.

The participants in this study, have, by most standards, "made something" of themselves but not necessarily in the ways that their parents had intended. In fact, for many of them, their successes have been accomplished *in spite of* what they learned during their childhoods about what it means to be successful; their successes have also sometimes come at the expense of the approval and acceptance of their families and childhood peers.

This chapter addresses the first period in our respondents' life histories—the period of childhood and adolescence. Their life histories tell a multitude of stories about particular circumstances and significant coincidences. Along with our more quantitative analyses of their responses, we will also quote some of their actual responses, not only to give voice to their uniqueness, but also to point out what they share in common.

Theoretical explanations about socialization within a class culture would lead us to make certain predictions about the social mobility of individuals who grow up in working-class families—that is, that working-class kids usually grow up to become members of the working class themselves. However, academics from working-class families have moved far from their families of origin to pursue

professional careers that place them firmly in the upper middle class. How can
we account for this? What is it about these individuals that makes them different
from other working-class kids? Does their mobility invalidate the theoretical
premises on which predictions about social mobility are based? Or is there some
way to reconcile the actuality of their exceptional leap in class status with the
theoretical assumptions that make such a leap so unlikely? Perhaps they were not
really working class in the first place; or perhaps, they are not *really* upper
middle class now, at least not in ways that count.

These are the questions inherent in our analysis—and the data we have
gathered are uniquely suited for addressing them. In the pages that follow, we
will lay out an explanation—one that is consistent with the theoretical framework
outlined in Chapter 1. We will first show that these individuals grew up
thoroughly working class, both materially and culturally. Yet, in contrast to
many of their peers, they somehow managed to overcome the material, cultural,
and social barriers to their mobility out of the working class. Our explanation
for their success is based on four important factors: (1) *they were smart*—most
respondents reported that they were certainly above average and many were
even high achievers in their early educations, despite their families' relative lack
of cultural capital; (2) they had the benefit of *encouragement and support* from
both parents and teachers; (3) their home environments taught them one of the
most fundamental of working-class values, *to respect hard work*—they were
taught to persevere and to be proud of themselves for their ability to work hard,
regardless of the task; and (4) most of them gained entry to colleges and
universities during the *expansion of public higher education* that has taken place
since the 1950s. The first three of these reasons—that the members of this
sample of sociologists from the working class were smart, that they received
support and encouragement from both parents and teachers, and that they
learned early the value of hard work—will emerge from our analysis of the data
about their childhoods and early educations. The fourth, the expanding
opportunity structure of post–World War II America, will be discussed in
Chapter 4.

GROWING UP WORKING CLASS

Family Background

Class Location of Parents.   Our first goal was to establish that our
respondents were, indeed, from working-class backgrounds. Recall that Wright's
(1985) perspective on class characterized working-class jobs as sharing three
attributes: (1) they possess no productive resources, (2) they possess no
organizational resources, and (3) they possess few skills/credentials resources.
We assessed our respondents' parents'[1] class locations in two different ways.
First, we employed responses to a series of closed-ended questions about these
three criteria for each parent's main job (see the items listed under questions 9

and 10 of the questionnaire in Appendix B). Using this approach, all but one of the parents of the respondents satisfied the three criteria that define working-class jobs.

Because this approach limited itself to each parent's *main* job and many members of the working class are likely to hold a number of different jobs during their work careers, we also asked respondents to provide a narrative overview of the work careers of their parents. Table 3.1 displays the distribution of the parents of our respondents across the four categories that emerged from our analysis of their responses to this question: unambiguously working class, where the parent spent his/her entire career in working-class jobs; mostly working class, where the parent spent a majority of her/his career in working-class jobs; ambiguously working class, where the parent spent some time in jobs that were not classified as working class, but also spent some time in working-class jobs; and other, where the parent worked mostly in jobs that were clearly not working-class jobs.[2] As displayed in Table 3.1, all but one of the male respondents' fathers and all but two of the female respondents' fathers held jobs that were (either unambiguously, mostly, or [at least] ambiguously) working class. The sole exception among the male respondents' fathers died when the respondent was very young, and, therefore, his occupation is not relevant to the study. The same is true for one of our female respondents' fathers; the second's father was a high school dropout who joined the navy, who later attended but did not complete college, and who was irregularly employed in lower-level white-collar jobs as a worker/manager in fast-food restaurants or who started various small businesses, all of which went bankrupt.[3]

For respondents' mothers, the situation was slightly different. As displayed in Table 3.1, approximately four in ten of the respondents' mothers' jobs were either unambiguously or mostly working class; the remainder were either full-time housewives (about half of the remainder) or they held lower-level white-collar jobs such as secretarial, clerical, or bookkeeping, or were lower-level professionals (two were nurses, a third was a dental assistant). As shown in Table 3.1, breaking down the work situations of both parents by the gender of respondent had virtually no impact on their distributions for fathers' jobs, but there were small differences for mothers' jobs. Table 3.1 also summarizes information about our respondents' grandparents. As displayed there, nearly nine in ten of the grandparents of our respondents were also employed in working-class jobs, the few exceptions were either small business persons or professionals. For example, one grandparent was a teacher and another was an attorney.

To summarize, these data demonstrate that our respondents spent their child- and early adulthoods in households whose male adults held working-class jobs during most, if not all, of their work careers and whose female adults were either homemakers or held working- or lower-level white-collar jobs (some of which were part time).[4] It is also noteworthy that almost all of our respondents' parents also grew up in working-class homes.

Table 3.1
Respondents' Perceptions of the Kind of Work Parents and Grandparents Did When Respondents Were Growing Up

N (%)

	Father			Referent	Mother	
Response	*Total*	*Males*	*Females*	*Total*	*Males*	*Females*
Unambiguously Working Class	25(64)	14(67)	11(61)	10(24)	8(33)	2(11)
Mostly Working Class	10(26)	6(28)	4(22)	8(19)	3(13)	5(28)
Ambiguously Working Class	1(03)	—	1(06)	2(05)	2(08)	—
Other	3(08)	1(05)	2(11)	12(29)	6(14)	6(14)
Housewife				10(24)	5(12)	5(12)
N(%)	39(100)	21(100)	18(100)	42(100)	24(100)	18(100)
NA	3			0		7

	Grandparents		
Response	*Total*	*Males*	*Females*
Unambiguously Working Class	23(66)	15(75)	8(53)
Mostly Working Class	7(30)	3(15)	4(27)
Ambiguously Working Class	2(06)	1(5)	1(17)
Other	3(19)	1(5)	2(13)
N(%)	35(101)	20(100)	15(100)
NA	7		

[Reliability = 96%]

Parents' Perceptions about Class. The second issue we explored with our respondents was their parents' perceptions of the class structure of society, their location within that structure, and their perceptions of the consequences of that location for their lives. These issues are important for the study since parents' attitudes and values have been shown to exercise a strong influence on those of their children and this intergenerational transference has important implications for the eventual class location of their children (Bourdieu 1984; Coleman 1988; Kohn and Schooler 1983).

We were aware that our respondents' parents were unlikely to have used the labels we, as sociologists, would apply. Americans generally do poorly at identifying themselves within social classes and we had no reason to believe that our respondents' parents were exceptional in that regard. As Halle (1984) points out, the working class in the United States is more likely to use the term "working man" to refer to the broad range of workers who work with their hands or perform menial and repetitive work.

We coded respondents' answers to the first of the class-awareness questions "yes" if they said that their parents were aware of the class structure of society, and "no" if they said they were not. Some respondents commented that their parents were (at least somewhat) aware of a hierarchy, whereas others stated that their parents clearly recognized themselves as working class. An example of the latter is the response of a thirty-nine-year-old female, who said: "My father recognized and continues to recognize himself as not only someone who is working class, but more respectfully as 'someone who actually works for a living.' Beyond his own class position, he is aware of the class structure of this society, although he has always emphasized power and influence over wealth." An example of a "no" response to parents' awareness of a class structure is that of a forty-four-year-old female who wrote: "My parents were not significantly aware of class positions in any manner that made this clear to the children. Further, in the community we lived in there were few rich people and all classes in the community participated in the same institutions (churches, schools) and lived in the same general areas." The distribution of our respondents between these two categories, displayed in Table 3.2, reveals that over four-fifths of them thought that their parents were aware of a class structure in American society.

We next examined respondents' answers to the question for evidence of their parents' awareness of their own location within this class structure. Here we also used two categories—"yes" for those who noted that their parents were aware of their location within the class structure and "no" for those who said that their parents were not aware of their location within this structure. The remarks of a thirty-four-year-old female concerning her parents' awareness of their location within the class structure are a good example of the former category: "I believe my parents were very aware of their location within the class structure. Since a house fire destroyed most of their possessions, it really took them the rest of their working lives to climb out of debt." An example of the latter category comes from a forty-four-year-old male who said: "I have the sense that my parents were generally unaware of the class structure and their position in it." As noted in Table 3.2, eight in ten of the respondents said that their parents were aware of their location within the class structure, whereas only two in ten said they were not.

Finally, we also asked respondents to comment on their perceptions of their parents' viewpoint(s) on the consequences of their class location. Here we coded their responses into three categories: "positive," if they answered that their parents felt that there were positive consequences to their class location within society; "negative," if they indicated that their parents felt that the consequences

Table 3.2
Respondent's Perceptions of Parents' Awareness of Class, Their Own Location(s) within the Class Structure and the Consequences of This Location When They Were Growing Up

N(%)

	Total	Males	Females
Awareness of Class Structure			
Yes	34(81)	19(83)	15(79)
No	8(19)	4(17)	4(21)
N	42(100)	23(100)	9(100)
Awareness of Location within Class Structure			
Yes	34(81)	20(87)	14(74)
No	8(19)	3(13)	5(26)
N	42(100)	23(100)	19(100)
Viewpoint on the Consequences of Class Location			
Positive	2(04)	1(04)	1(05)
Negative	20(48)	12(50)	8(44)
Few	20(48)	11(46)	9(50)
N	42(100)	24(100)	18(99)

[Reliability=89%]

of their location were mostly negative; and "few," if they indicated that their parents saw few consequences as resulting from their class location. An example of the first category comes from a thirty-nine-year-old female who remarked that "we were considered pretty well off. By the time I was five, my parents bought a brand new house, one of only a few in this very old neighborhood. . . .I had a greater sense of . . . feeling like a big fish in a little pond, rather than being a little fish in a big pond." This viewpoint contrasts sharply with that of a fifty-one-year-old male participant whose response to the question was coded "negative": "My father communicated a simple, embittered sense of class to us. He had canned phrases which I've forgotten that implied that the 'workingman was always getting the shaft.'" An example of a response that we coded as "few" comes from the remarks of a fifty-five-year-old male respondent about his parents' perspective on the impacts of class:

There was recognition that classes existed, but I don't recall anything that I would describe as strong class solidarity or identification. Although they seemed to recognize that not everyone got the same chances or start in life, differences in success and wealth were ascribed more to individual differences in work, worthiness, and perhaps luck than to life chances or opportunities determined by the class system.

As shown in Table 3.2, respondents were evenly divided between those who saw class as having mostly negative consequences and those who saw it as having few, if any, consequences. The fact that almost half of them (48 percent) viewed class as having mostly negative consequences (in contrast to the 4 percent who said class had positive consequences) contradicts functionalist scholars such as Parsons (1940) and Davis and Moore (1945) who have stressed the positive, motivational consequences of social inequality. Although gender did not have a large impact on responses to this issue, it should be noted that female respondents were slightly less likely to view their parents as being aware of their class location when compared with males.

Given the importance of the class variable for the research project, we also asked respondents a more global question about their perceptions of their parents' viewpoint on the class structure of the society and its relative importance. Three categories resulted from our inspection of their responses—that "classes don't exist"; that "classes exist, but they are not important"; and that "classes exist and are important." Typical of those respondents placed in the first category (classes don't exist) are those of a forty-three-year-old male who said in response to this question: "My parents did not discuss their perceptions of the class structure and seemed to simply accept the ideology that everybody in America got what they deserved." The remarks of a thirty-seven-year-old female are a good example of the second category: "This is difficult to evaluate, because they so rarely spoke about their own class in relation to others. When perceptions of differences were made, it was certainly never jealousy—to the contrary, the upper classes were revered." A typical response for a participant whose parents believed both that classes exist and that they matter comes from a forty-two-year-old female respondent who reported that "both my parents saw U.S. society as highly unequal. This was really felt by them at the local level, when they saw local elites get unfair advantages (such as lenient treatment by law enforcement authorities, educational advantages, other political advantages)." The distribution of our respondents across these three categories is presented in Table 3.3. As revealed there, nearly six in ten (57 percent) reported that their parents believed both that classes exist and that they exercise important influences on the life chances of their members. In contrast, fewer than 15 percent of the respondents noted that their parents did not think that classes exist in society. There are gender differences in response to this question—more male respondents reported that their parents believed that classes exist and are important, while females were more evenly divided in terms of these issues (for example, nearly one in five female respondents, compared with one in ten males, reported that their parents did not believe that classes even exist). As these data suggest, a majority of respondents' parents both believed that America has a class structure and that it has important consequences for peoples' lives. Such a viewpoint is consistent with the theoretical perspective that guides this study.

To summarize the findings concerning family background and class awareness, first, the data clearly show that the class background of the respondents was working class (and, more often than not, multigenerational working class). Second, the data indicate that our respondents' parents were aware of the class structure of American society, placed themselves within the working-class portion of that structure, and viewed the consequences of class on their lives and those of their children as either few in number or negative.

The Working-Class Home Environment

We were also interested in the home and neighborhood environments within which our respondents spent their childhood years because these environments play a large role in a child's socialization experiences (Rubin 1976). In this section of the chapter, we present data on a number of different aspects of the home environment including the nature of the gender division of labor within the household and the material and cultural circumstances within which the respondents' families lived.

The Domestic Division of Labor. The first issue is the nature of the division of labor within our respondents' households. Research has confirmed that working-class households are more likely to rigidly divide household labor along gender lines than are middle-class households (Collins and Coltrane 1995). Since we were interested in the extent to which our respondents' households were similar to or different from this pattern, we asked respondents to provide us with information about this issue. Our analysis of their responses generated three categories: "traditional" (when respondents noted that there was little overlap

Table 3.3
Respondents' Perceptions of Their Parents' Perceptions and Evaluations of the Class Structure of American Society

	N(%)		
	Sample		
Response Category	Total	Males	Females
Classes don't exist	5(14)	2(11)	3(17)
Classes exist but are not important	11(30)	4(21)	7(39)
Classes exist and are important	21(57)	13(68)	8(44)
N(%)	37(101)	19(100)	8(100)
NA	5		

[Reliability = 63%]

between parents in the household tasks performed); "modern" (when there was a great deal of overlap between parents in the household tasks performed) and "ambiguous" (when there was some, but not complete, overlap between the parents in the nature of the household tasks performed). A good example of a "traditional" response comes from the characterization of a thirty-eight-year-old male respondent, who noted: "In the household, the gender division of labor was such that my mother did all of the cooking, household maintenance, and most of the child-rearing. My father did nothing. The only thing he ever did was to take my siblings and I [sic] for an occasional trip to the park." A more "ambiguous" response to this question is that of a fifty-one-year-old male, who noted "My mother wasn't a great housekeeper, so my father did a lot of work at home. . . . He did the dishes frequently. He could make dinner . . . . Mother did all the clothes shopping." The remarks of a sixty-two-year-old female are typical of a "modern" response to this question: "[My family was] headed by two wage earners with stable jobs, and household responsibilities were shared by all members of the family." As displayed in Table 3.4, eight in ten of our respondents reported that there was a traditional division of labor in their households when they were growing up. When examining these responses by gender, female respondents were just as likely to view their households as traditional as were their male counterparts. From these data, it seems obvious that a large majority of the study's respondents, whether male or female, spent their childhoods within households whose domestic labor was heavily gender organized.

Table 3.4
Respondents' Perception of the Nature of the Gender Division of Labor in Their Household When They Were Growing Up

N(%)

Sample

Response Category	Total	Males	Females
Traditional	33(80)	18(82)	15(79)
Ambiguous	5(12)	3(14)	2(11)
Modern	2(05)	—	2(11)
One-Parent	1(02)	1(05)	—
N(%)	41(100)	22(101)	19(101)
NA	1		

[Reliability=97%]

The Family's Material, Social, and Cultural Resources. Given the strong emphasis that theorists such as Bourdieu (1984,1986) place on the role(s) that resources play in differentiating classes (and the accompanying opportunities afforded their members) within advanced capitalist societies, we were also interested in the material, cultural, and social circumstances of our respondents' childhoods. We first focused on the economic resources of our respondents' families by asking them if they had ever experienced a sense of material deprivation as children. In reading their responses to this question, it became immediately apparent that the material circumstances of the childhood homes of our respondents were diverse. In response to this, we devised a scheme that contained four categories. The first was "definitely yes," and we assigned our respondents to this category if they unequivocally said that they had felt a sense of material deprivation as a child. An example of a response classified in this category is from a twenty-five-year-old male who wrote: "In the early years, I often felt materially deprived. There never seemed to be enough money. We were always scrimping and getting by . . . . The food was always scarce; there was not much of it and it was always the cheapest . . . . The housing was dilapidated . . . . [One night] I was awakened screaming with my fingers bleeding from rat bites." The second category was "yes, but more a sense of relative deprivation." Respondents were placed here if they stressed that they had felt more a sense of relative rather than absolute deprivation. An example of a response placed into this category comes from a thirty-nine-year-old female who noted: "The concept of relative deprivation keeps floating up when I consider the answer to this question. For the most part I don't remember a sense of material deprivation when I was a child." The third category was labeled "no, but mentions relative deprivation." Respondents were placed here if they said no to the general question, but mentioned feelings of relative deprivation nonetheless. The response of a fifty-one-year-old male respondent is typical of those placed into this category:

High school was also a place where our relative material deprivation came home to us since it was a school that was comprised of working- and middle-class kids with a few children from very wealthy families thrown in as well. I think that both my sister and I really began to be aware of the relative circumstances in which we lived when compared with others at that point in our lives.

The last category was "no," and respondents were placed here if they denied feeling either form of deprivation during their childhoods. An example of a response that was placed here is from a forty-three-year-old female who put the matter this way: "I never felt a sense of material deprivation as a child. On the contrary I always felt that we lived very well. We always had enough to eat, although sometimes at the end of the week my mother struggled to put together a good meal."

As shown in Table 3.5, respondents were almost evenly divided between those who did not feel materially deprived and those who did (38 percent versus 36 percent). Still smaller groups reported that they had not experienced absolute material deprivation, but they had experienced a sense of "relative deprivation" and that they had experienced both, but more relative than absolute deprivation. These findings indicate that, though the families of the study's respondents were not uniform in terms of their levels of material resources, more than one-third of them did report suffering material deprivation at least at some point during their childhoods.

Given the importance that Bourdieu (1984) and others place on cultural resources in advanced capitalist societies, we were also interested in the cultural environments of our respondents' homes. As a result, we asked them to describe this environment. Based on their responses, we developed a coding scheme that contained a total of eighteen different cultural activities, including: (the presence of) books, newspapers, magazines in the home; listening to music (and the type of music as well); visits to museums and libraries; attending movies; going to plays/concerts; taking music or dance lessons; TV viewing, and so on. Following Bourdieu's (1984) distinction between "high" and "low" cultural activities, we then selected a subset of these activities to serve as an index of "high" culture. This group of activities included such things as listening to classical music, taking music/dance lessons, visits to museums, attending plays and concerts, and engaging in intellectual discussions with parent or older siblings. We then scored each individual in terms of the number of these

Table 3.5
Respondents' Perceptions about Being Materially Deprived as a Child

	$N(\%)$		
Response Category	Total	Males	Females
Definitely Yes	15(36)	7(30)	8(42)
Yes, but more relative deprivation	4(09)	3(13)	1(05)
No, but mentions relative deprivation	7(17)	4(17)	3(16)
No	16(38)	9(39)	7(37)
$N(\%)$	42(100)	23(99)	19(100)

[Reliability=82%]

activities in which he or she had engaged during childhood. The results are reported in Table 3.6. As displayed there, two-thirds of the respondents (67 percent) had experienced none of these activities during their childhoods, only two in ten had experienced even one of them, and no respondent had experienced four or more of them. In terms of gender, female respondents were no more likely to have experienced these activities than were male respondents (in contrast to the males, however, one female respondent had actually engaged in three of these activities during her childhood). These findings are consistent with Bourdieu's (1984) conclusion that the exposure to "high" culture is directly related to the family's position in the class structure of society, most particularly for him, the educational attainments of the parents.

Working-Class Neighborhoods

Because we believe that the environments immediately surrounding a child's home also provide important influences on her or his socialization experiences, we next queried our respondents about the character of the neighborhoods within which their households were located, their awareness of class differences between their family's neighborhood and other families's neighborhoods, and their reactions to these differences.

When we asked them about the class nature of the neighborhoods within which they grew to maturity, their responses led us to construct a total of eight categories that ranged from "lower class" to "upper middle class" (we also included a category labeled "unclear" for those whose responses could not

Table 3.6
Number of High* Cultural Activities in Which Respondent Reporting Engaging During Childhood

N(%)

Number of Activities	Total	Males	Females
4 or more	—	—	—
3	1(03)	—	1(06)
2	3(08)	1(05)	2(12)
1	8(22)	5(26)	3(18)
None	24(67)	13(68)	11(65)
N(%)	36(100)	19(99)	17(101)
NA	6		

[Reliability = 96%]

*High cultural activities include listening to classical music, taking music/dance lessons, visits to museums, attending plays or concerts, and engaging in intellectual discussions with parents.

unambiguously be placed into one of the other categories). These data are displayed in Table 3.7. As shown there, nearly half of the respondents (45 percent) indicated that they had spent their childhoods within homogeneous working- or lower-class neighborhoods (13 percent of the total placed themselves within the latter category), and nearly four in ten (38 percent) reported having lived in neighborhoods that were "mixed" and contained working- and (either "lower" or "just plain") middle-class households. There were no large gender differences in response to this question. These data indicate that a majority of the study's respondents spent their early lives surrounded by other children and adults whose location within the class structure was similar to, if not identical with, their own.

Children from the working class, given the negative cultural images of the working class and the responses of institutional actors to members of the working class described in Chapter 1, cannot help but contrast their material and cultural resources with children from other class groups (Rubin 1976). This awareness motivated us to ask respondents if they were ever ashamed of their family, home, or neighborhood environments. The remarks of a forty-three-year-old female provide a good example of being ashamed of family: "I am ashamed to say, yes, I have felt ashamed of my parents and others. From my

Table 3.7
Respondents' Perceptions of the Class Background of the Neighborhood in Which They Grew Up

N(%)

Sample

Class Level	Total	Males	Females
Lower class	5(13)	4(19)	1(05)
Blue collar/ working class	13(32)	7(33)	6(32)
Blue collar/ lower middle class	11(28)	6(29)	5(26)
Lower middle class	2(05)	1(05)	1(05)
Middle class	—	—	—
Upper middle class	1(03)	1(05)	—
Mixed	4(10)	2(09)	2(10)
Unclear	4(10)	—	4(21)
N(%)	40(101)	21(100)	19(99)
NA	2		

[Reliability=95%]

earliest recollections I remember not being proud of my mother, not wanting to introduce her to my teachers at school." A forty-four-year-old male respondent's comments about his home and neighborhood are a good example of responses placed in this category: "[In junior high school] I remember going to classmates' homes in the middle-class neighborhood, standing in awe of the luxurious, spacious, homes and realizing that I would not be inviting them to my home for parties and other social gatherings." The results are displayed in Table 3.8. As displayed there, six in ten of the respondents reported being ashamed of either family, neighborhood, or both. It is interesting that female respondents were more likely to report being ashamed of their families than were male respondents. Another 40 percent, by contrast, report not being ashamed of

Table 3.8
Respondents' Perceptions of Being Ashamed of Parents, Siblings, Home, Neighborhood, etc.

N(%)

Sample

	Total	Males	Females
Yes			
Of Family	17(45)	8(38)	9(53)
Of Neighborhood	4(11)	3(14)	1(06)
Of Both	2(05)	2(09)	—
No	15(39)	8(38)	7(41)
N(%)	38(100)	21(100)	17(100)
NA	4		

[Reliability=95%]

either.

We then broadened the scope of inquiry and asked our respondents if they had ever been or were currently ashamed of their class background in general. Based on their responses to this question, we divided them into two groups— "yes" if they said that they had been and "no" if they said that they hadn't been ashamed of their class background(s). A good example of a respondent placed in the "yes" category is a thirty-eight-year-old male, who noted: "As I became more aware of the position of my class in respect to others, I became ashamed of my class background. I saw 'us' as less educated, less refined, dirtier and cruder than the norm." A representative response from a respondent who claimed not to have been ashamed of his class background comes from a thirty-eight-year-old male respondent who observed: "I certainly do not remember being ashamed of my class background nor do I feel that way currently. On the contrary, I think that it has probably given me certain values and perspectives that have not only influenced my work as a sociologist but the specific focus of that work as well." These data, displayed in Table 3.9, show that the respondents are divided on this issue with a slight majority (59 percent) responding that they are/were not ashamed of their class background and the remainder (41 percent) indicating that they are/or were ashamed of their class background. There were no significant gender differences in response to this question.

Table 3.9
Respondent's Perceptions About Being Ashamed of Their Class Background

N(%)

Sample

Response	Total	Males	Females
Yes	16(41)	9(43)	7(39)
No	23(59)	12(57)	11(61)
N(%)	39(100)	21(100)	18(100)
NA	3		

[Reliability=92%]

LEARNING THE VALUE OF WORK AND OF WORKING HARD

Since there are generally negative stereotypes associated with manual labor in contemporary American society (cf. Aronowitz and Giroux 1991), it seems useful to look at the way in which members of the working-class rationalize their position in the socioeconomic hierarchy. We were interested in respondents' perceptions about their parents' viewpoints about their work and its relative importance for society. We wanted to determine whether our respondents' parents tended to accept or reject the overall culture's negative stereotype, and if they accepted it, how did they interpret their participation in manual-labor jobs?

In this context, Halle (1984) describes an orientation toward work held by a group of blue-collar chemical plant workers. These men (his observation included only males), in their everyday conversations, contrasted blue-collar work with other kinds of work. They portrayed "working man's" work as dirty, dangerous, closely supervised, boring, and routine. Yet, when they contrasted what they did with other types of work they found the latter lacking. Halle calls this a "moral and empirical theory about who really works in America" (Halle 1984:205). The main difference is whether the work is productive or not. In spite of the often unpleasant nature of blue-collar work, it is valued more by the "working man" than work that is seen as unproductive (i.e., work that produces no tangible product). A good example of this sentiment is reflected in the quote given above, in which a thirty-nine-year-old female respondent said that her father refers to himself as "someone who actually works for a living." One respondent summed up both the recognition of the unpleasantness of the work and the pride his parents took in it:

Both of my parents placed low value on laboring, manual, menial, or factory work. I can remember no time during my childhood when they did not preach and urge me and my brother and sister not to "get stuck in a factory job." It was not that they thought that the work was unworthy in itself; doing good honest work with your hands was respected; it just did not pay off well and it was a dead end.

Another issue that became evident from the responses was the extent of overlap with the intrinsic-extrinsic judgments about work that Kohn and Schooler (1983:15) have employed in their research. Intrinsic orientations toward work (those most characteristic of middle-class jobs), are those that value work for the opportunities it affords the individual for self-development and personal and/or intellectual growth. An example of a response from a fifty-one-year-old male participant about his dad's feelings about his work typify this orientation: "For my father his work as an electrician provided a livelihood and a sense of craftsmanship. I don't ever remember him complaining about work. It seemed to be a place where he had some control." An extrinsic orientation toward work (more closely linked to working-class jobs) sees work merely as a means to some other end such as income and benefits and as something that does not, in itself, bring pleasure to, or intellectually challenge, the worker. A typical response coded as extrinsic is from a thirty-four-year-old female respondent, who characterized her parents' orientation toward work as "something that had to be done to put food on the table."

We added a third category labeled "mixed" for respondents who combined elements of the two in their descriptions of their parents' orientation(s) toward work. A good example of a response that we placed into this category is that of a fifty-five-year-old male, whose remarks both note his father's pride in his work and his frustration at not being able to use his skills more often: "Dad took immense pride in his work whenever he was able to work on something, such as repairing a machine, that called for him to exercise some skill and 'figure things out.'. . . He was always chafing at not being able to exercise his own judgment enough." We also added a third referent category (in addition to father and mother) labeled "undifferentiated" for those respondents who combined both parents' work orientations into a single description. Table 3.10 displays the results of these coding efforts. As shown there, with the exception of fathers' work orientation (which was viewed as either extrinsic or mixed), most of our respondents reported that their parents' orientation toward work was extrinsic.

Gender differences in responses to this question were obvious. Male respondents were much more likely to characterize their fathers' and parents' work orientation(s) as extrinsic and their mothers' as intrinsic, whereas female respondents were much more likely to characterize their fathers' orientation as "mixed" and their mothers' as extrinsic. It is interesting that for mothers' jobs, the characterizations provided by the two gender groups are just the opposite— 60 percent of women said their mothers' orientations toward their jobs was "extrinsic," whereas 60 percent of men said their mothers' orientations were

Table 3.10
Respondents' Perceptions of How Their Parents Talked/Felt About Their Work

N(%)

		Father			Mother	
Parents' Orientation Toward Their Work	Total	Males	Females	Total	Males	Females
Extrinsic	9(36)	6(43)	3(27)	9(45)	3(30)	6(60)
Mixed	9(36)	4(29)	5(45)	3(15)	1(10)	2(20)
Intrinsic	7(28)	4(28)	3(27)	8(40)	6(60)	2(20)
N(%)	25(100)	14(100)	11(100)	20(100)	10(100)	10(100)
NA	17			22		

Parents' Orientation Toward Their Work	Undifferentiated		
	Total	Males	Females
Extrinsic	8(80)	5(17)	3(100)
Mixed	2(20)	—	—
Intrinsic	—	2(29)	—
N(%)	10(100)	7(100)	3(100)
NA	32		

[Reliability = 72%]

"intrinsic." What does this say about the different interpretations that male and female children have of the necessity, meaning, and interpretation of their parents' work? For example, does the greater contact and interaction between mothers and their daughters make the latter more aware of the former's perspectives about work when compared with their sons? We suspect that this is the case.

This question not only asked respondents about their parents' opinions about their jobs, it also asked them to comment on their parents' perception of the importance of their work for society as a whole. In response to this latter issue, most respondents noted that their parents did not dwell on the importance of the work they did for the society. A few reported that their parents felt pride in their work. There were statements like "My father was obviously proud about his craft as a machinist." But most reported that their parents were simply utilitarian about their work and placed more stress on its necessity for "keeping the wolf away from the door" rather than its importance for the economy, and so on.

Considering the physical, menial, repetitive, and often dirty or dangerous nature of many of their jobs, it is not surprising that our respondents' parents did not see them as opportunities for "self-development and personal and/or intellectual growth" as upper-middle-class professionals often view their jobs. But recognizing the unpleasant nature of job tasks is only part of the story. In fact, even in light of this recognition, most of our respondents' parents continued to work hard and to uphold the "moral and empirical" ideal of work in the United States (Halle 1984:205). This is evident in the characterization of a thirty-six-year-old male about his father's attitude toward his work: "My father clearly believed that working people were central to the economy." Another respondent remarked that his parents "seemed to believe that your work was more or less like your word—you were known by it and derived your status in society from it.

In this context, many of our respondents commented on the importance of their parents' work ethic. Part of the "working man's" ethos is pride in doing any job well, whether it is a big, important job, or a small, invisible one (Halle 1984). One respondent referred to the working-class ethic as "honorable and worthwhile. I know working class people work very hard for a living and do honest work for a day's wage." Another respondent, in discussing what was considered an appropriate way to spend one's time, said: "All of these activities [are] important work; 'sitting around' was not acceptable." There were numerous references to working-class attitudes about the value of hard work. A few of these follow:

(My father) had a strong sense of craft, what now goes by the name quality, doing it right the first time. In his work he did a quality job and could do it with speed. He did complain about other's sloppy, uncraftsmanlike work, but not a lot. He got fulfillment from doing things right, a la Veblen's instinct to craft.

My father is a perfectionist. He always overworked (hours, effort) because he did not want to be criticized for having done poorly. He would be constantly fatigued and ill due to the self-induced stress.

Father preached work ethic and authoritarian discipline.

In referring to working-class women in her family, one respondent said: "They were very proud women who worked hard and valued the quality of their work." Another respondent put it this way: "Both parents felt their work was important. My dad believed the working man did the real work while managers and engineers, (and) architects did not generally know what they were doing. My mother was proud of her work raising a family with four kids."

The work ethic was often tied to ideology, that is, a belief in individualism and striving. For example, a respondent said her parents "had a very strong work ethic and bought into the American dream completely. If you worked hard enough, you would make it." For some, the ideology of individualism provided insight into the social order, both justifying the position of those at the top and explaining the "failure" of those at the bottom. Several examples follow:

The upper classes were revered; the lower classes got that way because they didn't work hard...

I also recall very negative and even nasty comments by my family and neighbors about white trash and lazy white folks who would not put in a honest day's work. There was special disdain for those who would take a "hand-out" or depend on county welfare whether black or white.

They are extremely committed to the notion that they had to work hard to be successful and that if they can do it then everyone else can too.

To working-class parents, then, it appears that the best legacies to offer one's children are teaching them to value work and to work hard. From a parent's own experiences, and according to the working-class ideology, the ability to work hard and do a job well is the key to success in the world. In the working-class world, success means having a steady job and being able to support yourself and your family. The best training for working hard is hard work. Thus, many of our respondents remarked about working hard as children. Two examples follow:

I had always worked hard, having learned my work ethic on a farm, where there was always plenty of work to be done.

Since I was the oldest child (and only child for about nine years), I participated in ALL business and farm work: milking, field work . . . dressing turkeys, gathering and sorting and packing fruits and vegetables for sale on the routes, helping with books and often responsible for checks. . . . My father often said that he had wished for a boy as his first child, but that I was a good as any boy would have been!

Working as children often took the form of household labor, especially when both parents were employed. For example:

I was expected, as the oldest girl child, to baby-sit the younger children, clean house every week, do dishes, cook, help can food, mow the lawn, rake the leaves. Since I was a girl, it did not matter that I was in high school sports and held a part-time job, I was still expected to do my work around the house on top of everything else.

As soon as my brother and I were old enough, we started doing quite a bit of household work and by age six we could cook, wash dishes, etc.

Some of our respondents pointed to the positive side of this early training. In the following quote, a respondent draws a direct link between the values learned as a child within a working-class family and her success in an academic setting: "I acquired some positive skills because of my working-class roots. I have a persistence to my nature that is in part rooted in the heavy emphasis on work my parents drilled into me. This has served me well in a sometimes hostile academic environment."

To summarize, in this section of the chapter, our results have shown that our respondents generally believed that their parents' orientation toward work was extrinsic or a combination of extrinsic and intrinsic. More important from our point of view, however, although they did not see their jobs as being especially important for the larger society—a viewpoint that is consistent with society's generally negative image of manual labor—they did emphasize the importance of having a *good work ethic*. Because we think that this trait is an important part of our explanation for why our sample of sociologists from working-class backgrounds was able to succeed, we will return to this issue both later in this chapter and in the next.

BEING SMART

Early Educational Experiences

In addition to having been firmly socialized to appreciate the value of hard work, another important ingredient in the success stories of our respondents was their skills in the academic realm. A number of researchers (Bourdieu 1984; Bowles 1972; Coleman 1988) have emphasized the increasingly important role that formal educational credentials have begun to play in "locating" individuals within advanced capitalist societies; others have also stressed the "unequal" nature of the educational opportunities afforded America's children (Kozol 1991).

The Class Composition of Schools

The first issue we asked our respondents to address was the class composition of the schools they attended and any impact(s) that this composition might have had on their educational experiences. This issue is important because public education in American society is heavily class organized and the quality of the educational experience varies greatly according to the school attended (Kozol 1991; Lareau 1987). We coded the class composition of our respondents' schools into four categories: "lower," "working," "mixed," and "middle," and we also organized the data by level of school (i.e., whether elementary, middle/junior high, or senior high). As displayed in Table 3.11, during their elementary educations, slightly over half (54 percent) of the respondents reported that they attended schools whose student bodies were almost exclusively working class; another third said that they had attended schools with a mixture of students from different classes. These responses differed by gender in that male respondents were more likely to report that they had attended working-class elementary schools, whereas females were more likely to report that they had attended mixed-class elementary schools (for males 53 percent working class versus 35 percent mixed; for females 36 versus 57 percent). The pattern of the data for the class composition of middle/junior high schools was similar to that found for elementary schools in that approximately one-half (52 percent) of the respondents reported having attended schools whose students were predominantly from the working class, whereas another third (35 percent) reported having attended schools with a mixture of students from different class groups. Gender differences in response were more modest in magnitude for these schools than those observed for elementary schools, but they were in the same direction. In contrast, the distribution of respondents across the class categories for high schools differed from the other two levels. For this portion of their educational careers, the proportion of respondents who reported having attended working-class high schools declined to about one in four, whereas the proportion who reported having attended mixed-class high schools increased to nearly six in ten (63 percent). The gender differences in the class composition of schools attended that were present for lower levels of schools were less apparent for high school.

Since we were also interested in exploring the impact(s) that the class composition of the schools our respondents attended had on their educational experiences, we asked them to speculate about this subject as well. We divided their responses into three categories: "positive," "negative," and "no discussion" (when they did not discuss impacts). A good example of a respondent who felt that the class composition of his school had a positive impact on his educational experiences comes from a fifty-one-year-old male who wrote: "The school was expected to achieve this result [to prepare students for enrollment in good colleges]; students competed to achieve this result. . . . Although my parents were pro-education, this school environment established a strong expectation independent of our family influence to go to college." A quote from a twenty-eight-year-old female who moved from working-class elementary and middle/junior high schools to a mixed-class high school exemplifies a negative assessment of the impact of school: "I felt inferior in high school . . . like I wasn't as good as other people. . . . I knew that my grades were better than those middle class kids but I also knew that they would be the one to go on to university." As shown in Table 3.12, over half of our respondents (53 percent) reported that the class composition of the schools they attended had a negative impact on their educational experience, while another quarter (26 percent) felt

Table 3.11
Respondents' Perceptions About the Class Composition of the School(s) in Their Early Educations

Class Composition of School	N(%)	Samples	
Elementary School	Total	Males	Females
Lower	1(03)	—	1(07)
Working Class	19(54)	13(65)	6(40)
Middle Class	3(09)	3(15)	—
Mixed	12(34)	4(20)	8(53)
N*(%)	34(97)	20(100)	15(100)
Middle/Junior High School	Total	Males	Females
Lower	1(03)	—	1(07)
Working Class	16(52)	10(59)	6(43)
Middle Class	3(10)	3(18)	—
Mixed	11(35)	4(23)	7(50)
N*(%)	31(100)	17(100)	14(100)
High School	Total	Males	Females
Lower	1(03)	—	1(07)
Working Class	8(25)	5(28)	3(21)
Middle Class	3(9)	2(11)	1(07)
Mixed	20(63)	11(61)	9(64)
N*(%)	32(100)	18(100)	14(99)

[Reliability = 90%]

*Ns vary due to differences in ways respondents answered question.

Table 3.12
Respondents' Impressions of the Impact of Class Composition of School on Their Educational Experiences

N(%)

Samples

Impact	Total	Males	Females
Positive	9(26)	5(28)	4(25)
Negative	18(53)	10(56)	8(50)
No Discussion of Impact	7(21)	3(16)	4(25)
N(%)	34(100)	18(100)	16(100)
NA	8		

[Reliability=86%]

the impact(s) were positive (approximately 20 percent of our respondents failed to address the issue). Because we were interested in the linkage between the class composition of the school(s) attended and the issue of the impact of this composition on the educational experience of our respondents, we cross-classified the two assessments. The results are presented in Table 3.13. The data displayed there indicate a strong relationship between the two variables—the lower the class composition of the school, the greater the proportion of respondents reporting a negative impact on their educational experiences. For example, nine of ten students who spent their entire educational careers in working-class schools reported that the schools had a negative impact on their educational experiences! These findings are consistent with Kozol's (1991) linkage between the material circumstances of a school and its relative ability to provide a positive educational experience for its students.

Personal Educational Assessment

We next asked respondents to provide us with a global assessment of themselves as students between kindergarten and graduation from high school. Based on their responses to this question, we developed a four-category coding scheme: "mediocre;" "average"; "above average"; and "high achiever." The results are displayed in Table 3.14. These data show that four in ten of the respondents were coded into the "high achiever" category; if we combine this

Table 3.13
The Class Composition of School Respondent Attended by Respondents'
Reactions to Their Educational Experiences

N(%)

Reaction to Educational Experience

Class Composition of School Attended	*Positive*	*Negative*	*N(%)*
Lower Class	—	1(100)	1(100)
Working Class	1(10)	9(90)	10(100)
*Working Class to Mixed**	1(25)	3(75)	4(100)
Mixed	3(43)	4(57)	7(100)
Middle Class	1(50)	1(50)	2(100)

*Respondents reported moving from a working-class to a mixed-class school during the course of their educations.

group with those who were rated "above average," then more than eight in ten (85 percent) of the respondents were rated as either "above average" or "high achiever."

Gender impacted these self-descriptions. For example, four times as many male respondents' replies were coded as "average" when compared with those of female respondents, and twice as many females' responses were coded "high achiever" when compared to the responses offered by male respondents. Only one of the respondents—a female—chose to label herself a "mediocre" student during this phase of her educational career.

The evidence reviewed thus far in this section of the chapter might appear somewhat contradictory. For example, many of the findings presented earlier in the chapter—things like the relative or absolute material deprivation that a majority of respondents suffered as children; the meager cultural resources available to them via families, households, and neighborhoods; and the internalization of the larger culture's negative assessment(s) of their class of origin that many respondents reported experiencing—do not appear consistent with their eventual educational successes. Some of the results of this section of the chapter, such as the fact that most of the respondents attended schools that were working class or that contained a mixture of working- and lower-middle-class students, that more than half of them judged their "early" (K through 12)

Table 3.14

Respondents' Assessments of Self as a Student between Kindergarten and the Twelfth Grade

N(%)

Samples

Assessment	Total	Males	Females
Mediocre	1(03)	—	1(05)
Average	5(13)	4(20)	1(05)
Above Average	17(44)	11(55)	6(32)
High Achiever	16(41)	5(25)	11(58)
N(%)	39(101)	20(100)	19(100)
NA	3		

[Reliability = 77%]

educational experiences as negative, and the close linkage between the class composition of the schools they attended and their assessment(s) of their "early" educational experiences, also seem inconsistent with their eventual educational achievements.

On the other hand, the fact that eight in ten of them judged themselves to have been either above average or high achievers throughout their early educational careers is more consistent with their eventual educational successes. These successes, despite the obstacles presented by their working-class backgrounds, encouraged us to explore other factors that might have made a contribution to their relative successes.

THE INFLUENCE OF SIGNIFICANT OTHERS

In particular, we were interested in examining their perceptions of the role(s) that other individuals, such as members of their families (parents and older siblings) and institutional actors (teachers and administrators), played in encouraging their educational goal settings and achievements.

Parental Encouragement

We next examined data on each of these potential sources of influence. We first explored the issue of the relative influence(s) that parents and older siblings played in encouraging their early educational efforts. We wish to make the case here that parental/older sibling expectations and encouragement (and perhaps their achievements as well) may be especially important for the children of parents whose cultural capital resources (for these purposes, their formal educational credentials) are more modest. Coleman (1988) makes the point that the cultural resources of the adult members of a family must be effectively transmitted to the children through their social relations with parents for them to make a difference in the child's acquisition of human capital skills. At the same time that we acknowledge the importance of Coleman's argument, one of the indicators that he uses in his empirical example is parental (mother's) expectations for the child, and the effects of this variable are statistically *independent* of his indicators of parental human capital skills in his empirical model. Furthermore, his example of Asian families purchasing two copies of schoolbooks, one for the student and one for the parent(s), also points to a role for parents that may operate *independently* of their own human capital skills achievements. Given the important role that Coleman (1988), Lareau (1987), and others assign to parents, we asked our respondents to comment on any role(s) that their parents had played in encouraging their early educational efforts. We coded their response into three categories: "encouraging"—when the respondent made direct reference to a parent's encouraging her/his educational efforts; "indifferent"—when the respondent indicated that there was no overt effort on the part of either parent to encourage or discourage educational efforts; and "discouraging"—when parents made overt efforts to discourage the educational efforts of the respondent. Table 3.15 displays a summary of their replies to this question. As shown there, over eight in ten of our respondents remarked that their parents played an important role in encouraging their early educational efforts (about 13 percent ranked their parents as indifferent, whereas only 2 percent ranked their parents as having discouraged their educational efforts). A good example of an "encouraging" response is that of a forty-one-year-old female who said: "To them [her parents], education was the most meaningful aspect of one's life. Although my parents only graduated high school . . . both my parents and my maternal grandparents encouraged my early education."

Since Bourdieu (1984), Coleman (1988), and Lareau (1989) have linked parents' educational attainments to children's successes, we were interested in the relationship between our respondents' parents' own attainments in this realm and the (perceived) encouragement they provided for their children. To explore this issue, we divided the respondents' parents into four groups:(1) both parents with less than high school educations (24 percent of the total); (2) father with less than high school, mother with high school or more (27 percent of the total); (3) father with high school or more, mother with less than high school (11 percent of the total); and (4) both parents with high school or more (38 percent of the total). We then examined the association between parental educational attainment(s) and the amount of encouragement provided for respondents' early educations (see Table 3.16). The results clearly show that

Table 3.15
Respondent's Perceptions of Parents Encouraging (or Discouraging) Their Early Educations

N(%)

Encouraging	Total	Males	Females
Dad	1(02)	1(05)	—
Mom	8(20)	2(09)	6(32)
Both	25(63)	16(76)	9(47)
Indifferent			
Dad	—	—	—
Mom	2(05)	—	2(11)
Both	3(08)	2(10)	1(05)
Discouraging			
Dad	1(02)	—	1(05)
Mom	—	—	—
Both	—	—	—
N(%)	40(100)	21(100)	19(100)
NA	2		

[Reliability = 90%]

the two are related. Generally, the higher the educational attainments of parents, the more likely they were to encourage the early education of their children. Despite this linkage, however, even the lowest level of encouragement provided by any parental group in the table (composed of fathers who had high school educations or more and mothers who had less than high school) was still 50 percent. Previous research (Coleman 1988; Kohn and Schooler 1983; Parcel and Menaghan 1994) finds that the socialization of working-class children is heavily influenced by the occupational experiences of their parents. Parents tend to re-create components of their work environments at home; for example, when parents work in jobs that provide little opportunity for autonomy and

Table 3.16
Parental Educational Attainment Level and Encouragement of Respondents' Early Educational Efforts

N(%)

Level of Encouragement

Parents' Educations	Encouraged	Indifferent	NA	N
Both with Less Than High School	7(78)	2(22)	—	9
Father with Less Than High School/Mother with High School or More	9(90)	1(10)	—	10
Father with High School or more/ Mother with Less Than High School	1(50)	1(50)	2	4
Both with High School or More	10(93)	1(7)	3	14

independent thought, they are likely to encourage their children to conform rather than to think independently. Despite the fact that most parents stress "independence" in their children, what they mean by it often differs. While middle-class parents may be more interested in creativity and self-determination, the primary concern of working-class parents is that their children be able to support themselves, that is, to do a "day's work for a day's pay" and to avoid appearing weak by asking for help. To the extent that a high level of conformity is required in most working-class jobs, "independence" may come to mean just the opposite of what middle-class parents expect. In making comparisons such as these, it is necessary to recognize that the differences between class cultures means there is also a lack of agreement on meanings and values—differences that may be masked by the use of similar language.

Parental encouragement to "do well" in school, in many working-class families, means to follow the rules, keep out of trouble, and so on. A working-class parent sees a "good" report card as equivalent to a satisfactory evaluation at work. Getting good grades was an outward sign that you were able to fit into a system and accomplish what was expected. One respondent referred to his father's efforts to teach him "industrial discipline" in the following way: "He explained that I would always have a 'boss' and that I would have to obey authority without question or reason." And in a similar vein, a respondent talks about her parents' concern that she "do well" in school: "This urgent need for conformity could be attributed in part to the working-class attitudes toward work. For the types of work that everyone did and that I was expected to do when I was grown, it was very necessary that one develop the 'proper' attitude toward authority."

Note the gender differences that are reflected in the response pattern presented in Table 3.15. Nearly one-third of the women (32 percent) isolated their mothers as a major source of encouragement (and none said that their fathers were) compared with only 9 percent of men; and more women than men rated their parents' as either indifferent to or downright discouraging to their efforts. These latter findings are compatible with more traditional notions about the appropriate roles that men and women should play in society and with the gender-specific parental reinforcement patterns reported by some researchers (Barker 1993; Higginbotham and Cannon 1988). They are also consistent with the traditional divisions of household labor that we noted earlier as present in the childhood homes of our respondents. Consistent with the gender differences observed in the table, we also found, in female responses to this question, a certain ambivalence in parental attitudes. The remarks of a forty-three-year-old female respondent demonstrate this tendency: "Despite the fact that my parents encouraged me to perform well at school, I certainly got the message . . . that a good education was not as important for a girl because one day she would marry and have children." These gender differences notwithstanding, our analysis of the responses of our participants revealed that a sizable majority of their parents provided them encouragement during their early educational careers.

Older Siblings' Encouragement

We were also interested in any role(s) that older siblings might have played in encouraging respondents' early educational efforts. Nineteen respondents reported having older siblings, so the analysis below will be confined to these respondents. Our analysis of their responses yielded three categories: "positive influence;" "negative influence;" and "indifferent."

Following is a response we coded in the "positive influence" category. A twenty-seven-year-old female respondent remarks about her older brother: "He was the only relatively persistent person who would ask what my plans were after high school. He encouraged me to visit him [at college], convinced me that I could find a way to pay for college, and even suggested that I could live with him if the money ran out." On the other hand, the remarks of a thirty-four-year-old female led us to place her in the "indifferent" category: "My eldest brother, _____, has a [college] degree and is currently a _____. I do not believe his experiences influenced my own goals and plans." An example of a "negative" sibling influence on a respondent's educational goals is from the remarks of a thirty-eight-year-old male who noted:

All of my siblings graduated from high school but none went directly to college. My older brother started business school to avoid the draft, but he dropped out voluntarily and eventually was drafted. All three of my sisters took jobs immediately after high school. If my older brother or sister would have paved the way and gone to college, it may have been easier for me. However, that didn't happen.

The distribution of respondents across these categories is presented in Table 3.17. As shown there, approximately four in ten (42 percent) of respondents with older siblings reported that their own educational plans/goals were influenced positively by those of their older siblings; nearly half (47 percent) claimed that the educational attainments of their older siblings had no effect one way or the other on their plans/goals; and slightly more than one in ten reported that their older siblings experiences had a negative influence on their plans/goals. Gender of respondent had an impact on the pattern of response, with female respondents more likely to claim an "indifferent" or "negative" influence of older siblings' educational experiences on their own educational goals/plans, while males were more evenly split between "positive" and "indifferent."

Since we were also interested in how the levels of older siblings' educational success might influence respondents' opinions about these influences, we divided older siblings' educational experiences into "high school graduate" and "more than high school graduate" and then cross-classified the respondents' answers to the question by this educational attainment variable. These data are displayed in Table 3.18. The pattern of response at the top of the table demonstrates that older siblings' levels of education did not have a strong influence on the patterning of response to the question. Those respondents with older siblings with more than a high school education were almost evenly divided between "positive" and "indifferent" in their assessments of the impacts that their older siblings' educational experiences had on their own educational goals/plans. The effect of gender of respondent reported above is present in these data as well. Slightly more female respondents, even those whose older siblings had gone beyond high school, were either "indifferent" or "negative" in their assessments of the impact(s) of their older siblings' educational experiences on their own goals/plans in this area of endeavor.[5] Thus, in contrast to the positive influences of parents' on respondents' educational goals/plans reported earlier in this section of the chapter (even if they were somewhat colored by gender), respondents were more evenly divided as to whether their older siblings' experiences in the educational system had a positive effect on their own goals/plans regarding education or were simply indifferent to those goals/plans.

Table 3.17
Respondents' Perceptions About Impact of Siblings on Their Educational Goals or Plans

N(%)

Samples

Nature of Impact	Total	Males	Females
Positive	8(42)	6(46)	2(33)
Indifferent	9(47)	6(46)	3(50)
Negative	2(11)	1(8)	1(17)
N(%)	19(100)	13(100)	6(100)
NA	23		

[Reliability=92%]

Teachers' Encouragement

A third group that might have had an influence on our respondents' early educational goals/plans/successes was teachers. We asked our respondents if there were any of their teachers who were important in encouraging their educational growth and development. After reading their responses to the question, we coded them into several categories including "one;" "several;" "all;" or "none." The results of our coding are displayed in Table 3.19. If the first three categories are combined (each of which is one of the "yes" categories), we find that two-thirds of the respondents (67 percent of males, 69 percent of females) indicated that one, several, or all of their teachers had exercised positive influence in directing their paths toward higher education. In contrast, nearly one-third of the respondents (32 percent) answered "no" to the question. Gender of respondent had no impact on the pattern of response to this question. A typical "yes" response to this question comes from a fifty-seven-year-old male respondent: "Most of my high school teachers encouraged me to make plans for going to college. Two of them, who were from middle-class backgrounds, provided valuable guidance when it came time to choose a college." A good example of respondents who indicated that their teachers had no influence on their educational goals/plans/successes, was that of a thirty-four-year-old female respondent: "No, unfortunately none of my teachers were particularly encouraging. I think that they didn't feel someone with my particular background would go on to university so they didn't bother to encourage me in any way." We also queried respondents about their perceptions of the class

Table 3.18
Formal Educational Attainments of Older Siblings and Their Influence on the Educational Plans of Respondents

N(%)

Total Sample

Older Sibling's Education	Positive	Indifferent	Negative	N
High School Graduate	1(25)	2(50)	1(25)	4
More than High School	7(47)	7(47)	1(6)	15
N(%)	8(100)	9(100)	2(100)	19

By Gender

Education of Sibling	Positive		Indifferent		Negative	
	Male	Female	Male	Female	Male	Female
High School Graduate	—	1(17)	—	2(33)	—	1(100)
More than High School	5(100)	2(83)	4(67)	3(69)	1(100)	
N(%)	5(100)	3(100)	4(100)	5(100)	1(100)	1(100)

background of the teachers who had been supportive, and although few remembered enough about their teachers' backgrounds to respond to this request, three out of the four who did mentioned that they suspected that their teachers had, themselves, come from working-class backgrounds.

Several of the findings reviewed above concerning the influences that other persons such as parents, siblings, and teachers might have had on the educational careers of respondents seem especially important. First, and perhaps most important, the data indicate that the parents of our study's respondents were an important—perhaps the single most important—source of encouragement for their early education efforts, and, moreover, the data show that the more formal educational training the parents had themselves acquired, the more supportive of their childrens' efforts they were (although a majority of all parents, regardless of level of education, were supportive). Second, the support that parents were acknowledged to have provided was tempered by the gender of the respondent, with males claiming more support from parents than females. Third, in contrast to the important role that parents played in encouraging our

Table 3.19
Respondents' Perceptions of Any Teachers Who Were Particularly Important in Directing Their Path toward Higher Education

N(%)

Number of Important Teachers	Sample		
	Total	*Males*	*Females*
One	6(17)	3(19)	3(17)
Several	13(38)	7(44)	6(33)
All	4(12)	1(06)	3(17)
None	11(32)	5(31)	6(33)
N(%)	34(100)	16(100)	18(100)
NA	8		

[Reliability=86%]

respondents' educational efforts, their older siblings seem to have had a more ambivalent influence on their efforts. A majority of the respondents viewed their older siblings' educational experiences as having an "indifferent" influence on their own plans/goals, with about 40 percent viewing them as "positive" (with a few of our respondents viewing their older siblings' influences as negative). Male respondents were slightly more likely to rate their older siblings' influence as "positive" or "indifferent," whereas female respondents were more likely to rate them as "indifferent" or "negative." Fourth, two-thirds of the respondents, both male and female, also rate their teachers as having made a positive contribution to their early educational experiences (although the remaining third indicated just the opposite). The few respondents who did mention the class background of their teachers noted that they believed them to have come from either working-class or lower-middle-class backgrounds.

CONCLUSIONS

In this chapter, we have examined aspects of the child- and early adulthoods of our sample of sociologists from working-class backgrounds. By all outward appearances, these are people who have "made something" of themselves, thus fulfilling the expectations laid out for them by their parents since their early childhoods. Having achieved a considerable measure of social mobility, their accomplishments challenge the tenets of theories explaining the intergenerational reproduction of social class and, thus, offer us an interesting explanatory challenge.

On the one hand, it seems clear that these respondents spent their child- and early adulthoods within working-class environments and that these environments impacted their lives in a number of ways, most of them negative. For example, they lived within households whose domestic labor was heavily gender organized, many of them reported suffering either absolute or relative material deprivation as children, the cultural environment(s) of their homes (and neighborhoods) contained few of the elements of "high" culture that are more typically found in middle- and upper-middle-class homes (and neighborhoods), and many of them reported having been ashamed of parents, family, neighborhood, and of the working class in general at some point in their lives. Furthermore, most of the respondents attended schools that were either working class or a mixture of working class and lower middle class, and many of them reported that these early educational experiences were more negative than positive.

If we were to view the particular subset of the chapter's findings summarized in the previous paragraph through the theoretical lenses of scholars such as Aronowitz and Giroux (1991) Bourdieu (1984,1986) Coleman (1988) and Kohn (1969) who have stressed the important role that a family's relative material, cultural, and social resources play in the intergenerational transmission of class, we would likely conclude that the probability that children and young adults from such backgrounds would achieve substantial upward mobility from the class of their parents is negligible.

Yet, despite the limitations of many aspects of their working-class backgrounds described above, the subjects who are the focus of this investigation are either in the process of, or have already moved into the upper middle class of American society. How can this be explained? From our viewpoint, two of the chapter's other findings offer important clues that help us offer, at this point in the study at least, a partial explanation for how these children from working-class backgrounds were able to move, as Dews and Law (1995) put in the title to their book on working-class academics, "so far from home." First, a large majority of our respondents rated themselves as either "above average" or as "high achievers" when asked to characterize themselves as students during their early educational careers. Being "above average" or a "high achiever," especially when coming from a background that was limited in terms of material and cultural circumstances, must be part of the answer. A second piece of evidence that we uncovered that is consistent with the successes of the members of our sample of sociologists from working-class backgrounds is that most of them reported having received a great deal of support and encouragement from parents and teachers.

A third piece of evidence that is also a part of our explanation, and which we will explore in greater detail in the next chapter, is the fact that most of our respondents also reported that they learned early the *value of hard work.*

Combining these three—being a strong student, receiving support from significant others, and being willing to work hard to reach one's goals—seems like an ideal combination of ingredients for success, perhaps even enough to overcome the material, cultural, and social limitations of a working-class background.

We should also remind the reader that there were a number of gender differences in response to the questions we raised and that these, too, must be a part of any explanation that we construct. On the negative side, female respondents were more likely to report being ashamed of their families than were men, and they were also more likely than men to report having been discouraged by their parents and older siblings from setting their educational goals too high when compared with their male counterparts. On the positive side, female respondents were also more likely than their male counterparts to report being high achievers; they were also more likely to identify their mothers in particular as important sources of support in their educational efforts.[6] To conclude, if the evidence presented thus far in the study—both that which is more consistent with and that which is less consistent with the eventual academic and professional successes of the subjects of our research—has any larger meaning, it is that it should remind us that social mobility, like many other aspects of human behavior, is the end product of a complex process that mixes personal, interpersonal, and structural influences in ways that often defy theoretical simplification or summarization. In the next chapter, we continue our exploration of the lives of this sample of academics from working-class backgrounds by examining their perceptions of the impact(s) of class on the second period in their life cycles—their experiences in college and graduate school.

NOTES

1. We include in this category not only parents but also other adult significant others such as stepparents who were a part of the household when our respondents were maturing. We will henceforth use the term "parent" to refer to these individuals, since most of our respondents grew to maturity in households that were headed by their biological parents—the few exceptions to this pattern either lived alone in a single-parent family following a divorce or the death of one of their biological parents, or they shared a home with a biological parent and a nonbiologically related adult.

2. For mothers, we added a fifth category—housewife—so that we could distinguish between those mothers who worked outside the home and those who did not.

3. We decided to leave this respondent in the data set despite the marginal middle-class status of her father. We based this decision on, among other things, the unpredictable (and often materially deprived) standard of living of the family, its frequent geographic mobility in search of employment opportunities for the father as he lost one job after another, the fact that the family's residences were usually located within working-class neighborhoods, and the respondent's own strong self-identification as a daughter of the working class.

4. The formal skills/credentials resources of the parents of our respondents offer additional evidence to support this conclusion. The average educational attainment for our respondents' fathers was 10.3 years, whereas that for their mothers was only slightly higher at 11.3 years. Furthermore, nearly half (more than 45 percent) of our respondents' parents had no more than a high school education.

5. The fact that female respondents got less encouragement from their older siblings, even those with advanced educations, than their male counterparts, is consistent with the finding above that their parents did not encourage them as much as did the parents of male respondents. Our interpretation of this difference offered above—that it reflects the larger culture's assessment of appropriate roles for males and females—seems to apply equally well in this situation.

6. Although we view these gender differences as important, we should also remind the reader that female and male respondents' perceptions on the various issues addressed in this chapter overlapped more than they diverged; this suggests that their common background within the working class exercised a powerful influence on their lives despite the gender differences we observed.

4

Realizing That We Could "Make the Grade"

Being a white, working-class male in a stable household made me secure and comfortable. I believed in the "American Dream," which meant that I could do or be almost anything I wanted. That I didn't aspire to be a professional or manager was like not thinking that I could fly, it wasn't a possibility. I figured I was going to do some type of blue-collar work, get married, have children, and own my own house—a fifty-four-year-old male respondent.

Ironically, one of the most imposing obstacles to higher education facing the group we studied was not their lack of ability but rather their *unawareness* of the routes to college and the possibilities connected to a college education. Although children of middle-class families are brought up with the expectation that college will unquestionably follow high school, this idea is foreign to many working-class families. For most working-class kids, finishing high school means coming of age, being "on your own," no longer under parental control. Given the emphasis on obedience in the child-rearing practices of working-class families, children are understandably anxious to become independent. But aside from the issue of parental control of the household, the children of working-class families are presented with a different set of expectations. Pursuing a "profession" is not a part of their family histories. There are no doctors or lawyers or college professors in their families. Their only contacts with such people are formal. It is not clear to them how someone reaches such a position, and the social distance imposed by superior social rank prohibits the sort of informal interaction that would allow them to discover how to do so.

BEYOND THE THREE KEY INFLUENCES OF CHILDHOOD

This chapter focuses attention on the second period in the life cycles of our respondents—the period during which they attended college and went on to receive their graduate training. We hypothesized in the last chapter that, for these individuals, success in achieving unusual social mobility can be explained by looking at three important factors: (1) they were smart, (2) they were encouraged by significant others to excel in school, and (3) they were taught to value hard work. In this chapter, we show how these factors continued to have an effect during their undergraduate and graduate educations, even as one of them began to change; we also introduce here a fourth factor in our equation that explains the successes of the members of our sample of sociologists from working-class backgrounds.

Although the first two of these factors remained closely tied to the success of our respondents, the third (the level of encouragement received from significant others) began to take on a different character during this period of their lives. Graduation from high school usually means, for working-class kids anyway, the beginning of one's work life. That may mean attending a trade school, working as an apprentice, or even joining the military. But it does *not* mean spending any more years than necessary being supported by your parents, especially if the goal is not clearly justifiable. Within blue-collar culture, the only justification for continuing one's education is to qualify for a job that pays more. Goals as unspecific or ambiguous as "furthering" an education are simply outside of the realm of comprehension for most of the members of the working class. Indeed, U.S. society in general and blue-collar culture in particular has a history of anti-intellectualism (Hofstadter 1963). To encourage one's children to do well in elementary and high school is to encourage them to become good citizens, to show that they know how to behave themselves and work hard. But to encourage adult children to postpone accepting the responsibility of earning their own living is, in some ways, to neglect the parental responsibility to prepare those children for adult life.

Many of our respondents' parents *did* encourage them to attend college, though certainly not out of a well-informed understanding of the process of getting a college degree and its consequences. Their encouragement was much more general, similar to the advice to "make something" of themselves. Such parental encouragement often came from their own dissatisfaction with the conditions of a blue-collar job or the more generalized idea that a college degree was an opportunity for more money and a better life. But even those parents who encouraged their children to continue their educations beyond high school became increasingly less able to comprehend their child's continuing education beyond some point, in the case of our respondents, usually the bachelor's degree.

The choice of sociology as a major was perhaps the first indication to the parents that their working-class child had gotten off course. Many working-class parents have never heard of sociology and, even with repeated explanations and the passage of many years, some never understand exactly what the field is that their son or daughter finds so engrossing.

Thus, the encouragement to do well in school that these individuals received from their families diminished with their increasing years of formal education. For some, their family's expectation was that high school was enough; for others, it was a bachelor's degree. But all, at some point in their educational paths, as they moved beyond the point in their educations that made sense to their families, were forced to venture on alone, into unfamiliar territory. Perhaps there was some consolation in knowing that if one failed, the family wouldn't grasp the full impact of that either. On the other hand, however, many successful children from the working class have had to deal with the disappointment of not being able to truly share their successes with many of their closest relatives. Some were fortunate enough to receive encouragement from their instructors; some report the significant influence of mentors. For many, the years during which they received their undergraduate, and *especially* their graduate education, were lonely ones in several respects, not the least of which was this shift in familial recognition and encouragement of their efforts.

THE FOURTH KEY TO SUCCESS

One of the reasons that so many parents, both working class and middle class, encouraged their children to attend college during this period is that higher education was expanding and becoming available to many who had never had access before. Thus, we add a fourth factor to the equation explaining the success of this group of academics from working-class families: the growth of higher education since World War II.

The history of higher education in the United States since World War II is a picture of massive expansion. The postwar economic boom, the GI Bill, the baby boom in the population, all are factors that had an encouraging effect on the growth of American colleges and universities in the second half of the twentieth century (Ryan and Sackrey 1984).

The postwar economic boom and its accompanying rapid scientific and technological advancement created a demand for a more educated work force. During this time the United States inaugurated a system of mass higher education that raised the proportion of eighteen to twenty-one-year-olds enrolled in institutions of higher education from 15 percent in 1940 to over 50 percent by 1970 (Trow 1977). Thanks to the GI Bill, over one million veterans entered college by the early 1950s and another million used the bill to start their own businesses (Heilbroner and Singer 1994). Among the effects of this expansion of opportunity was a "creaming process" (Gilbert and Kahl 1993). This is a process whereby, in an environment of limited access, there is a pool of potential students, contenders for access to higher education that form a kind of queue. The best students from the most advantaged families, heading up the queue, are most likely to enroll when access begins to open up.

As the door opens wider, the most ambitious and talented, as well as those individuals from the higher socioeconomic status families who were previously excluded, take more advantage of the opportunities as they become available. The "cream of the crop" of children from working-class families are *only then* able to gain entry, but the most disadvantaged remain outside the door (Gilbert and Kahl 1993). In the period following World War II, with the advent of mass access to higher education, a growing number of children from working-class backgrounds became the *first* in their families to ever attend college. As more members of the working class entered colleges and universities and became teachers, they, in turn, encouraged others to follow in their paths. Thus, this was a peculiar period in the history of higher education. It was a time when class boundaries became more fluid than ever before. However, the individuals who crossed those boundaries, while achieving unusual upward mobility, were cast into the uncertainty of trying to maneuver in the unfamiliar terrain of the middle-class culture that they encountered in college. Much previous research has documented that the cultural differences between the working and the middle class exacerbate the problems that working-class children face in adapting to the middle-class-dominated world of the university (cf. Rubin 1994; Ryan and Sackrey 1984; Sennett and Cobb 1972; Shostak 1969). In this chapter we explore the undergraduate and graduate careers of the members of our sample.

THE UNDERGRADUATE YEARS

The Source of the Undergraduate Degree

The first question we asked respondents about their undergraduate careers was the source of their undergraduate degree and how they chose the institution from which it was granted. The rationale for this question stems from the point raised by researchers that the family environments within which working-class students are socialized not only provide less information about the importance of choosing a good college/university but also are less able to provide the material resources that could make it possible to entertain a wider range of choice among institutions (Bourdieu 1984; Bowles 1972; Rubin 1994; Shostak 1969).

The importance of the long range effects of one's choice of a college cannot be overstated. As Rubin (1994:128) points out, "our optimistic statistics about the benefits of a college education obscure fundamental truths about class and gender differences." Moreover,

[They] make no distinction between the kind of low-prestige school a working-class youth is likely to attend and the elite college or university that educates the child of a professional family. But it's clear to anyone who is not blinded by our myth of classlessness, that the education is superior and the opportunities for mobility greater with a degree from Harvard or Princeton than one from Clearview State. If the average earnings of college graduates were broken down by school—which would, by and large, reflect a breakdown by class—the annual income of the Clearview graduate would be significantly less than the one from Princeton.

Although we have no direct measure of the relative prestige of the undergraduate institutions our respondents attended, we were able to rank institutions according to the highest level of degree offered by the sociology program. We coded these institutional sources of the respondents' degrees into four different levels, ranging from those who were graduated from four-year colleges that offered bachelor's degrees in sociology, to those whose undergraduate degrees came from a research university (i.e., one that offered the Ph.D. in sociology). Table 4.1 displays these data. As shown there, despite the predictions of previous research, half of the respondents completed their undergraduate degrees at research universities; approximately a third of them were graduated from four-year colleges with undergraduate programs in the discipline; and the remainder were graduated from universities that offered the M.A. degree. The impacts of gender on the source of the undergraduate degrees of our respondents were minimal.

It is an intriguing coincidence that some of our respondents, by attending state universities, were exposed to sociology departments with research emphases. Many upper-middle-class kids were attending small, expensive, liberal arts colleges like Swarthmore or Brown. Their ideas about graduate school were, for many, already formed before attending college at all. But for these young college students from working-class backgrounds (who had probably never even heard of places like Swarthmore or Brown), having a chance to attend *any* college at all was remarkable. Had it not been for their exposure, often in state universities, to graduate students and graduate programs, many of them would not have known about such possibilities. We next look at why particular institutions were selected and, as will become apparent, the prestige or stature of the institution was only a small part of the decision.

Choosing a College/University

Examining the responses to a question asking how our respondents chose their undergraduate institutions, revealed a total of eleven major reasons that received at least one mention (because most respondents mentioned more than one reason and there was no way to select the best or most important reason for many of them, we simply coded each reason mentioned). As displayed in Table 4.2, a total of fifty-eight reasons were mentioned—the two most frequent were "proximity to home" (thirteen nominations) and "affordability" (twelve nominations). Six respondents mentioned both these factors as being important, whereas four mentioned these two along with "live at home" (six nominations)

Table 4.1

Respondents' Self-Reports of the Source of Their Undergraduate Degrees

	N(%)		
	Samples		
Source of Degree	*Total*	*Males*	*Females*
Four-Year College with B.A. in Sociology	12(33)	7(33)	5(33)
University with M.A. in Sociology	6(17)	3(14)	3(20)
University with Ph.D. in Sociology	18(50)	11(52)	7((47)
Totals	36(100)	21(99)	15(100)
Foreign University	3		
NA	3		

as major motivations for their choice.[1] When the responses to these three categories were combined into a single group, it received a total of thirty-one (or 53 percent) of the nominations offered by our respondents. The category "quality of education or program" was the third most frequently mentioned reason for choice of undergraduate institution; it received eight nominations (or 14 percent of the total). There were modest gender differences in response to this question: Males were more likely than females to mention "affordability" as a major criterion (28 percent versus 17 percent); females were more likely to mention "quality of education or program" than males (21 percent versus 10 percent); and males were more likely than females to mention "easy admissions" as a criterion that influenced their choice (three male respondents listed this factor, whereas none of the female respondents did so). The fact that over half of the reasons mentioned as important influences on respondents' choices of undergraduate institutions were either "proximity to home," "affordability," or "live at home," when combined with the fact that "quality of education or program" received only 14 percent of the total nominations, is compatible with the notion advanced in Chapter 1 (and reinforced by the data reviewed in Chapter 3) that children from the working class, because of their family

Table 4.2
Respondents' Reasons for Choice of Undergraduate Institution

N(%)

Samples

Reason for Choice	Total	Males	Females
Proximity to Home	13(22)	7(22)	6(23)
Affordable	12(21)	8(25)	4(15)
Quality of Education	8(14)	3(9)	5(19)
Live at Home	6(10)	3(9)	3(12)
Scholarship/Aid	5(8)	2(6)	3(12)
Family/Friend History	5(8)	3(9)	2(8)
Lack of Guidance	1(2)	1(3)	—
To Get away from Home	1(2)	—	1(4)
Low Aspirations/ Doubts about Abilities	1(2)	—	1(4)
Easy Admissions	3(5)	3(9)	—
Unclear	1(2)	—	1(4)
Other	2(3)	2(6)	—
Totals*	58(100)	32(98)	26(101)
NA	2		

[Reliability = 84%]

---

*"Totals" refers to total mentioned by all respondents and is greater than the number of respondents since they could mention more than one reason for choosing their undergraduate institution.

background, are likely to have at their disposal fewer resources to assist them in acquiring higher educational credentials than do many middle-class children. This fact is compatible with choosing schools based on more "practical" criteria.

Revisiting the Value of Hard Work

We next explored the issue of how respondents supported themselves during their undergraduate careers. Recall from Chapter 1 that Bourdieu (1984), Bowles (1972), and Rubin (1994), among others, have noted that working-class families simply do not, as a rule, have the economic resources necessary to support their children's higher educational efforts. Our review of respondents' answers to this question yielded a six-category scheme that included "work," "loans/grants," "family," "scholarships," "welfare," and "unclear" (reporting the findings for this issue is made more complicated by the fact that many respondents mentioned that they had supported themselves by more than one means; as a result, we coded each means mentioned). We report these findings in Table 4.3. Notice first the total number of times each means of support was mentioned (in rank order): work (thirty-three nominations), loans/grants (ten nominations), family (eight nominations), scholarships (eight nominations), welfare (one nomination, and unclear (one nomination). Also note the number of factors mentioned as the *sole* means of support (again, in rank order): work (fourteen); and scholarships (one). These findings indicate that work was nominated by a majority of the respondents as at least *one* of the major means by which they supported themselves during their undergraduate careers and as the *sole* means of support for fourteen of them. There were modest gender differences in response to this question: Females were more likely than males to mention loans and grants as at least one of their major means of support (21 percent versus 12 percent), and males were slightly more likely than females to mention work as at least one of their major means of support (58 percent versus 50 percent).

What impressed us most about the responses to this question was just how much effort our respondents were willing expend in order to pursue and obtain their undergraduate degrees. For example, one of them mentioned that she had to rely on welfare for support during a portion of her undergraduate studies, and another (also a female) offered the following response to this question: "Work, work, work. I have held a multitude of jobs since high school, including but not limited to truck driver, bartender, secretary, blueprinter, delivery driver, dispatcher, loading-dock worker, and nurse's aide." A number of respondents also mentioned having held full-time jobs; several stated that they worked for more than forty hours per week during portions of their undergraduate educational careers. It is also clear from the data (as we anticipated, given the literature on the resources of working-class families) that these respondents got little financial assistance from their families during this period in their educational careers (only eight of the forty mentioned family as

Table 4.3
Respondents' Reports of How They Supported Themselves during
   Undergraduate Studies

N(%)

Samples

Means of Suppport	Total	Males	Females
Work	33(54)	19(58)	14(50)
(only)	14	6	8
Loans/Grants	10(16)	4(12)	6(21)
(only)	—	—	—
Family	8(13)	4(12)	4(14)
(only)	—	—	—
Scholarships	8(13)	5(15)	3(11)
(only)	1	—	1
Welfare	1(2)	—	1(4)
(only)	—	—	—
Unclear	1(2)	1(3)	—
	—	—	—
Totals*	61(100)	33(100)	28(100)

[Reliability=93%]

---

*"Totals" refers to total mentioned by all respondents and is greater than the number of respondents since most mentioned more than one means of support.

one of their means of support and none said that family was their sole means of support).

Continuity in the Undergraduate Career

Given the important role that material resources play in enabling a student both to attend college and to complete the degree and our knowledge about the relative material circumstances of the families of these respondents (see Chapter 3 above), we next asked them whether they had gone straight from high school to college or whether they had to make some "stops" along the way. Our inspection of their responses to this question yielded a three-category scheme: "no interruptions between completing high school and the college degree," "interruption between completing high school and entering/completing the college degree," and "interruption during the college career." Nearly two-thirds (63 percent) of our respondents went "straight through" from completion of high school to their undergraduate degree, about a quarter did not immediately begin college after graduating from high school, and about 10 percent interrupted their college career for one reason or another (see Table 4.4). When we examined the distribution of respondents across these three categories by gender, there were no differences among those who went "straight through" from high school graduation to their undergraduate degrees, yet, among those who did not go straight through, there were some differences—females were more likely than males to have a "break" between the completion of high school and the beginning of college, and males were more likely to have had an interruption in their college careers once they had begun them. When we examined the reasons for those who had "interrupted" careers, we found various factors cited by those who did not begin college immediately upon completion of high school. For example, four of the respondents cited "low aspirations/ignorance" as the reason. A typical response from this group is that of a thirty-nine-year-old female: "I did not go directly from high school to college. Nobody ever mentioned college to me when I was in high school. I had no idea what college was until I enrolled in [a] vo-tech program." Two (both women) cited "family issues" (i.e., they got married in the interim), and a third said she didn't feel comfortable about the idea of attending college. For those who interrupted their college careers at some point between entry and earning the degree, three cited insufficient financial resources as the major reason, and a fourth said he felt guilty about attending college. This last respondent, a male, reported: "I dropped out . . . . due to guilt, inability to admit to my peers/coworkers that I was taking course[s]." These data show that a majority of the respondents were able to move from high school through their undergraduate degrees without interruption. This finding would be somewhat surprising given the relative paucity of material resources of many of their families (as noted in Chapter 3), were it not for the fact that most respondents reported working their way through college and/or depending heavily on loans, grants, and scholarships. We should also remind the reader that one of the respondents whose remarks led us to place her in the "not interrupted" category nonetheless took thirteen years to finish her undergraduate degree.

Characterizations of the Undergraduate Careers

In order to include a truly "open-ended" question on this subject, we asked our respondents to describe their undergraduate careers in their own words. We felt that such a question would give them maximum flexibility in constructing their answers without any preconceptions about how they should answer it (thus, these responses might give us different insights into their undergraduate careers than we might get through more "structured" questions). As might be expected, given the approach we took to the issue, the responses we got were diverse and

Table 4.4
Respondents' Self-Reports on Interruptions in Their Undergraduate Studies

	N(%)		
	Samples		
Career Paths	*Total*	*Males*	*Females*
No Interruption Between Completing High School and the College Degree	24(63)	12(63)	12(63)
Interruption Between Completing High School and Entering/Completing College Degree	10(26)	4(21)	6(32)
Interruption During College Career	4(11)	3(16)	1(5)
Totals	38(100)	19(100)	19(100)
NA	3		

[Reliability = 97%]

this diversity made it impossible to summarize them in tabular form. However, our analysis of their responses led us to select seven "themes" that seem to pervade their responses.[2] The first was the problem of limited finances. A twenty-seven-year-old male wrote:

A tightrope. I believe now that I was lucky to make it through. At any given time I could have fallen through the cracks, either monetarily, academically, or social-psychologically. At one point, due to lack of money, I ate peanut butter sandwiches for an entire week and nothing else. This sounds funny now, but at the time I was so embarrassed I would not tell anyone.

A second theme that stood out from the respondents' remarks about their undergraduate careers was the realization that they were less well prepared than their classmates. A fifty-seven-year-old male put it this way: "My undergraduate educational career was both challenging and exciting. Even though I had graduated from high school at the head of my class, I was not adequately prepared for a rigorous academic program. I had to work harder than many middle class students who had graduated from better high schools." A second respondent, a forty-one-year-old female, offered this response: "My first shock in college was that most of my peers had received a better high school education than me. I was always top in my class, but in college I realized what a poor education I really received." In this context, remember that most of the respondents had attended schools, at least early in their public educational careers, that were working class. Such schools, as Willis (1977) reminds us, often do not often have as a goal the preparation of their students for college-level work; they are often also inferior to those schools in which a majority of the students are middle class.

The third theme is the fact that very few of our respondents initially chose sociology as a major when they entered college. Most of them selected more applied fields such as engineering, nursing, teaching, or medicine as their majors. This is not surprising since others have mentioned that first-generation college students are much more likely to pick what might be called "applied" careers when compared with their middle-class counterparts (cf. Ryan and Sackrey 1984; Shostak 1969). The remarks of a twenty-eight-year-old female respondent are typical of those who took this path: "I began my career in engineering. . . . I then moved to pre-pharmacy, pre-business . . . etc. During my pre-business stage I took my first sociology course. I finally transferred into sociology"[3]

The fourth theme in the respondents' descriptions of their college careers was the conflict between their need to work and their academic careers and social lives. A forty-four-year-old female's remarks on the subject are typical: "I did not participate in school activities because I was working so many hours off campus." A forty-two-year-old female wrote: "As I mentioned above, there was a great deal of difference between me and most of the other students. I worked part time as well as went to school and never had the time to socialize and at times to afford the types of activities that the other students could."

A fifth issue that struck us as important in our examination of our respondents' characterizations of their undergraduate careers was that a number of them spent many years acquiring their undergraduate degrees. A sixty-four-year-old female respondent noted: "I took about thirteen years to compete the undergraduate degree. This was because of working full time, commuting, and also because not all courses I needed for fulfilling degree requirements were offered every time I had a time slot available." Another, forty-four-year-old female remarked that: "It took me ten years to achieve my undergraduate degree: The first eight years were part-time and the last two years I went to college were full time. . . . I never had the luxury of just "being" a college student." This particular theme resonates with findings noted earlier in the chapter concerning the necessity for our students to mix school and work.

A sixth issue that emerged from these respondents' characterizations of their undergraduate careers was their realization that there were important class differences between themselves and their classmates. In the words of a thirty-one-year-old male: "I was alienated and felt totally out of my element since my undergraduate school was relatively elite and had a student body made up overwhelmingly of middle/upper-middle-class students."

The final issue that caught our attention when reading our respondents' replies to this question was their perception(s) that they were far more interested in and involved in social activism than many of their undergraduate peers. A forty-four-year-old male makes note of the transformation he underwent during his undergraduate years:

Upon entering college my political views were on the far right. I also felt a growing sense of responsibility to become politically active. It began with my membership in the Young Americans for Freedom and student government. . . . This awakening of political activism and ideological shift became key aspects and motivators for my continued education as well as professional career.

From this evidence it appears that, while this sample of sociologists from working-class backgrounds, no doubt, shared many common experiences with other students from different class backgrounds during their undergraduate years, there also appear to be have been some important differences between themselves and their classmates that are related to their class backgrounds.

THE GRADUATE YEARS

Deciding on a Professional Career

The first issue we asked respondents to address about their graduate careers was *when* and *why* they decided that they wanted to pursue a career in sociology. We coded their responses to the first part of the question into four categories: "during undergraduate studies," "in between undergraduate and graduate studies," "during graduate studies," and "other." The distribution of respondents across these categories is presented in Table 4.5,A. As shown there, more than eight in ten reported that they had decided on their careers as academic sociologists either during their undergraduate studies (44 percent), in-between undergraduate and graduate school (6 percent) or during graduate school (36 percent). A fourth category, labeled "other," with 14 percent of the total, contained those who had different routes to their decision that included careers in the nonacademic sector (both "secular" and "sacred"), serving as a VISTA volunteer, and serving as a high school teacher. There were sizable gender differences in response to this question—females were much more likely than males to have decided to pursue a career in sociology while they were still undergraduates (56 versus 33 percent), whereas more males made their decisions during graduate school or after they had pursued another career for a number of years (these two categories sum to 66 percent for males and to 34 percent for females).

We were also curious as to why respondents decided to embark on careers as sociologists. In this second part of the question, for purposes of comparison, we divided our respondents into two subsamples based on their responses to the

Table 4.5
Respondents' Perceptions of When (and Why) They Decided to Become a College Professor and Sociologist

N(%)
A. When the Decision Was Made

	Total	Males	Females
During Undergraduate Studies	16(44)	6(33)	10(56)
"In-between" Undergraduate and Graduate Studies	2(6)	—	2(11)
During Graduate Studies	13(36)	8(44)	5(28)
Other*	5(14)	4(22)	1(6)
Totals	36(100)	18(99)	18(101)
Not Applicable	1		
No Answer	3		

B. Why the Decision was Made

Reason for Decision	Decision Made "Earlier"			Decision Made "Later"		
	Total	Males	Females	Total	Males	Females
Interest in Subject Matter	9(50)	4(67)	5(42)	5(38)	3(38)	2(40)
Early Experience with Role	4(22)	1(17)	3(25)	4(31)	2(25)	2(40)
Life Style	2(11)	1(17)	1(8)	2(15)	1(13)	1(20)
Mentoring	2(11)	—	2(17)	2(15)	1(13)	1(20)
Unclear	1(6)	—	1(8)	1(8)	1(13)	—
Totals	18(100)	6(101)	12(100)	13(100)	8(102)	5(100)

[Reliability = 90%]

---

*This category included two who had "finished" their educations and held full-time jobs in the private sector, one who had spent a year as a VISTA volunteer, one who was a minister, and one who had taught high school for a number of years before accepting a position as a college professor at a new college.

first half of the question—those who had made their decisions either during their undergraduate years or in between undergraduate and graduate school, and those whose decisions were made during graduate school (See Table 4.5,B). For the eighteen respondents who said they had made their decisions to pursue the career either during their undergraduate years or in between those and graduate school, nine (fifty percent) said their choice was motivated by their interest in sociology as a subject matter and the remainder mentioned early experiences with the academic role (22 percent), the professorial lifestyle (11 percent), or mentoring (11 percent). Gender had a modest impact on the responses of this group to this question—males were more likely than females to mention interest in the subject matter (67 percent versus 42 percent), whereas females were more evenly spread across the various categories. Two females also mentioned the importance that mentors played in their decision, but no male mentioned this motivator.

For those who made the decision while in graduate school, the modal response was also interest in the subject matter (38 percent mentioned this reason), but early experience with the academic role was nearly as important a reason for the decision (31 percent claimed this reason). In terms of gender, the only noteworthy differences were that more women than men mentioned early experience with the role, the academic lifestyle and mentoring as motivating factors.

The second set of issues we explored concerning the graduate educations of our respondents were the factors that influenced their choices of graduate institutions. Our expectation was that, since the families of working-class children have fewer economic, cultural, and social resources than their middle-class counterparts, their childrens' choices of institutions of higher education should be based on more "practical" criteria than those of their middle-class counterparts (Bourdieu 1986; Bowles 1972; Coleman 1988; Ryan and Sackrey 1984). Our inspection of their responses to this question resulted in a seven-item coding scheme that included: "convenience/location," "financial support," "affordable," "specialties/programs," "class environment," "institutional prestige," and "other." (since we did not constrain respondents' choices to a single factor and a number of them mentioned more than one, we coded each factor mentioned). Table 4.6 displays the distribution of our respondents' choices among these categories. As shown there, the two most frequently mentioned factors influencing respondents' choices of graduate programs were convenience/location (24 percent) and the availability of financial support (22 percent). The third most frequently mentioned factor was the specialty or program offered by the department (16 percent chose this factor). There were gender differences in response to this question—the modal category mentioned by females was financial support, but for males it was convenience/location (but financial support ranked a close second for them). Males were also slightly more likely than females to mention the specialties/programs offered by departments as an important influence on their choices of graduate programs.

Respondents were also asked whether they felt that their class background

Table 4.6
Respondents' Perceptions of Factors Influencing Choice of Ph.D. Program

N(%)

Samples

Reasons for Choice	Total	Males	Females
Convenience/Location	12(24)	7(28)	5(21)
Financial Support	11(22)	4(16)	7(29)
Affordable	6(12)	3(13)	3(13)
Specialities/ Programs	8(16)	5(20)	3(13)
"Class Environment"	4(8)	2(8)	2(8)
Prestige	2(4)	3(12)	3(13)
Other*	6(12)	3(12)	3(13)
Totals	49(98)	25(100)	24(101)
NA	2		

[Reliability = 76%]

---

*"Other" category includes six respondents whose motives for choice included such things as working with African-American students, getting the "best" education possible, departmental atmosphere, advice of mentors, and so on.

had played any role in influencing their choice of a graduate program. We coded their responses to this question into one of three categories: "yes," "no," or "did not mention." Of the total sample, fifteen (44 percent) responded that their class background had impacted their choice of graduate program, two (6 percent) said that it had not, and seventeen (50 percent) did not mention the issue (gender did not impact responses to this question). A typical response from a participant who said that class had impacted his decision is from a thirty-eight-year-old male who said:

I selected _____ University because it was the only affordable university in the _____ commuting area that offered a graduate program in sociology. _____ has a history, tradition, and reputation of being an avenue for working/lower middle class people to obtain degrees. I'm certain that my selection of _____ was influenced by my class background.

An example of a "no" response comes from a thirty-four year old female, who wrote:

At the doctoral level, three factors were important in my selection. First, how close the school was to _____. I applied primarily to schools within a day's drive. Second, the areas of specialization they had. I was interested in the area [*sic*] of the family and methodology at the time. The third factor was whether or not they would give me funding. I do not feel that class was a factor in any of these choices. Marriage seems to have been the deciding factor.

These findings generally support our theoretical expectations concerning the choice of a graduate institution since "practical" reasons were nominated more frequently than were "academic" reasons.

Quality of the Graduate Program

Given the fact that earlier research has hypothesized that academics from working-class backgrounds tend to graduate from institutions ranked lower in the academic prestige hierarchy than do sociologists from other class backgrounds (Ryan and Sackrey 1984:77), we were also interested in the sources of the doctorates of our respondents and in how they compared with those of the larger sociological community in terms of relative disciplinary prestige. After first identifying the sources of the respondents' doctorates, we assigned them disciplinary prestige rankings.[4] We then collapsed these rankings into six categories: "Top 5," "6-10," "11-25," "26-50," "51-75," and "76 or higher." As shown in Table 4.7, column 1, the modal prestige category for the sources of the Ph.D. for this sample of sociologists from working-class backgrounds is the 26–50 category (slightly more than one-third of the members of the sample's doctoral institutions were located there). If we use the top of this category as a bench mark, then 30 percent of our sample received Ph.D.s from departments ranked in the top twenty-five departments in the country, whereas the remaining 70 percent received their Ph.D.s from departments ranked lower than the top twenty-five.

When we compare these data with similar data from a sample drawn from the membership of the ASA, we find, in contrast, that 62 percent of the members of the latter group received their Ph.D.s from departments ranked in the top twenty-five, whereas only thirty-eight percent received their doctorates from departments ranked lower than the top twenty-five.[5] The large differences between the two samples in terms of the prestige of the source of the Ph.D. support the claim of earlier researchers that sociologists from working-class backgrounds are more likely than other sociologists to receive their graduate degrees from departments that are ranked lower in the disciplinary prestige

Table 4.7
A Comparison of the Relative Rank of the Source(s) of the Ph.D. for Our Sample of Sociologists from Working-Class Backgrounds and a Sample of the Membership of the American Sociological Association

N(%)

Samples

Prestige Ranking of Ph.D.-Granting Institution	*Sample of Working-Class Sociologists*	*Sample of Membership of the ASA*
Top 5	6(16)	8(17)
6–10	1(3)	5(11)
11–25	4(11)	16(34)
26–50	13(34)	11(23)
51–75	11(29)	6(13)
76 or higher	3(7)	1(2)
Totals	38(100)	47(100)

hierarchy (since gender differences did not impact these rankings, we do not include a breakdown by gender in the table).[6]

Source(s) of Material Support

Our next topic was how respondents supported themselves during their graduate educations. Once again, this question was motivated by the relative material circumstances of working-class families when compared with those of other classes (cf. Bourdieu 1984). Our inspection of respondents' replies to thisquestion yielded a total of eight categories: "work," "teaching/research assistantships," "fellowships/scholarships," "loans/grants," "family," "work-study," "welfare," and "unemployment insurance" (as with several earlier questions, since we did not restrict respondents to a single choice, a number of them mentioned more than one, and we coded each means of support mentioned). As noted in Table 4.8, a total of fifty-seven nominations were made by the respondents (the range of factors mentioned by each respondent was from one to four). More than four in ten mentioned work as an important means of

Table 4.8
Respondents Self-Reports of How they Supported Themselves during Graduate School

	N(%)		
	Samples		
Means of Support	Total	Males	Females
Work	25(44)	13(39)	12(50)
Teaching/Research Assistantships	12(21)	7(21)	5(21)
Fellowships/ Scholarships	9(16)	6(18)	3(13)
Loans/Grants	4(7)	2(6)	3(13)
Family	4(7)	2(6)	2(8)
Work-Study	2(4)	2(6)	—
Welfare	1(2)	—	1(4)
Unemployment Insurance	1(2)	1(3)	—
Totals	57(100)	33(99)	24(100)
NA (for grad)	4		
NA (for either)	3		

[Reliability=98%]

support, two in ten mentioned various types of graduate assistantships, and 16 percent mentioned fellowships and awards. There were gender differences in response to this question. For example, more females mentioned work and loans/grants than did men, and slightly more men mentioned fellowships/awards as their major means of support during their graduate studies. These findings closely parallel those for the respondents' undergraduate careers (see Table 4.3) with the exception that some of the burden of support for the respondents' graduate careers was lessened somewhat by the availability of teaching/research assistantships. Despite the availability of these various forms of support, however, it seems clear that material resources were a constant preoccupation for many of these respondents during their entire higher educational careers. In fact, one of them noted that she had borrowed $50,000 to support her higher education. Note as well that respondents' families' contributions did not rank nearly as high as the various forms of personal effort for either our respondents' undergraduate or graduate careers. This particular finding is consistent with research cited earlier that has stressed the marginal material resources of working-class families (cf. Bourdieu 1984; Rubin 1994; Shostak 1969) and the impacts of this marginality on their relative abilities to financially assist their children in acquiring higher educational credentials.

Continuities in Graduate Education

This knowledge about the modest material resources of working-class families (Rubin 1994; Shostak 1969) and the impact(s) of these modest resources on their abilities to assist their children materially during their pursuit of higher educational credentials motivated us to ask our respondents about the continuity of their graduate educational careers. We coded their responses to this question into three categories: "no interruption between the B.A. and the Ph.D." "interruption between the B.A. and entry into graduate school," and interruption during graduate school." Table 4.9 displays the distribution of our respondents across these categories. As displayed there, respondents were about evenly split between those who had no temporal interruption between graduating from college and finishing their graduate degrees (49 percent) and those who, for various reasons, experienced some sort of interruption either between the completion of college and entry into graduate school (11 percent) or during their graduate educations (40 percent of our respondents). For those who experienced educational interruptions of either kind, although there were a number of motives mentioned, the most persistent was their relative inability to support themselves (and sometimes their dependents) and continue their educations at the same time.

Themes in Graduate Educational Careers

Finally, in a manner similar to the way we asked our respondents to describe their undergraduate careers, we did the same for their graduate careers. As was the case with their undergraduate years, the question was worded to provide maximum freedom of response—it was put to them simply: "Describe your graduate educational career." Again, our approach to coding this question was to search for important themes present in their responses. For this portion of the respondents' higher educational experiences, we identified seven important themes that were present in their responses.[7] The first of these was the precariousness of their financial resources and the correlated necessity for work. In the words of a forty-four-year-old male respondent: "Upon entering the Ph.D.

Table 4.9
Respondents' Self-Reports about the Continuity of Their Graduate Careers

N(%)

Samples

Career "Type"	Total	Males	Females
No Interruption between B.A and Ph.D.	17(49)	10(53)	7(44)
Interruption Between B.A. and Graduate School	4(11)	3(16)	1(6)
Interruption during Graduate School	14(40)	6(32)	8(50)
Totals	35(100)	19(100)	16(100)
Did Not Respond to Graduate Portion of Question	4		

[Reliability = 95%]

program I again was confronted by insecurities and these were reinforced because I was one of those graduate students who came in *without* money." Although almost all respondents mentioned that they received some form of departmental/university support for at least some portion of their graduate careers, many of those who mentioned this issue did not have consistent support from the department/ university throughout their careers and, thus, had to seek other, external sources of financial support. Additional remarks of the same respondent just quoted above also apply here: "The second semester of my first year I picked up a job teaching an urban sociology course at a nearby state college. . . . I got a summer assistantship. The second year I began again without assistantship money but picked up some money by being admitted to the specialty program in alcohol and drug abuse and by working work-study for a social work professor." Similar patterns of support were reported by a number of other respondents for this portion of their higher educational careers; this finding supports the notion that they knew how to *work hard*.

The second theme that emerged from respondents' descriptions of their graduate careers was their perception that they were not as well prepared as their classmates. The response of a fifty-one-year-old male respondent is a good example of those who mentioned this problem: "My undergraduate education in the social sciences was very weak despite the fact that I did switch to, and get my undergraduate degree in sociology. As a result . . . I entered graduate school with a very marginal knowledge of the discipline." This particular theme is consistent with two different findings of previous research. The first is the notion that the resources of working-class homes, neighborhoods, and schools put their students at a relative disadvantage when compared with middle-class students. The second is that this same background leads students from the working class to "feel" less well prepared (whether or not they, in fact, are so) when compared with their middle-class counterparts (cf. Bourdieu 1984; Coleman 1988; Sennett and Cobb 1972; Shostak 1969).

A third theme identified was the notion that a number of respondents felt that their cultural and social skills were not as adequate as those of their classmates. The remarks of a twenty-eight-year-old female respondent provide a good example: "During my graduate career I first began to realize that getting advanced degrees involves a high level of politics in the sense that you have to network, to go to parties, etc. where the right people will be. You have to learn to hobnob. I found this very hard . . . because I didn't have the social skills required to go about this kind of thing properly." Another who mentioned this problem wrote: "I'm just seriously lacking in middle class social skills, and people are not very tolerant of this." This particular theme resonates with Bourdieu's (1984) notion that the "embodied" cultural capital of the home environments (and neighborhoods and schools as well) of working-class students puts them at a relative disadvantage when compared with middle-class students.

The fourth theme or issue that a number of our respondents mentioned was the inordinate length of time it took them to finish their graduate degrees. Since more females than males made direct reference to this issue, we calculated the average length of time from the date of the awarding of the B.A. to that of the Ph.D. for our respondents—the figure was nine-and-one-half years (the range was from three to twenty-four years). When we divided the sample by gender, we found that males took, on the average, about nine-and-one-half-years, whereas females took ten-and-one-half years, not as great a difference as our initial reading of their responses led us to expect. To further explore this issue, we also looked at the proportion of respondents who took five or fewer years to complete their graduate educations by gender. Here we found that only about two in ten (18 percent) went straight from the B.A. through the Ph.D. without interruption and that the proportions of males and females who followed this pathway were nearly identical. While nine-and-one-half years between the completion of the undergraduate degree and the awarding of the Ph.D. seems to us a long time to complete a graduate education, we do not have data from nonworking-class students with which to compare this finding. What is clear is that many in our sample did not begin their professional careers until they were in their thirties.

A fifth theme that emerged from our respondents' descriptions was the fact that some mentioned they were older than many of their classmates. Some who mentioned this fact noted that it was an advantage in their relations with professors, while others noted that it was a disadvantage because they felt isolated (and even alienated) from their classmates and programs (this was particularly true for some of those who were older and who either had family responsibilities or who were part-time students during some portion of their graduate studies).

A sixth theme that was present in the remarks of our respondents was that, for some, there was also a sense of "redefinition of self" that occurred during their graduate studies as they began to "catch up" with their classmates in terms of knowledge, to "redefine" themselves as capable of competing with them, and, finally, to believe that they were capable of finishing the Ph.D degree and successfully pursuing a career as a professional academic. The remarks of a thirty-seven-year-old female reflect this transformation in self-definition:

I was [initially] floored by how many of the graduate students, and especially, of the professors, were second or third generation college educated. . . . I have always felt at a practical disadvantage, that I didn't . . . belong, that I'd be found out and my presence [would be] questioned. But as I started teaching, I discovered that I loved it and was good at it; as I took classes I found myself equal to and excited by the intellectual discussions; I did often enjoy a life where I was very much engaged in intellectual pursuits.

The seventh and final theme was the important role that mentoring played in the successes of a number of our respondents. Since this issue is the focus of a more detailed question that will be discussed in the next section of the chapter, we will defer discussion of it here.

From our point of view, the findings of this section of the chapter, even more than those for the respondents' undergraduate careers, are compatible with our theoretical expectations and with the findings and speculations of other research that has examined the lives of academics from working-class backgrounds. Students from working-class backgrounds simply encounter an "alien" world when they go to college/graduate school; they attend less prestigious schools; and they also have to work harder than their middle-class peers to obtain their professional credentials.

THE LINGERING EFFECTS OF CLASS BACKGROUND

This section of the chapter is devoted to an examination of respondents' perceptions about a number of general educational issues about which earlier researchers have found differences between academics from the working class and their middle-class counterparts. Among the issues discussed here are respondents' perceptions about feeling somehow different from their classmates, the influences of their class backgrounds on their pursuit of higher education, having to work harder than their classmates, the roles that mentors played in their higher educational careers, and the relative impact(s) of class background when compared to other salient structural attributes on their higher educational careers.

On "Feeling" Somehow Different from Other Students

One of the most consistent findings of earlier research is that academics from working-class backgrounds feel that they are different, in many ways, from their classmates (Dews and Law 1995; Ryan and Sackrey 1984; Tokarczyk and Fay 1993; Shostak 1969). To explore this issue, we asked our respondents the following question(s): "Did you ever feel somehow "different" from your classmates? If so, how?" We coded the first part of this question "yes" or "no," and the distribution of respondents between these two categories is presented in Table 4.10,A. As displayed there, over three-quarters (77 percent) of respondents' replies to the question led us to place them in the "yes" category; males were more likely than females to be placed there (89 percent versus 63). For those who answered "yes" to the first part of this question, we also coded their rationales for feeling different from their classmates. These reasons are displayed in Table 4.10,B. Although there were a number of different rationales mentioned, most fell into two categories: eleven of the thirty respondents (37 percent) who said that they felt somehow different from their classmates mentioned perceived class differences as the reason, and ten of them (a third of the total) mentioned that being older and/or a nontraditional student was the reason that they felt different. When we added the members of two additional categories our respondents mentioned that overlap most with class differences—"class/ethnicity" and "material differences"—to the total for class differences, the revised percentage of the total group that chose rationales related to class as their reason for feeling different from their classmates increased to half of the total. There were modest gender differences in response to this part of the question in that women were more likely than men to mention being older than their classmates and to stress the role that material differences played in making them feel different from their classmates. These findings support the notion that college students from working-class backgrounds do indeed feel themselves to be different from their classmates and that they identify factors related to class as major sources of the differences they perceive between themselves and their classmates. Such findings are compatible with earlier research that has examined the problems that children of the working class face in higher education (cf. Rubin 1994; Ryan and Sackrey 1984; Shostak 1969).

Impact(s) of Class Background on Graduate Education

Because the issue of class background is so central to this study, we also asked our respondents a direct question about their perceptions of any impediments that their class background might have had on their efforts to acquire their higher educations, and, if they perceived an impediment, we also

Table 4.10
Respondents' Perceptions of Feeling Somehow "Different" from Other Students during Their Higher Education Careers

N(%)

A. Did you feel somehow different from other students?

		Samples	
Response	*Total*	*Males*	*Females*
Yes	30(77)	16(89)	12(63)
No	9(26)	2(11)	7(37)
Totals	39(99)	18(100)	19(100)
NA	2		

B. If yes, how so?

Class Differences	11(37)	6(38)	5(38)
Older or other Nontraditional Student	10(33)	5(31)	5(43)
Class/Ethnicity	1(3)	1(100)	—
Material Differences	3(10)	1(6)	2(15)
More Motivated	2(7)	1(6)	1(7)
Cultural/Intellectual Differences	1(3)	1(6)	—
More Insecure	1(3)	1(6)	—
Regional Differences	1(3)	1(6)	—
Totals	30(100)	16(99)	13(100)

[Reliability=98%]

asked them to describe the nature of the impediment(s). We coded the first part of this question either "definitely yes," "yes and no," or "definitely no." The distribution of respondents across these three categories is presented in Table 4.11,A. The results displayed there show that over eight in ten (81 percent) indicated that their class background had, indeed, been an impediment to their pursuit of higher education. An additional 14 percent provided ambivalent answers that were coded into the "yes and no" category—only two of our respondents (5 percent) said that class had no impact on their higher educational careers (the impact of gender on the nature of our participants' responses to this question was minimal). For those whose responses to the question were coded into either of the first two categories (i.e., "definitely yes" or "yes and no"), we next examined the reasons they offered for their assessments (as noted above, since we did not confine our respondents' to a single reason and a number of them provided more than one, we coded each reason offered); we collapsed these into six categories as shown in Table 4.11,B. The most frequently mentioned reason was "lack of financial resources" (three in ten mentioned this reason). A representative quote for respondents who mentioned this reason is that of a forty-four-year-old female who responded: "The major impediment to my pursuit of a higher education was finances; I felt the continual, pressing requirement to work (usually full-time) and depended upon student loans to supplement my lifestyle."

The second most frequently mentioned reason why our respondents' class backgrounds impeded their pursuit of higher education was a "lack of knowledge about opportunities/options" (29 percent mentioned this option). A typical response for this reason is from a sixty-four-year-old female, who, after lamenting the length of time it took her to complete her higher education, remarked that: "This, again, was probably a result of the class background and lack of contacts or knowledge about opportunities and options: I believed that working full time and paying for tuition as it was due was the only way to get through school, I would have never considered taking out student loans or going into debt for this education, nor did I know about these opportunities."

The third reason given by these respondents had to do with their perception that they had limited cultural resources when compared with their classmates (19 percent mentioned this reason). A typical response placed into this category is that of a fifty-five-year-old male: "While I was accepted for graduate work, it became apparent from both professors and fellow students that a 'mechanic' knew nothing of the real world. Their world was a mystery to me. I did not know anything about classical music, foreign countries, or art. I did not read poetry. If I talked about what I did—I was proud if I fixed a carburetor. . . . I was tuned out."

Inadequacies in early education was the fourth most frequently mentioned impediment of class background (12 percent mentioned this reason). A thirty-eight-year-old male put it this way: "While I did well in secondary school, the curriculum in math and writing was poor. This put me at a continuing disadvantage

Table 4.11
Respondents' Perceptions about Whether Their Class Backgrounds Have Been an Impediment to Their Pursuit of Higher Education and, if so, the Nature of its Impacts

N(%)

A. *Class Background Has Been an Impediment to Respondents' Pursuit of Higher Education*

Response	Total	Samples Males	Females
Definitely Yes	30(81)	15(79)	15(83)
Yes and No	5(14)	3(6)	2(11)
Definitely No	2(5)	1(5)	1(6)
Totals	37(100)	19(100)	18(100)
NA	4	2	2

B. *How has class background impeded your pursuit of higher education?*

Response	Total	Males	Females
Lack of Financial Resources	18(31)	9(28)	9(35)
Lack of Knowledge about Opportunities/Options	17(29)	6(19)	11(42)
Limited "Cultural" Resources	11(19)	9(28)	2(6)
Inadequate Early Education	7(12)	4(13)	1(4)
Negative Impacts on Personality/Self-Confidence/Self-Esteem	4(7)	3(9)	1(4)
Lack of Adequate Role Models	1(2)	1(3)	—
Totals	58(100)	32(100)	26(99)

[Reliabilities "A"=95%; "B"=83%]

and continues to do so."

Two other factors offered by respondents as reasons why their class backgrounds had impeded their pursuit of higher education were personality factors such as "The biggest problem has been self-confidence [and] . . . the lack of social skills" and the lack of adequate role models—one respondent said "My class history also meant that I had no role model or guide." There are important gender differences in response to this part of the question. Females were more likely than males to mention two of the reasons why class background impeded their pursuit of higher education—lack of financial resources and limited knowledge about opportunities and options—and males were more likely than females to mention two others—limited cultural resources and personality issues. It is also interesting to note that, for those five members of the sample included in this group who said "yes and no" when asked whether or not class had been an impediment to their higher educations, two of them said their class background had positive effects as well, such as encouraging them to devote greater efforts to their studies; a third observed that his background within the working class had also provided him with a different and useful perspective when he studied class issues during the course of his graduate studies.

To summarize, a large majority of respondents agreed that their backgrounds within the working class had definitely impeded their pursuit of higher education. Among the reasons mentioned were the lack of financial resources, the lack of an adequate fund of information about higher education, and perceived cultural and social skills deficits. There were also gender differences in the reasons given for the negative impacts of class, with males more likely to mention limited cultural resources, and females more likely to mention limited financial resources and inadequate knowledge about higher education as impediments. Finally, several respondents (those who we placed in the "yes and no" category of the first part of the question) also mentioned benefits that derived from their class backgrounds, including a strong "work" ethic and unique insights into portions of the subject matter of the discipline.

On Having to Work Harder Than Others

The next question we asked respondents to address was whether or not their class background had made it necessary for them to work harder at any time during their higher educational careers when compared to their classmates. Our coding of this question was made somewhat more difficult by the fact that the referent "work harder" was interpreted differently by various respondents. Some thought we were referring to working harder in general, others thought we were referring to academic work, and still others thought we meant work as a means of financial support.[8] No matter the interpretation they chose to employ, however, our coding scheme reflected their responses. As presented in Table 4.12, nearly three-quarters (74 percent) of our respondents answered that

Table 4.12
Respondents' Perceptions about Having to Work Harder Than Other Students because of Class Background

N(%)

Samples

Response	Total	Males	Females
Yes	26(74)	13(76)	13(72)
(undifferentiated)	1	—	1
(stressed academic)	8	3	5
(stressed both)	9	5	4
(stressed work)	8	5	3
No	9(26)	4(24)	5(28)
Totals	35(100)	17(100)	18(100)
NA	6		

[Reliability = 92%]

they did feel that they had to work harder (in the various ways noted above) than their classmates; in terms of gender, males and females were almost equally likely to hold this viewpoint. Second, the respondents who answered " yes" to the question were almost equally divided in terms of the particular interpretation of "work harder" they offered (i.e., academic work, work to support their studies, or both).

And, although gender differences were not large, females were slightly more likely to stress having to work harder academically, whereas males were more likely to emphasize work either as a means for financial support, or for both reasons. A good example of a positive response to the question that stressed having to work harder academically is that of a forty-six-year-old female who said in response to the question: "Yes, I did have to work harder than other students because of my class background. The students at _____ were much better academically prepared in some respects. For example, I did not know how to use the library system until I was a graduate student. . . . I acted, thought and spoke differently than most of the students." An example of a respondent that "mixed" the two meanings of work in her response is that of a forty-four year old female, who noted: "I often felt that I had to work harder than many other students . . . for two reasons: (1) since employment was a necessity, I never had the luxury of just 'being' a college student and (2) since I didn't have some of the life experiences that my more "cultured" counterparts seemed to have. . . . I felt the need to at least prove that I was intelligent and trainable."

A typical response from a respondent who stressed the "work for support" version is from a thirty-five-year-old female, who noted: "So, the answer to this question is yes and no—I had to work harder financially because of my class background but [I] did not have to work harder scholastically. I chose to work harder scholastically." Finally, a good example of a respondent who said "no" to this question is the response of a thirty-nine-year-old female who said: "I felt if I chose an academic career, I would always be working, so to always work was a means of growing. I knew people who had everything paid for by their parents, and they still didn't do any better academically, so I never felt put-upon or over-burdened. Work is something you do to learn, to grow." Despite differences in interpretation of the precise meaning of the phrase "work harder," and the fact that a quarter or so of the respondents answered "no" to the question, it seems clear that a large majority of them agreed that, because of their working-class backgrounds, they had to work harder, in one way or another, during their higher educational careers, than did many of their classmates. This finding is consistent with those reported earlier (see Chapter 3) that stressed both the financial hardships faced by the families of students from working-class backgrounds and shortcomings in the cultural/social resources of their families of origin, the neighborhoods within which they grew up, the schools they attended, and so on.

The Role(s) Played by Mentors

The next issue that we asked respondents to address about their general educational careers was the role played by mentors in influencing their educational and career paths. Our motivation here stems from the fact that a number of researchers have noted the paucity of adequate role models within working-class culture for occupations outside the working class as well as the incompatibilities between working-class socialization and success in higher education—not to mention life as an upper-middle-class academic (cf. Dews and Law 1995; Ryan and Sackrey 1984; Tokarczyk and Fay 1993). The question we put to them was in two parts: "What role did mentor(s) play in your educational success? What do you know about the class background(s) of your mentor(s)? Our coding of the responses to the first part of the question yielded two categories: "mentors important in respondents' educational successes" and "mentors unimportant in respondents' educational successes." The distribution of respondents between these categories is displayed in Table 4.13,A. As shown there, more than eight in ten (82 percent) indicated that mentors had played an important role in their educational successes. Breaking down respondents' replies to this question by gender reveals that women were slightly more likely to claim

Table 4.13
Respondents' Perceptions about the Role(s) That Mentors Played in Their Educational Careers and the Class Background of these Individuals

N(%)

A. Role(s) of Mentors in Respondents' Successes

Samples

Responses	Total	Males	Females
Mentors Important	31(82)	15(75)	16(89)
Mentors Unimportant	7(18)	5(25)	2(11)
Totals	38(100)	20(100)	18(100)
NA	2	1	1

[Reliabiity = 100%]

B. Respondents' Perceptions about Class Background of Mentors

Samples

Mentors' Class Background	Total	Males	Females
Middle Class/Professional	13(42)	9(60)	4(25)
Some Middle Class/ Professional, Others Working Class	5(16)	2(13)	3(19)
Working Class	8(26)	3(20)	5(31)
Uncertain	5(16)	1(07)	4(25)
Totals	31(100)	15(100)	16(100)

[Reliability = 82%]

an important role for mentors than were men (89 percent versus 75 percent). Table 4.13,B. displays respondents' perceptions about the class background(s) of their mentors (the sample here is confined to those respondents who agreed that mentors had been important for them). Since a number of respondents mentioned more than one mentor and their class identities were not always the same, we developed a coding scheme that contained four categories: "middle class/professional," some middle class/professional and others working class," "working class," and "uncertain." As shown in the table, the largest proportion of respondents (about four in ten) reported that their mentors were from the middle class/professional ranks; about one-quarter (26 percent) claimed mentors from working-class backgrounds; 16 percent claimed mentors from both of these groups; and an additional 16 percent of our respondents could not classify their mentors' class background. Notice that the sum of the latter two "active" categories of mentors' class backgrounds (i.e., "some middle class/professional and others working class" and "working class") is equal in size to that of the first category ("middle class/professional"). There are also gender differences present for this question—women were more likely to identify their mentors' backgrounds as working class, whereas men were more likely to identify their mentors' backgrounds as middle class/professional. Notice as well that the sum of the latter two categories for women is much larger than the sum of the same two categories for men (50 percent versus 33 percent). From these data, it seems clear that mentors played an important role in the successes experienced by most of our respondents.

Class versus Ascriptive Influences

Finally, we asked our respondents to compare the impact(s) of their class backgrounds on their higher educational careers with those of other important structural locations they also occupy such as gender, race, ethnicity, and religion. Our interest in asking this question was to see how the members of various ascriptive groups would rank the influences of their class backgrounds when compared with their ascriptive statuses. Because of this interest, we broke the sample down not only by gender but also by race and ethnicity. We also coded each respondent's perceptions of the relative influence of each factor when more than one was mentioned.[9] Table 4.14 displays these data. The categories in the table are confined to those mentioned by the respondents (for example, there is no category in the table for race as primary followed by class as secondary [and several other combinations of factors as well] because none of the respondents mentioned it [them]). Inspecting the data, as we suspected, male respondents overwhelmingly mentioned class alone (72 percent) as the most important influence on their higher educational careers. Two males mentioned class as primary followed by religion, a third mentioned religion alone, a fourth mentioned religion as primary followed by class, and one male said that none of these factors had influenced his higher educational career. For females, over

Table 4.14
Respondents' Perceptions of the Relative Influence of Class Background on Their Higher Educational Careers when Compared with Ascriptive Attributes such as Gender, Ethnicity, Race and Age

N(%)

| | | Samples | | | | | |
| | | European Americans | | | African Americans | | |
Factor	Total Sample	Total	Males	Females	Total	Males	Females
Class(alone)	19(53)	18(56)	13(72)	5(36)	1(50)	1(100)	1(100)
Class/Gender	4(11)	3(9)	3(21)	1(50)	1(100)		
Class/Religion	2(6)	2(6)	2(11)				
Class/Age	1(3)	1(3)	1(7)				
Gender(alone)	1(3)	1(3)	1(7)				
Gender/Class	3(8)	3(9)	3(21)				
Race(alone)	2(6)				2(100)	1(100)	1(100)
Religion(alone)	1(3)	1(3)	1(6)				
Religion/Class	1(3)	1(3)	1(6)				
None	2(6)	2(6)	1(6)	1(7)			
Totals	36(99)	32(98)	18(101)	14(99)	2(100)	1(100)	1(100)
NA	4	4					

Hispanic Americans

	Total	Males	Females
Class(alone)	1(50)	1(100)	1(100)
Class/Gender	1(50)		1(100)
Totals	2(100)	1(100)	1(100)

[Reliability=95%]

one-third (36 percent) mentioned class alone, and an additional 21 percent mentioned class as primary followed by gender, one mentioned class as primary followed by age, one mentioned gender alone as the most important influence, while three mentioned gender as primary followed by class. Finally, one female respondent mentioned that none of these factors had been influential. What interests us about the patterning of response among the females was that over half of them (56 percent) ranked class as the most important factor or class as primary followed by gender. This compares with only a single respondent who said gender alone was most important and three who said that gender was primary followed by class (these two groups total 28 percent). These figures indicate to us that our female respondents, as a group, felt that class background was more important than gender in influencing their higher educational careers. The two African Americans in the sample both nominated race as the *only* important influence on their higher educational careers as we would expect given the schisms between European Americans and African Americans in American society. The two Hispanic American respondents, in contrast to the African Americans, did not mention their ethnic status as an important influence on their higher educational careers. The male Hispanic American said his class background alone was the most important influence; the female Hispanic American nominated class followed by gender.

The nature of the findings reviewed in this section of the chapter—things like the fact that the respondents felt themselves to be different from their classmates, that a large majority of our respondents agreed that their class backgrounds exercised an important influence on many aspects of their higher educational careers, that most of the respondents noted that they found it necessary to work harder than their contemporaries, both academically and in order to support themselves while in school, that many respondents' higher educational careers were facilitated by their relationships with mentors, and that most respondents, regardless of gender or ethnicity, still felt that class was the major influence on their higher educational careers—are all compatible with the argument advanced in Chapter 1 that the influences of class background are hard to leave behind and remain potent influences far beyond childhood and early adulthood.

CONCLUSIONS

In this chapter we have focused attention on the second period in the life cycles of our respondents—the period during which they attended college and went on to receive their graduate training. We revisited the three factors leading to their success that we outlined in Chapter 3: (1) they were smart, (2) they were encouraged by significant others, and (3) they were taught to value hard work. These factors continued to have important effects during their undergraduate and graduate educations. The first two remained closely tied to the success of our respondents, whereas the third began to take on a different character during this period. We introduced a fourth factor for consideration, the timeliness of the expansion of higher education that has taken place in this country over the last forty years. We summarize our findings in the following paragraphs.

When we examined the undergraduate careers of our respondents, we found that respondents chose their undergraduate institutions more for "practical" than for "academic" reasons. Half of our respondents attended undergraduate schools with a research emphasis—usually state universities. Such choices are consistent with the relative material, cultural, and social resources available to the children of working-class parents (Bourdieu 1984; Shostak 1969). We also found that most respondents were forced to support themselves through their undergraduate studies and that they did not receive much material assistance from their families. Once again, these findings are consistent with the resource base available to working-class families (as described in Chapter 3). Our analysis of respondents' descriptions of their undergraduate careers yielded a number of themes that are insightful: most suffered financial difficulties during their undergraduate careers and were forced to work; most felt that they were less well prepared than their classmates; most began in more "applied" majors and then switched to sociology; most mentioned conflicts between work and their academic and social lives; some were forced to interrupt their undergraduate careers and thus took longer than four years to complete their degrees; many felt themselves to be different from their classmates and a number of these linked these differences to their class background; and, finally, many remembered themselves to be more politically active than their classmates. Each of these themes resonates with the findings and conclusions of earlier research on students from the working class (cf. Ryan and Sackrey 1984).

Gender also proved to be an important source of difference for respondents' undergraduate careers. Males were more likely than females to mention affordability as a major criterion influencing their choice of an undergraduate institution, while females were more likely to stress the quality of the program. Females were more likely to depend on loans and grants to support their undergraduate educations, whereas males were more likely to depend on work as a major means of support. Finally, although most of our respondents went straight through from high school graduation to the college degree, for those who did not do so, gender made a difference in the path they took. Females were more likely to have an interruption between graduating from high school and entry into college, whereas males were more likely to experience their interruption after entry into college but before the awarding of the degree. These findings resonate with earlier research that has examined the intersection between class and gender in higher education (Barker 1995; Tokarczyk and Fay 1993).

Our examination of the graduate careers of the respondents also generated findings that are compatible with our theoretical expectations. For example, the motives mentioned as influencing our respondents' choices of graduate institutions, like those of their undergraduate institutions, were more practical than academic. Second, respondents also mentioned that class factors had played an important role in these choices. Third, a comparison between the sources of the doctorates of this sample with those of a sample of the membership of the ASA revealed that far more of these respondents attended graduate programs ranked lower in disciplinary prestige hierarchy than did the members of the ASA sample. Fourth, as was the case with their undergraduate degrees, most respondents supported themselves by what might be labeled "private" means, such as work, loans/grants, graduate assistantships, and scholarships. Importantly, they did not report depending heavily on their families' resources for financial support. Similar to their undergraduate careers, a number of important themes emerged from our analysis of responses to an open-ended question about their graduate careers: ever-present financial need; feelings of being less well prepared than their classmates; perceived cultural and/or social skills deficits; taking a long time to complete graduate training; and the role that mentoring played in many of our respondents' educational successes. Each of these themes is compatible with the circumstances that confront students from the working class who manage to pursue higher educational credentials (Dews and Law 1995; Ryan and Sackrey 1984).

Gender also played a role in structuring respondents' perceptions about their graduate educations. Women were more likely than men to mention the academic lifestyle as a major motive for choosing a career in academia, whereas men were more likely to mention interest in the subject matter. Men were more likely to mention the programmatic specialties offered by graduate departments as a major criterion influencing their selection, whereas women were more likely to mention the availability of financial support as being more important. Men were more likely to have available fellowships or scholarships to assist them in supporting themselves while in graduate school, whereas women were more likely to depend on work and grants/loans to support themselves (Barker [1995:67] has made the point that working-class women receive less support than working-class men during their graduate studies). Finally, women were more likely to stress the importance of mentoring during their graduate careers than were men.

Respondents' answers to a number of more general questions about their higher educational careers also provided support for our theoretical expectations. First, a majority felt themselves to be somehow different from their classmates during their entire higher educational careers and class differences were the most frequently mentioned source for these differences. When asked specifically the way(s) that their class background impacted their higher educational careers, respondents mentioned precarious finances, limited cultural and social skills, and less-than-adequate early educational training as reasons.

These findings are consistent with research that has argued that working-class children are less well equipped than their middle-class counterparts with the material, cultural, and social resources that facilitate the acquisition of higher educational credentials (Barker 1995; Bourdieu 1984; Coleman 1988). Most respondents also agreed that they had to work harder (either academically, as a means of supporting themselves, or both) than their classmates as well. Once again, this finding is consistent with earlier research that argues that the resource base that a family is able to offer its children is a crucial ingredient in their eventual successes (Barker 1995; Coleman 1988; Lareau 1986).

Another influence on the successes of these respondents that can be linked to their class backgrounds is the important role that mentors played in their eventual educational successes. Eight in ten agreed that mentors had played a crucial role in their higher educational careers; it seems logical that mentors would play a particularly important role for students from working-class backgrounds who are less likely to be exposed to professional role models and who possess marginal information about the "ins" and "outs" of higher education.

Finally, when asked to compare the relative influence of class when compared with other structural locational attributes on their higher educational careers, most said that class was more important than gender, race, or ethnicity. The only exception to this generalization was that African American respondents were more likely to identify race as the only influence on their careers, while all other groups mentioned either class or class combined with some other attribute such as religion or gender.

We also found gender differences with regard to the lingering effects of class on higher educational differences. Male respondents were more likely to feel themselves to be somehow different from their classmates than were females and their reasons for feeling different varied according to gender—males were more likely to mention cultural and social skills differences, while women were more likely to mention being older and/or having far fewer material resources than their classmates. With regard to the question about having to work harder than their classmates during their higher educational careers, women were more likely to mention having to work harder academically, whereas men were more likely to stress having to work to support themselves and their families as well as academically. Women stressed the importance of mentoring more frequently than men and they were also more likely to identify the class background of their mentors as working class than were men. Finally, it is interesting that women were almost as likely as men to stress that class was most important, *even when compared with gender*, on their higher educational careers. This finding is somewhat surprising even though it is consistent with class-based arguments. It is also consistent with a quote from Law (1995:6): "Class poses different dilemmas than posed by either race or gender. . . . We do not cease being men and women, for instance, when we become doctors of philosophy. But most of us cease being working class when we become professors."

The respondent we quoted at the beginning of this chapter describes a view of his world as having a range of possibilities limited only by his imagination. His imagination, however, placed the possibility of his ever becoming something like a college professor within the realm of the impossible—akin to the idea that he "could fly." Thus, as we have shown in this chapter, not only are children from working-class families socialized in family (and neighborhood and school) environments that provide them with fewer material, cultural, and social resources, but also these resource deficits constrain their efforts to acquire higher educational credentials in a number of ways that have important consequences, not only for their relative levels of success, but also for their social and psychological adjustment(s) to this success. Thus, once again, the findings of these two chapters support Rubin's (1976:13) conclusion that "no matter how far we travel, we can never leave our roots behind."

NOTES

1. These totals probably underestimate the number of respondents who were motivated by a combination of these three reasons since some of the respondents who mentioned only one of the three—say "proximity to home"—may have been motivated to select an institution close to home in order to live there and/or to cut expenses. Since we only coded those factors explicitly mentioned, we missed those who only mentioned one of the three but whose motivations may have included all of them.

2. As should be obvious, although our selection of these themes was informed, we make no claim that they were "unbiased." We selected things that struck us, given our own backgrounds within the working class and our knowledge of the literature on the working class in general and on academics from working class backgrounds in particular, as important. See Strauss (1987) for a description of "open coding."

3. As a brief aside here, we should add here that a number of our respondents also mentioned that their first exposure to the discipline marked an important turning point in their undergraduate careers. A thirty-four-year-old female put it this way: "Just to be different, I enrolled in an introductory sociology course and loved it. I took another course from the same instructor, and loved it. I took another course, and changed majors."

4. We used the National Research Council's *Research-Doctoral Programs in the United States: Continuities and Change* (1995) as a source for the rankings of the departments. We took an average of the 1992 and the 1982 rankings for each department because we felt that the average ranking over the decade would be a better indicator of a department's relative location in the prestige hierarchy than either of the single-year rankings.

5. Given these differences, we entertained the notion that membership in the ASA might have a class bias—that is, sociologists from working-class backgrounds *may not* join the ASA as frequently as do sociologists from other class backgrounds. If this were to be the case, then perhaps some of the differences between the two samples that we observed could be explained by that fact. In order to check this out, we took our list of respondents and checked it against two ASA membership directories (two because we suspected that there might be some variability in membership because of changes in status such as moving from student to professor or from active employment to retirement). We discovered that 89 percent of our sample were in one or both of these directories and that if we excluded the student members of our sample, the percentage

climbed to 92 percent. This finding gives us more confidence that the differences observed are not an artifact of (class) membership bias.

6. We used the *1990 Biographical Director of Members* (American Sociological Association 1990) as our source of information about member characteristics. This particular directory was chosen over more recent once because it is the last directory to date that published biographical information on members. We randomly sampled a total of 60 of the 13,853 members of the association using a skip-interval sampling method.

7. Three of these themes are identical to those offered by the respondents when asked to describe their undergraduate careers: financial problems, feeling less well prepared than classmates, and the length of time taken to finish degrees.

8. It should go without saying that questions should be formulated in such a way as to avoid such misinterpretations. Ironically, we thought that the context in which the question was asked clearly called for an assessment of the extent to which our respondents felt that they had to work harder *academically* than their classmates to make up in some way for the shortcomings in their earlier educational careers that were linked to their class backgrounds. Obviously, this was not the case for some of our respondents.

9. By this we mean that if respondents mentioned more than one factor, we scrutinized their responses carefully in order to determine the relative weight they gave to each of the factors they mentioned. These rankings are reflected in the way we organized the categories in the table.

5

Life As a Professional Sociologist

This chapter focuses attention on the professional lives of our sample of sociologists from working-class backgrounds. It is here and in the personal lives of our respondents (the subject of Chapter 6) that the impact(s) of the contrast(s) between growing up within a working-class environment and then attempting to adjust to, and survive in, an upper-middle-class academic world should be most apparent.

Erik Wright (1976) has used the term "contradictory class locations" to describe positions located between the working class and the owning class in advanced capitalist societies, that is, to those class positions that require their occupants to act on behalf of the owning class even though they do not, themselves, belong to that class.[1] As he has put it, they are "objectively torn between two classes" (Wright 1976). They are tied to the working class because they share with it a lack of control over the means of production. Yet, they are also tied to the owning class because the nature of their work requires them to act on its behalf, often in ways that are detrimental to the interests of the working class.[2] Ryan and Sackrey's (1984:112–113) assessment of the academic work process explicitly acknowledges this latter point: "Our conclusion is that the academic work process is essentially antagonistic to the working class, and academics, for the most part, live in a different world of culture, different ways that make it, too, antagonistic to working class life." As the second part of their assessment makes clear, in contrast to Wright's (1976) focus on the objective contradictions inherent in these "middle class" locations and their consequences for the interests of the incumbents of these classes, Ryan and Sackrey (1984) are also interested in the cultural consequences for the incumbents of these positions as well.[3]

We share with them and others who have studied academics from working-class backgrounds (Dews and Law 1995; Tokarczyk and Fay 1992) the belief that upwardly mobile members of the working class experience both personal/psychological (i.e., cultural) and structural consequences in the form of diminished opportunities as a result of the numerous contradictions between their class of origin and their class of destination. For example, at the personal/psychological level, academics from working-class backgrounds are hindered when they enter the upper-middle-class world of the academy, because, though they have achieved the "institutionalized" cultural capital (in the form of academic credentials) necessary for entry, at the same time they lack much of the "embodied" cultural capital that is almost unconsciously transmitted to children who grow up in a middle or upper-middle-class environment.[4] As noted below, the relative personal/psychological costs of these cultural deficiencies can be minor, such as embarrassment over a minor violation of middle- (or upper-middle-) class attitudinal or behavioral norms; moderate, such as believing one's self to be less worthy than one's colleagues; or major, such as feeling one's self to be a permanent "stranger" or "outsider" to the academic culture.

In this same vein, membership in the academy also forces the working-class expatriate to perform "sifting and sorting" functions that contribute to the reproduction of the class hierarchy. Thus, no matter how sympathetic they are to students who share their class of origin, or how much they "agonize" over the assignment of grades, the rules for inclusion within the academy require that assessments of students' performances be based on normative expectations that are more compatible with the childhood and early educational experiences of their middle- and upper-middle-class students than they are with those of their working-class students. Their actions, in this context, can have important personal/psychological consequences for academics from working-class backgrounds.

We are also convinced that academics from working-class backgrounds suffer structural consequences in the form of diminished opportunities as well. When we say that students from working-class backgrounds are "disadvantaged" by their lack of "embodied" cultural capital, we are not just referring to the "symptoms" of this problem, which we we described in the previous chapter (i.e., experiencing higher levels of stress or continued feelings of "angst"). We are also talking about what Bourdieu (1986:242) refers to as the: "immanent structure of the social world . . . the set of constraints, inscribed in the very reality of that world, which govern its functioning in a durable way, determining the chances of success for practices." What our respondents have told us goes beyond their psychological distress. Their collective experience shows us that growing up in a working-class family has also had concrete effects on their market viability. Thus, not only have these academics fought the uphill battles associated with trying to navigate in the foreign terrain of the middle- (or upper-middle-) class culture in higher education (as recounted in the life histories portrayed in earlier research by Dews and Law [1995]; Ryan and Sackrey [1984]; Tokarczyk and Fay [1993]), but they have also worked harder for, and they have received less return on, their educational investments than have sociologists from other class backgrounds. As will be demonstrated in this chapter, we see two prime (and, obviously, interrelated) factors that help to explain the relative levels of professional success enjoyed by our respondents—the sources of their graduate degrees and their relative lack of "embodied" cultural capital when compared with their middle- or upper-middle-class colleagues.

CLASS BACKGROUND AND PROFESSIONAL CAREERS

As noted in its introduction, the goal of this chapter is to explore key aspects of the professional careers of our sample of sociologists from working-class backgrounds, giving special attention to reports of the personal/psychological and structural costs associated with their class backgrounds. Our discussion below is grouped into four broad areas of interest. First, we examine the career histories of our respondents. Here, we are interested in our respondents' perspectives on how a variety of aspects of their careers such as the choice and nature of their first and current positions, the relative location of their current institutional affiliation within the disciplinary prestige hierarchy, the association between the relative prestige of the institutions from which they received their doctorates and those of their current institutional affiliations, their relative satisfaction with their current professional employment situations, and their assessments of the role that class (and other factors) has played in influencing their careers to date.[5] Second, we examine our respondents' perceptions about salient aspects of their professional lives. Explored here are such issues as the proper balance among the roles of the academy (i.e., research, teaching, and university community service/action), relations with academic authority, the correspondence between their initial expectations and the realities of life within the academy, relations with colleagues and students, and the extent to which they feel that they fit into the academic role. Third, we explore our respondents' sociological perspectives and the influences of factors such as class, gender, and race and/or ethnicity on their political/ideological outlooks, their orientations toward social action, their theoretical preferences, and well as their general assessments of life within contemporary American society. Finally, we assess the extent to which the members of our sample are happy with their choice of sociology as a career. As was the case with earlier life-cycle stages, we will continue to explore the impacts of gender on our respondents' perspectives on each of these issues.

Professional Career Histories

Choosing the First Professional Position. Our first goal was to examine the professional career histories of our sample. The first question we asked our respondents dealt with the influences that were important in choosing their first position following the completion of the Ph.D. degree. Our interest in this issue was motivated by speculations of previous researchers that academics from working-class backgrounds may, often of necessity, be motivated by more practical concerns when choosing a position when compared with other academics (Barker 1995; Ryan and Sackrey 1984). In response to this question, six in ten of our respondents mentioned only one factor; about three in ten (31 percent) mentioned two; two respondents mentioned three; and one mentioned four. The results of our coding of these responses are presented in Table 5.1.[6] As displayed there, we grouped the factors into three general categories: university and/or department characteristics; characteristics of the position's geographic/climatic/social location; and other factors. Of the forty-seven nominations made by our respondents, almost half (45 percent) involved various characteristics of the university and/or department in question such as the balance between teaching and research and the opportunities for research that the position offered; various locational factors such as closeness to home and region of the country were nominated by slightly more than a quarter of our respondents (30 percent); and another quarter mentioned other factors such as networks, family ties, and/or economic necessity as important influences on their choices of their first professional positions. It is interesting that the two most frequently mentioned individual factors—closeness to home (mentioned by seven respondents) and economic necessity (mentioned by six)—were not factors within the modal group (university and/or departmental characteristics), nor are they consistent with a "career" (versus a "job") orientation. The choice of factors such as these is compatible with the findings of earlier research on academics from working-class backgrounds.

When we classify our respondents' nominations by gender, some differences are immediately apparent. First, though half of our male respondents mentioned factors that dealt with university and/or departmental characteristics, fewer of our female respondents (42 percent) mentioned such factors. Second, our female respondents were almost as likely to mention factors within the "others" grouping that includes networks, family ties/peer pressures and economic necessity as important influences on their choice of first professional career position as they were university and/or departmental characteristics. These gender differences, although modest in magnitude, nonetheless invite speculation: Are they suggestive of the existence of different pressures operating on males and females within this particular part of the academic environment (not to mention their lives in general)? Other research has shown, for example, that maintaining family ties is often more difficult for upwardly mobile individuals (Barker 1993), and that women in general take more responsibility

Table 5.1
Respondents' Perceptions of Factors Influencing Choice of First Professional Position*

Factor Groups	Total N	(%)	Samples Males N	(%)	Females N	%
University/Departmental Characteristics	21	(45)	13	(52)	8	(42)
Ranking/Reputation	2		1		1	
Degrees Offered	1		1			
Department Climate, Size	2		2			
Diverse Student Body	3		3			
Teaching/Research Balance	5		3		1	
Research Opportunities	5		4		1	
Salary, Fringe Benefits	3		1		2	
Location	14	(30)	10	(40)	4	(21)
Region	5		4		1	
Closeness to Home	7		5		2	
Size of Community	1				1	
Climate	1		1			
Others	12	(25)	2	(8)	7	(37)
Networks	4		2		2	
Family Ties/Peer Pressure	2				2	
Economic Necessity	6		3		3	
Totals	47	(100)	25	(100)	19	(100)

[Reliability=92%]

*Totals exclude nine students—two irregularly employed and two respondents who failed to respond to the question.

for, feel more stress about, and feel more guilt about family issues than do men (Belle 1987). The last line of the response of a forty-nine-year-old female to this question is a good example of responses we placed into this "other" category: "that I was married and my husband had a position at a local university also influenced my decision." There is also ample evidence that women are materially disadvantaged when compared with men (in any social class) and that they receive less support and encouragement (both material and nonmaterial) than do men in their pursuit of higher education (see Barker [1993] and the materials reported in Chapter 3).

Characteristics of the First Position. The second issue that we explored was the rank and location of our respondents' first professional positions. Recall that one of the conclusions of Chapter 4 was that the members of our sample as a whole, when compared with a random sample of the membership of the ASA were more likely to have graduated from departments ranked lower in the academic hierarchy. Previous research on this subject (Ryan and Sackrey 1984:29; Tokarczyk and Fay 1993) also makes this point with regard to their samples of academics from working class backgrounds. For these reasons, we would be surprised if these differences in the relative prestige of the source of the Ph.D. did not impact the nature of the first job of our respondents. Data concerning the rank of our respondents' first professional position are presented in Table 5.2. These data indicate that nearly half (47 percent) of our sample of sociologists from working-class backgrounds began their professional careers in tenure-track assistant professor positions within their respective institutions. The second most frequent first job for the members of our sample was as a visiting or an adjunct professor. When these data are stratified by gender, males were somewhat more likely to have begun in tenure-track positions than were females, who were more evenly divided between tenure-track assistant professor positions and various forms of research appointments (i.e., postdoctorates, research assistants, research associates, etc.).[7]

Institutional Locations of First Positions. We next examine the institutional locations of our respondents' first professional positions. These data are presented in Table 5.3. They show that our respondents were equally likely to have begun their professional careers in one of three types of institutions: four-year colleges without bachelor's degrees in sociology, four-year colleges with bachelor's degrees in sociology, and universities that offer Ph.D. degrees in sociology. When we break these responses down by gender, the modal employer for male respondents becomes the four-year college without a bachelor's degree in sociology (although various types of institutions that rank higher in terms of their sociology programs are not far behind in terms of relative frequencies). The first professional positions for our female respondents were in research positions (both public and private). Since four-year colleges and research appointments do not, as a group, rank high within the academic hierarchy, these data indicate that most of our sample of sociologists from working-class backgrounds did not begin their careers at prestigious institutions.[8]

Table 5.2
Nature/Rank of First Professional Position of Our Sample of Sociologists from Working-Class Backgrounds*

N(%)

Samples

Position	Total	Males	Females
Instructor/Lecturer	2(6)	1(5)	1(8)
Visiting/Adjunct Professor	6(18)	5(24)	1(8)
Assistant Professor (non tenure track)	5(15)	3(14)	2(15)
Assistant Professor (tenure track)	16(47)	11(52)	5(38)
Research Position	4(12)	—	4(31)
Administrative Position	1(3)	1(5)	—
Totals	34(100)	21(100)	13(100)

*Students omitted.

The Relative Location of the Current Professional Position. We next examine the current positions of our respondents and the relative location of these positions within the academic hierarchy. Table 5.4,A, contains data on the distribution of our sample of sociologists from working-class backgrounds' current positions within their universities. As can be seen there, nearly three in ten of the members of our sample hold the rank of professor at their institutions, whereas a quarter are associate professors and another quarter are in research/ administration. There are modest gender differences in the table. Notice that more males than females hold the rank of associate or professor, more females are assistant professors than males,[9] more females fall into the research/ administration category than do males, and that those females who are not in research/administration are much more likely than males to hold nontenure-track appointments.

When we compare our sample with a sample drawn from the membership of the ASA in terms of current professional position (see Table 5.4,B), we find that a far larger percentage of the members of the ASA hold the rank of professor than do the members of our sample.[10] The only other large difference

Table 5.3
Institutional Location of the First Professional Position of Our Sample of Sociologists from Working-Class Backgrounds*

	N(%) Sample		
Institution Type	Total	Males	Females
Research (Public Private	4(14)	—	4(31)
Community/Junior College	2(8)	2(13)	—
Four-Year College without BA in Sociology	6(21)	4(27)	2(15)
Four-Year College with BA in Sociology	6(21)	3(20)	3(23)
University with MA in Sociology	4(14)	3(20)	1(8)
University with Ph.D.	6(21)	3(20)	3(23)
Totals	28(99)	15(100)	13(100)

*Students, those with administrative appointments, and those who did not provide this
information have been omitted.

is that proportionately fewer of the sample of the ASA membership hold research/administrative appointments than do the members of our sample. The gender differences that we observed within our sample are even larger for the members of the ASA sample. The most important of these is that over six in ten males in the latter sample hold the rank of professor, when compared with fewer than three in ten females. This "gender gap" is almost twice as large as that present in our sample. Notice as well that women in the ASA sample are also more likely to hold research/administrative positions than are males, a finding that also suggests important gender differences.

Location of Current Institution. Since we were also interested in the distribution of our sample in terms of where they were currently employed, we requested this information as well. As noted above, this interest was motivated by Ryan and Sackrey's (1984) conclusion that academics from working-class backgrounds often end up affiliated with institutions ranked lower in the academic prestige hierarchy than do academics from other class backgrounds. Table 5.5,A displays these data. As shown in the first column of the table,

Table 5.4
Nature/Rank of Current Professional Position of Our Sample of Sociologists from Working-Class Backgrounds and a Sample of the Membership of the American Sociological Association*

N(%)

A. Our Sample

Position	Total	Males	Females
Instructor/Lecturer	2(6)	2(10)	–
Visiting/Adjunct Professor	2(6)	1(5)	1(8)
Assistant Professor (not tenure track)	2(6) (18)	1(5) (10)	1(8) (31)
Assistant Professor (tenure track)	4(12)	1(5)	3(23)
Associate Professor	8(24)	6(33)	2(15)
Professor	10(29)	7(33)	3(23)
Research/Administration	8(24)	4(19)	4(31)
Totals	34(101)	21(101)	13(100)

B. Sample of ASA Members

	Total	Males	Females
Instructor/Lecturer	1(2)	1(3)	–
Visiting/Adjunct Professor	—	–	–
Assistant Professor	6(13)	1(3)	5(28)
Associate Professor	10(21)	8(28)	2(11)
Professor	23(49)	18(62)	5(28)
Research/Administration	7(15)	1(3)	6(33)
Totals	47(100)	29(99)	18(100)

---

*Students omitted.

about a third (34 percent) of our sample is currently employed by four-year colleges, fourteen percent are employed in universities that offer the M.A. degree in sociology, and nearly a fifth (17 percent) is currently employed at universities that offer the Ph.D. degree in sociology.

When these responses are broken down by gender, about half of our male respondents (47 percent) are currently located at four-year colleges with another third located at graduate-level institutions (13 percent at M.A. schools and 20 percent at Ph.D. schools). Our female respondents, on the other hand, are rather evenly spread across four of the five types of institutions (none of them is located at community or junior colleges), with fully half of them being currently located at graduate-level institutions. We also gathered identical data from the membership of the ASA so that we could compare our sample with the membership of the discipline as a whole in terms of current institutional locations. As is clear from a comparison of sections A and B of Table 5.5, there are significant differences between the two distributions in terms of current institutional affiliations. Although the members of our sample are nearly evenly split between those who are located at four-year colleges and those who are located at universities that offer graduate degrees in sociology (34 versus 33 percent), fully half of the ASA sample is located at institutions that offer the Ph.D. degree, and six in ten are located at institutions with graduate programs.

These differences suggest that our sample of sociologists from working-class backgrounds is relatively disadvantaged when compared with the general membership of the ASA in terms of the relative prestige of their current institutional affiliations.[11] When we look at the impact of gender for the ASA sample, we find the opposite differences between males and females in terms of proportions currently located in Ph.D. departments than was present in our sample—in the ASA sample males have the advantage in that six in ten of them as compared to slightly more than four in ten females are currently located in Ph.D. departments. Note as well that proportionately more females in this sample are classified in the other (research/administration) category than are males (this finding is consistent with their respective distributions in our sample). Although these differences are more difficult to interpret theoretically (because gender appears to operate differently in the two samples), they do clearly show that gender impacts the institutional affiliations of these two samples of sociologists.

Prestige of Source of Doctorate and Current Professional Position. To further explore the issue of institutional affiliational differences between the two samples, we next cross-classified the relative prestige ranking of the institutional source of our respondent's doctorate degrees with the type of employment for both our samples.[12] Table 5.6 presents these data. When we compare the ranking of the source of the Ph.D. with the current employment status of the members of the two samples, not surprisingly, we find that the two are associated. Note that, generally, for our sample of sociologists from working-class backgrounds, the higher the ranking of the source of the Ph.D., the higher

Table 5.5
A Comparison between the Institutional Locations of Our Sample of Sociologists from Working-Class Backgrounds and a Sample of the Membership of the American Sociological Association

N(%)
A. Our Sample(s)

Type of Employer	Total	Males	Females
Community/Junior College	1(3)	1(7)	—
Four-Year College	10(34)	7(47)	3(25)
University with M.A. Degree in Sociology	5(14)	2(13)	3(25)
University with Ph.D. Degree in Sociology	7(17)	3(20)	3(25)
Other	6(14)*	2(13)	3(25)
Totals	29**	15**	12**

B. ASA Sample(s)

Type of Employer	Total	Males	Females
Community/Junior College	4(9)	3(11)	1(6)
Four-Year College	7(16)	5(19)	2(12)
University with M.A. Degree in Sociology	3(7)	2(7)	1(6)
University with Ph.D. Degree in Sociology	23(53)	16(59)	7(44)
Other*	6(14)	1(4)	5(31)
Totals	43**	27**	16**

*This category includes members whose job descriptions were either researcher or administrator.
**Total sample sizes exclude students.

Table 5.6
A Comparison between Our Sample of Sociologists from Working-Class Backgrounds and a Sample of the ASA Membership in Terms of Relative Rank of Source of Ph.D. and Current Employment
$N(\%)$

Current Employer

Rank of Ph.D. Institution	Junior College	4-year University	M.A. University	Ph.D. University	Other University	N	%
Sociologists from Working-Class Backgrounds Sample (N=29)*							
Top 5			1(20)	2(40)	2(40)	5	(17)
6-10							
11-25		1(25)		1(25)	2(50)	4	(14)
26-50	1(11)	4(44)	1(11)	2(22)	1(11)	9	(31)
51-75		3(38)	3(38)	2(25)		8	(28)
76+		2(67)			1(33)	3	(10)
Total (%)	(3)	(34)	(14)	(17)	(14)		
ASA Sample (N=41)*							
Top 5		1(3)		7(87)		8	(20)
6-10				5(100)		5	(12)
11-25	1(7)	3(22)	1(7)	9(64)		14	(34)
26-50		2(18)	1(9)	6(54)	2(18)	11	(27)
51-75	1(33)	1(33)	1(33)			3	(7)
76+							
Total (%)	(5)	(17)	(7)	(66)	(5)		

*Students and graduates of foreign universities omitted.

the ranking of the current institutional affiliation of the respondent. The same pattern holds true for the members of the ASA sample, but the linkage between the two is much stronger for them. For example, nearly nine in ten of the graduates of top-five schools, all of the graduates of schools ranked six through ten, and nearly two-thirds of the graduates of schools ranked between eleven and twenty-five in the ASA sample are currently affiliated with institutions that have doctoral programs. In contrast, only four in ten of the members of our sample whose Ph.D. came from a top five school have ended up at a Ph.D. school, whereas a quarter or fewer of the graduates of schools at the next two levels in the prestige hierarchy are currently located at such schools (note also that only 17 percent of our total sample is located at Ph.D. institutions, whereas two-thirds of the ASA sample is located at such schools). If we focus attention on the lower end of the prestige continuum of current institutional affiliations—four-year colleges and universities—we see that the members of our sample of sociologists from working-class backgrounds, except for the five whose doctorates came from top-five schools, are concentrated there in far larger numbers than are the members of the ASA sample (over a third of our sample is at such schools, whereas fewer than 20 percent of the ASA sample are located at schools at this level in the prestige hierarchy). These data point to two conclusions. First, that the current institutional affiliations of our sample of sociologists from working-class backgrounds, when the rank of the Ph.D source is controlled, are not as prestigious as those of the membership of the ASA. In other words, the members of our sample do not seem to have gotten as much mileage out of their source of degree as have the members of the larger group.[13] Second, despite the differences between the two samples, it is clear that, for both groups, the lower the prestige ranking of the source of the Ph.D., the greater the likelihood of being employed at an institution without a graduate program.[14]

Next, we wanted to examine the linkage between source of the graduate degree and the current institutional affiliation in greater detail; we did this by focusing our attention only on those from the two samples who are currently employed in Ph.D. granting departments and comparing the distributions of the two samples in terms of the rankings of the two. These data are presented in Table 5.7. Athough our sample is small (only seven of its members currently work in departments that grant the Ph.D. degree), the differences between the two distributions are, nonetheless, quite large. Ignoring for a moment the rank of the source of the Ph.D., only 14 percent (one!) of those sociologists from working-class backgrounds work in schools ranked in the top fifty among U.S. Ph.D.-granting departments. This compares with the two-thirds (eighteen) of the members of the ASA sample who work in Ph.D.-granting departments who are located at schools ranked in the top fifty departments in the country. Notice as well that, for the ASA sample at least, there is a clear association between the prestige ranking of the source of the Ph.D. and that of the current employer (i.e., the cells toward the top left of the table have cases in them—for example,

Table 5.7
A Comparison between Our Sample of Sociologists from Working-Class Backgrounds and a Sample of the Membership of the ASA in Terms of Relative Status of Source of Ph.D. and of Current Ph.D.-Granting Employer

N(%)

Sociologists from Working-Class Backgrounds Sample (N=7)*
Rank of Ph.D. Employer

Rank of Ph.D. Department	Top 5	6–10	11–25	26–50	51–75	76+	N
Top 5				1(50)	1(50)		2
6–10							
11–25					1(100)		1
26–50					1(50)	1(50)	2
51–75				1(50)	1(50)		2
76+							
Totals (%)				(14)	(43)	(29)	7

ASA Sample (N=27)*

Rank of Ph.D. Employer

Rank of Ph.D. Department	Top 5	6–10	11–25	26–50	51–75	76+	N
Top 5	4(57)	1(14)		1(14)	1(14)		7
6–10		1(20)		1(20)	3(60)		5
11–25			4(44)	2(22)	1(12)	2(22)	9
26–50			1(17)	3(50)		2(33)	6
51–75							
76+							
Totals(%)	(15)	(7)	(19)	(26)	(15)	(15)	27

*Samples reduced to those with (U.S.) Ph.D. degrees who are employed in Ph.D.-granting institutions.

four of the seven members of the ASA sample who were graduated from top five schools are currently employed in top five schools). Looking at the portion of the table that displays the data for our sample of sociologists from working-class backgrounds reveals that these upper left-hand cells are empty. Thus, no matter the relative ranking of the source of the Ph.D., the institutions that employ the members of our sample are clustered toward the right side of the table (i.e, toward the lower end of the prestige scale of sociology departments that offer the Ph.D. degree). These data provide additional evidence to support the conclusion that our sample of working-class sociologists (when compared with members of the ASA sample, at least), tend to work at institutions that are lower in disciplinary prestige. It also appears that the sources of their graduate degrees appear to have less influence on the locations of their current institutional affiliations within the disciplinary prestige hierarchy than they do for the members of the ASA.[15]

Feelings about Current Professional Position. Our final subject concerning the professional careers of our sample of sociologists from working-class backgrounds is their own feelings about the relative location of their college or university within the academic prestige hierarchy and their perceptions about why they have ended up where they have at this point in their careers. Previous research is ambivalent about the reactions of academics from working-class backgrounds to the relative prestige of their current location within the disciplinary hierarchy. On the one hand, some lament the fact that they are teaching at schools "beneath" their abilities; on the other hand, some have actually chosen such schools on purpose (Ryan and Sackrey 1984). Pursuing this issue, we first asked about our respondents' feelings about their current position (i.e., the position of their college or university) in the academic hierarchy. After carefully reading the responses to this question, we divided them into three categories. The first category, "generally satisfied," was for respondents who had only good things to say about their current employment situation. The reply of a fifty-five-year-old male provides a good example of responses placed in this category: "I am pleased with it. Sociology at _____ ranks in the top 40 departments in the country. . . . This gives me an especially good feeling because . . . I have been able to play some role in it." The second category is "mixed" and contains responses that voiced both positive and negative assessments of their current situation. A good example here comes from a forty-five-year-old male: "Mixed. I am happy to have a tenured position at a research university with a graduate program in sociology. The wages suck though. My name was the last one mentioned in the list of jobs secured by _____ alumni after I took this job, but my goals and career path were not exactly the same as most of my cohorts." The third response category is labeled "generally dissatisfied" and the response of a twenty-eight-year-old female is a good example of those placed here: "I am teaching at a junior college and really I feel that it's way beneath me. I feel that I am overeducated for the job I have and I'm very resentful of my colleagues who are less educated and yet have the kind of job security that I can only dream about." The distribution of our respondents across these three categories is presented in Table 5.8. As shown there, although slightly over four in ten of our respondents were generally satisfied with their current professional situation/position, the remainder either had mixed feelings or were dissatisfied. Gender has a strong association with responses to this question—two-thirds of our female respondents were classified as generally satisfied with their current employment situation, whereas slightly more than a quarter of our male respondents were. In contrast, nearly six in ten of our male respondents either had mixed feelings about their current situation or were generally dissatisfied with it (in comparison, only a quarter or so of our female respondents were placed into these two categories). As an aside here, as one might expect, the level of satisfaction expressed with a current employment situation was also correlated with the nature of that situation. In general, among our respondents, those located in departments with graduate programs in sociology were much more likely to offer a positive assessment of their current situation than were those located at institutions that only offered the baccalaureate degree or less. Although this association was observed in the data, it is, by no means, a perfect one. The response of a forty-six-year-old female located at a university with a limited sociology program is a case in point: "_____ is predominantly a working-class university, with a growing number of middle-class students. It is the perfect place for me to teach. I have at no time in the last 10 years tried to or wish to leave and work at a more prestigious college or university." Several other respondents located toward the bottom of the academic prestige hierarchy expressed satisfaction that they were able to concentrate on teaching and interaction with students and on having a positive influence on the paths that their students took. Others at this level, however, were more critical and dissatisfied with their current positions. Typical of these latter responses is that of a fifty-five-year-old male respondent who noted that "I teach now—and have for 17 years—at a minor league institution that is an intellectual desert. The job is to keep people paying tuition and not to flunk anyone."

The Impacts of Class Background on Professional Life. Given the study's interest in the intersection between class background and relative success within the academy, we also asked our respondents for their impressions about the role(s) that class (and other ascriptive) factors might have played in influencing their careers to date. Earlier research on this subject has argued for a strong association between class background and career trajectories (Dews and Law 1995; Ryan and Sackrey 1984; Tokarczyk and Fay 1993). These data are discussed in the paragraphs that follow.

We first asked our respondents to comment on any relationship between their backgrounds within the working class and their career trajectories. Table 5.9 divides our respondents into two groups—those whose remarks indicated that they believed that their class background had influenced their careers and those whose remarks suggested to us that it had not. As shown there, for those who

Table 5.8
Nature of Respondents' Assessments of Location of Current Employer/Position within the Academic Hierarchy*

N(%)

Sample

Response	Total	Males	Females
Generally Satisfied	10(42)	4(27)	6(67)
Mixed Feelings	7(29)	6(40)	1(11)
Generally Dissatisfied	7(29)	5(33)	2(22)
Totals	24(100)	15(100)	9(100)

[Reliability = 83%]

*Excludes student respondents and eight nonstudents who did not address the question.

answered the question, slightly more than seven in ten believed that their class background has had an important impact on their careers, whereas slightly less than three in ten indicated that it has not.[16] Examining the pattern of response to the question by gender of respondent reveals that males were convinced in greater numbers than females (82 percent versus 58 percent) that their class background has had an important influence on their careers to date.[17]

In light of the fact that most of our respondents agreed that their class backgrounds had impacted their careers, we wanted to examine their perceptions of the nature of these impacts. In exploring their responses to this issue, it became clear from their answers that most of our respondents felt that the influences of their working-class backgrounds were more *negative* than *positive*. It was also clear that the impacts our respondents mentioned in their answers were diverse. For example, several of our respondents noted that their class backgrounds had limited their knowledge about role models and the options available to them as they started to prepare for their careers. A forty-nine-year-old female stressed the lack of role models in her early life as a negative influence: "As I had no role models in my direct family for intellectual development, I have been held back by my poor reading speed, attention span and other intellectual skills. . . . These are definitely limitations which class can have on one." In this same context, a fifty-one-year-old male noted that "I actually did not know much about the academic business, the implications of taking certain jobs as opposed to others, the specifics of how to get jobs, the

Table 5.9
Respondents' Perceptions of Linkage between Career Trajectory and Working-Class Origins

	N(%)		
		Samples	
	Total	*Males*	*Females*
Class Background Important	21(72)	14(82)	7(58)
Class Background Unimportant	8(28)	3(18)	5(42)
Totals*	29(100)	17(100)	12(100)
		[Reliability = 98%]	

*Excludes students, no answers, and not applicables.

importance of networks or any of it. I attribute this to being working class." A number of respondents mentioned the relative lack of material resources as a major negative consequence of their working-class background on their career opportunities. In the words of a fifty-four-year-old male: "If I had more economic resources, i.e., had higher social class origins, I think that I would probably have a doctorate and be teaching at a university." Others mentioned the impact of their origins within the working class on their self-confidence and self-esteem. In the words of a fifty-one year old male: "I think that coming from the working class impacts a person's sense of self confidence and worth. Often when I could be working on some idea, I spend a lot of time trying to convince myself that I have something to offer. I think that many academics from the working class spend a lot of time dealing with self-doubts instead of pushing forward with more potentially productive activities."

Although many of the impacts discussed above are, in many ways, negative and potentially detrimental to the careers of those affected, several respondents chose to stress the positive influences of their class backgrounds on their careers and work. One of the most frequently mentioned of these latter influences of class on career was its impact on *choice of substantive interests*. A forty-one-year-old female put it this way: "Many of the basic questions I ask as a sociologist and how I understand the world are rooted in my class background.

I want to understand social inequality and understand what are the structures that keep some people on the bottom and others on the top. . . . My left politics . . . are clearly related to my class background." A second positive influence that was mentioned by several respondents was their ability to work with and, in some senses, to "reach out to" first-generation students from working-class backgrounds. In fact, some of our respondents deliberately chose employment at institutions whose student bodies were mostly from working-class backgrounds for this reason. These data show clearly that many in our sample feel that their backgrounds within the working class have had impacts, many of them negative, but some of them positive as well, on various features of their careers as professional sociologists. It is also clear that a number of the same influences of class that they mentioned in response to a similar question about their higher educational careers in Chapter 4 were highlighted by our respondents here as well.

Impacts of Class versus Ascriptive Characteristics. Because our sample contains not just male sociologists of European American descent from working-class backgrounds but also women and (a small number of) African Americans and Hispanic Americans, we were also interested in our respondents' perceptions of the relative impacts of class on their careers when compared with these other ascriptive variables. So, in a second question, we widened the scope of our inquiry and asked our respondents to include gender and race/ethnicity in addition to class as potential career influences. As might be suspected, several of our "minority" respondents thought that their particular minority status (i.e., gender or race/ethnicity) had exercised a greater influence on their careers than had class. Both an Hispanic American female and an African American male, for example, specifically mentioned the role that affirmative action had played in influencing their career opportunities, whereas a number of female respondents mentioned that the burdens of family responsibilities had a large role in "defining" the parameters of their careers. The statement of a thirty-nine-year-old female who finished her Ph.D. twenty years after she finished her B.A. provides a good example of the role that gender plays for many academic women: "My current position reflects more on my gender. Out of the number of 'Moms' in my program, we've all had delays from motherhood, no matter what our class background.[18]

This section of the chapter has explored a number of features of the professional careers of our sample of sociologists from working-class backgrounds, at times simply by examining the characteristics and responses of the members of our sample alone, at other times by comparing them with a sample of the membership of the national sociological association, the ASA. Although most of its findings are consistent with the findings of previous research on the subject, some of them are not. For example, we found that, though most of the members of our sample selected their first postgraduate job based on academic criteria, a number of them, more women than men, selected them based on other criteria such as economic necessity and closeness to family support systems. With regard to their first professional positions, we found that the modal position for both genders was assistant professor, but we also found that females were more likely to have begun their careers in research/ administrative positions than were males. This difference is consistent with Barker's (1993) finding that female academics from working-class backgrounds are subject to both class and gender effects, both of which are negative. Our comparisons between the current positions and institutional affiliations of our sample with a sample of members of the ASA revealed that sociologists from the working-class are disadvantaged in a number of ways: Their current ranks were lower; they are employed at institutions that rank lower in the disciplinary prestige hierarchy; and, for those few members of our sample who were currently employed in doctoral departments, these departments were ranked lower in academic prestige than those of the members of the ASA sample. When we asked our respondents to assess their satisfaction with their current job, most either had mixed feelings or were dissatisfied (male respondent were more likely to be dissatisfied than were females). Finally, most of our respondents felt that their class background was implicated in their careers, and many of them felt that the impacts of their class background were more negative than positive. We now turn to an examination of the academic/professional lives of our respondents.

PERCEPTIONS OF ACADEMIC/PROFESSIONAL LIFE

Our second topic concerning the professional careers of our sample of sociologists from working-class backgrounds focuses on their perceptions about life as a member of the upper-middle-class professional academic community. Here we are interested in things such as their perceptions about the proper balance among the various roles of a professional academic (i.e., teaching, research, and service), the nature of their relations with academic authority, the correspondence between their early expectations about what it would be like to be a college professor and the daily realities of life as a member of a college/university faculty, their relations with their colleagues and students, and, finally, the extent to which they feel comfortable with the academic/intellectual role. Each of these topics will be addressed in the paragraphs that follow.

Perceptions about Balance among Academic Roles

The first issue we examine is our respondents' perceptions about the current balance among the traditional roles of a faculty member in the academy (i.e., teaching, research, and service), and any changes that they would make in the relative importance of these roles if they were able to do so. This particular question was motivated by the notion developed by earlier researchers that academics from the working class have different goals within the academy when compared with many of their colleagues (Dews and Law 1995; Ryan and Sackrey 1984; Tokarczyk and Fay 1993). Coding these responses proved especially difficult because we were really asking two questions here and some respondents chose to answer both, whereas others answered either one or the other of the two. This made organizing their responses for presentation and discussion somewhat more difficult. The one finding that clearly emerged from our analysis of their responses, however, is that most of our respondents felt, although often for different reasons, that the current balance among the various roles within the academic enterprise was not ideal for them. For example, nearly half (45 percent) of those who were currently employed in academic positions and who responded to this question felt that there was too much emphasis on research within the academy and far too little on other activities such as teaching, departmental, university and community service, and community involvement. One extreme critic, a fifty-five-year-old male, put things this way: "Academic life is a fraud. It is all 'research.' It should be teaching and service. It is ridiculous to assume that there are that many new ideas each year to promote so much publication." Another, somewhat less extreme, viewpoint that reaches the same conclusion is that of a forty-four-year-old male, who noted that:

If I could change anything regarding my professional roles, it would be a reduction of importance of the research activity and more emphasis on teaching, as my institution is clearly a teaching institution in function. I do like the ability (and encouragement) to be research active, although the level of publication activity expected here casts such activity as the primary rewarded activity.

This opinion is mirrored in the remarks of a forty-one-year-old female respondent who observed that: "It is clear that research is regarded much higher than teaching or service in academic circles. I would like to see teaching taken more seriously."

A second group of respondents had the opposite reaction to the question. This group (approximately 30 percent of the total) felt that teaching took up far too much of their time and that research was not sufficiently encouraged. A typical response from this group is that of a fifty-four-year-old male who wrote: "At the community college level teaching and community service are stressed with very little encouragement or assistance given to research. I would encourage more research at this level and more stress on teaching at the four-year college and university level."

A third type of response to this question is both critical of the lack of attention given to *all* the various roles within the academy in general, and, most particularly, of its unwillingness to become more of an agent of social change in the community. In the words of a thirty-eight-year-old female respondent:

I believe colleges need to further support the research efforts of their faculty, universities need to further insist upon quality teaching efforts by all of their faculty, and both settings need to expand the "praxis" of public contributions and/or community services. I believe that professional academics (and especially sociologists) are in a unique position and have special responsibility to take an active role with regard to public policy.

As these remarks suggest, our respondents expressed general dissatisfaction with the current balance among various roles within the academy (in contrast, fewer than 20 percent of our respondents approved of the current balance among the various roles at their institutions); at least some of this dissatisfaction reflects the particular career histories or current institutional locations of our respondents (e.g., those teaching at the junior college level were particularly chagrined that their teaching loads were too high and their opportunities for research too meager); and the prescriptions for change that our respondents offered were diverse in nature. It is also interesting that despite the few who felt that the current balance of roles was good, most of our respondents felt that the particular balance among the various roles at their institution (whatever its nature) made it more difficult for them to be the kind of sociologist (whether teacher, scholar, departmental/community citizen, or social activist) that they preferred to be. It should also be noted here that gender differences did not play a major role in structuring our respondents' assessment(s) of this issue.

Orientation toward Authority

Our second major interest in our respondents' perceptions about their professional lives is their general orientation toward authority within the academy. Earlier research has suggested that working-class academics often have more difficulty dealing with authority than do their middle-class colleagues (Ryan and Sackrey 1984). Our examination of our respondents' remarks concerning this issue led us to divide them into two categories—positive, when respondents indicated that they accepted the necessity for authority and generally stressed its positive consequences; and negative, when the respondents noted that they were afraid of, resentful toward, felt constrained by, mistrusted, or even hated academic authority. Typical of a response placed in the first category is that of a thirty-eight-year-old male who responded: "I'm comfortable with authority in academia and I respect those who hold power. However, as in any other profession, I recognize all as human beings, imperfect, selfish, and hungry for power, fame, and money." One of the responses we placed in the "negative" category is that of a thirty-eight-year-old female respondent who said: "With regard to authority within the academic enterprise, I have a similar relationship to authority regardless of setting: I am generally troubled by it, and tend to resent it."

Table 5.10 contains the distribution of our respondents across these categories. As presented there, a majority of our respondents were more likely to have a negative assessment of academic authority, although the margin of

Table 5.10
Respondents' General Orientation toward Academic Authority

		N(%)	
		Samples	
Response To Authority	*Total*	*Males*	*Females*
Generally Positive	10(45)	7(47)	3(43)
Generally Negative	12(55)	8(53)	4 (57)
Totals*	22(100)	15(100)	7(100)
NA	5		
Inapplicable	5		
		[Reliability=100%]	

---

*Excludes students.

difference was only ten percentage points; moreover, gender of respondent did not have a large impact on the responses to this issue. As might be suspected, those with negative assessments of academic authority were more explicit and detailed in their condemnations of its deleterious effects. A good example of this latter group of respondents is the remarks of a forty-year-old male respondent who wrote:

My general orientation toward authority in the academy—a strange mixture of the necessary deference combined with incredible rage. As I have said, I have figured out how to "get by"–"get along"—to be pleasant to those in charge (deans, senior colleagues, etc.), do what I need to do to get and keep an appointment, etc. However, I often feel that this is merely a "mask" behind which I feel anger at having to be nice to people who have contempt for my students (and people like me) and who have little or no moral, political, or intellectual character.

Perceptions about Everyday Academic Life

We next turn to an examination of our respondents' answers to a question that asked them to assess the extent to which the realities of everyday life in the academy correspond to their early perceptions of what it would be like. This question is based in part on the relative lack of exposure of children from the working class to adequate role models for middle-class jobs in particular and for professional academic jobs in general (Tokarczyk and Fay 1993). After examining the responses to this question, we divided them into two groups—the first for those who felt that their expectations about life as an academic correspond fairly closely to their experiences and a second for those who felt that their experiences have fallen short of their early expectations. Most respondents who were placed in the first category gave fairly brief and simple answers like "Most of the realities of everyday life in the academy correspond to my expectations" and "My early perceptions of what academic life would be have not been jolted by the reality of everyday life." Those placed in the second category were also likely to be brief in their response to this question with such remarks as "I suppose the lack of value to teaching and discussing ideas is my major disappointment about academia." When we sorted out our respondents into these two groups (Table 5.11), we found that almost six in ten of them (59 percent) reported that their initial expectations and their everyday realities were about the same, whereas slightly more than four in ten viewed the realities of everyday life in the academy as different from, and, falling somewhat short of their expectations about what it would be like.[19] When these responses are stratified by gender, we found that male respondents were evenly split between those whose early anticipations and realities are comparable and those for whom the two differ, whereas females were far more likely to indicate that their early expectations and their current realities are in closer agreement (three-fourths of the female sample fell into this category). As a follow-up to this question, we also gave our respondents the opportunity to note any major disappointments they had experienced as members of the academy. Interestingly, most of them mentioned one or two things about which they were disappointed, no matter the tenor of the answer they gave to the first part of the question. Among those things mentioned were such things as workloads, departmental politics, having to deal with institutional bureaucracies, endless and meaningless meetings, inadequate salaries and resources, careerism and elitism among colleagues—in short, the very things that we suspect most academics complain about, regardless of their class backgrounds, particularly during the more difficult times of recent history. A couple of our respondents, however, more explicitly linked their disappointments to class issues. For example, a fifty-five-year-old male made the following remarks about his colleagues: "But my 'friends and enemies'. . . are constantly 'dis-ing' me and telling me that I do not belong in this department and I don't know what I'm doing. Of course, with typical middle class arrogance, most of them have no idea of what I do." A forty-seven-year-old male summarized his reactions to this issue this way: "In some ways, I expected all of this when I entered academia. But in other ways, it comes as a shock. I think that in graduate school in particular, I really believed that hard work and intellectual originality could overcome the 'disadvantages' (in the eyes of the academy) of being working class and a Marxist. My experience, especially in the last decade, has proved that incorrect."

Table 5.11
Respondents' Perceptions of Fit between Academic Role and Early Perceptions of What Should/Would Be

N(%)

	Samples		
Responses	*Total*	*Males*	*Females*
Expectations and Reality about the Same	13(59)	7(50)	6(75)
Reality Does not Live Up to Early Expectations	9(41)	7(50)	2(25)
*Totals**	22(100)	14(100)	8(100)
NA	4		
Not in Academic Employment	6		

[Reliability = 94%]

---

*Students excluded.

Perceptions about Fitting into Academic Role

Because earlier research has noted that the contradictions between the early lives of academics from working-class backgrounds and their contemporary realities as members of the intellectual elite of society generate a number of contradictions for them, including feeling like an "outsider" (cf. Dews and Law 1995; Ryan and Sackrey 1984; Tokarczyk and Fay 1993), we also asked our respondents to give us an estimate of how well they see themselves as "fitting into" the role of an academic sociologist. Examining their responses led us to divide them into three categories: "uncomfortable with the role/feel like an 'outsider' most of the time," "ambivalent/feel (or have felt) both 'inside' and 'outside,'" and "comfortable with the role/feel like an 'insider' most of the time." A good example of the "uncomfortable/outsider" response is that of a forty-four-year-old male respondent, who wrote: "As a professional sociologist, I have always felt like an outsider to the profession. This lack of fitting in stems from two sources. First, I have always felt academically less well prepared than most sociologists. . . . The second source of alienation comes from life in a strange [class] culture." Our example of an "ambivalent" position on the issue comes from a forty-three-year-old female, who responded:

I don't see myself as fitting in well. But I think I have the feeling that I am a stranger only when I am interacting with other academics. When I teach, I feel as though I have adapted well to the role. When I am doing research, I feel comfortable. It is only when I must present myself in a social situation with others (specifically, outside my department; at professional meetings, etc.) that I feel insecure and out of place.

Our example of a "comfortable/insider" response comes from a fifty-five-year-old male, who remarked that "I have always felt 'at home' in sociology. I have gained enormous satisfaction in the academic role and have felt accepted and appreciated by colleagues. I have never had a sense of being an unwanted 'outsider.'" The distribution of our respondents across these three categories is presented in Table 5.12. As shown there, almost half (45 percent) of our sample was placed, based on their responses to this question, in the "uncomfortable/outsider" category, with the remarks of another third suggesting that they are "ambivalent" about their sense of fitting adequately into the role. The responses of the remaining fourth of our respondents led us to place them in the "comfortable/insider" category. If we combine the respondents coded into the first two categories, we find that fully three-quarters of our respondents indicated either that they have always felt themselves to be uncomfortable with, or feel ambivalent about the extent to which they "fit into" the academic role.

When the distribution is broken down by gender, we find that half our males were placed into the "uncomfortable/outsider" category, and nearly eight in ten (78 percent) of them were classified as either uncomfortable with or ambivalent about the academic role. For females, only a third were placed into the "uncomfortable/outsider" category, but more than seven in ten (seventy-two percent) were classified as either uncomfortable with or ambivalent about the academic role. In short, although males were more likely to be placed into the uncomfortable/outsider category than were females, when the two categories (uncomfortable/outsider and ambivalent) are combined, their percentages become more equal—nearly three-quarters of both groups expressed opinions that led us to classify them as either uncomfortable with, or ambivalent about, the extent to which they feel that they fit into the academic role. These results are consistent with the findings of earlier research on the subject.

Relations with Academic Colleagues

Because earlier research has noted that academics from working-class backgrounds also have difficulty in their relations with colleagues (Ryan and Sackrey 1984; Tokarczyk and Fay 1993), we also asked our respondents to characterize their social and interpersonal relations with their fellow faculty members. After reading their responses to the question, we divided them into three categories—generally positive and close, more ambiguous or a "mixed

Table 5.12
Respondents' Perceptions of "Fitting into" the Academic Role and of Feeling Like an "Outsider" in the Role

N(%)

Samples

Response	Total	Males	Females
Uncomfortable with Role/ *Feel Like "Outsider Most* *of the time*	13(45)	9(50)	4(36)
Ambivalent, Feel (or have *Felt) Both "Inside" and "Outside"*	9(31)	5(28)	4(36)
Comfortable with Role/Feel *Like "Insider Most of Time*	7(24)	4(22)	3(27)
Totals*	29(100)	18(100)	11(99)

[Reliability = 100%]

---

*Excludes students, three respondents who did not address the question, and one who does not
  occupy a professional role.

bag," and generally more negative and distant. The remarks of a fifty-five-year-old male are a good (if somewhat extreme) example of the first category of our scheme: "All are very good. I have no colleagues with whom I have poor relations or conflict and am on friendly terms with all. I respect my colleagues and without exception find them to be personally very congenial." An example of a "mixed-bag" response is that of a thirty-eight-year-old male: "I mostly interact with friends and people I meet through friends. I do not 'network' and this is a direct consequence of class background. In my department I am certainly something of a 'crank,' but fortunately there are several others in the department." Our example of the generally more negative and distant category is a bit extreme in tone but clearly gets the message across: "I never socialize with my professional peers—except when they force themselves on me. . . . I have been to one social event with sociologists in the past ten years and I refuse all invitations and none of my friends and enemies at this institution are welcome in my home or office."

When we examine the distribution of our respondents across these categories (see Table 5.13), we find that a large majority (approximately seven in ten) viewed their relations with colleagues as generally positive and close; a couple of respondents were more ambiguous about them, and two in ten characterized their relations with colleagues as generally negative and more distant. There are

Table 5.13
Respondents' Perceptions of Relations with Professional Colleagues

N(%)

Samples

Respondent's Perception of Relations with Colleagues	Total	Males	Females
Generally Positive, More Close	18(72)	9(60)	9(90)
Ambiguous, More a "Mixed Bag"	2(8)	1(7)	1(10)
Generally Negative, More Distant	5(20)	5(33)	—
Totals*	25(100)	15(100)	10(100)

[Reliability = 100%]

*Omitted were students, a respondent currently employed in a working-class job, and five respondents who failed to adress the question.

gender differences in response to this question. Whereas nine in ten females saw their relations with colleagues as generally positive and close, only six in ten males did; furthermore, 20 percent of the males'characterizations of their relations with colleagues led us to place them in the generally negative, more distant category, but not a single female respondent was placed into this category. About a quarter of our respondents (five males and three females) explicitly mentioned class differences as an important influence in their relations with colleagues, but there was no association between whether or not they mentioned class and the nature of their characterization of their relations with colleagues (i.e., whether they saw them as positive, ambiguous/mixed, or negative in character). The remarks of a forty-six-year-old female provide an example of the linkage between class and these associations. Despite the fact that her overall response was coded as generally positive and close, she observed: "I tend to relate better to professors and administrators who share my class background. . . . unfortunately most don't!"

Another indicator of the nature of a respondent's relations with colleagues is the extent to which on-the-job social relationships carry over after work. Once again, previous research on the subject suggests that academics from working-class backgrounds would not feel as comfortable with their upper-middle-class associates as friends as they would with others from the working class (Ryan and Sackrey 1984). To pursue this aspect of the situation, we asked for our participants' reflections about their after-hours social relationships. Our inspection of their responses resulted in four categories. The first was "solely/mostly with colleagues." A typical response placed in this category is that of a forty-four-year-old female who observed: "With the exception of dating, I socialize mostly with other faculty members. Mostly, we go out to dinner and/or movies, to college plays or to local classical concerts." The second category was labeled "with colleagues, but also with others outside the academy." Typical of responses located in this category is that of a forty-four-year-old male who responded: "Outside of the typical departmental parties and other university-based social events, I tend to socialize with only two or three colleagues on a somewhat regular basis. . . . Otherwise, most of the people I socialize with are not colleagues, although some of them may be students or staff." The third category is "rarely/never with colleagues." The remarks of a fifty-five-year-old male (mentioned already in another, related context) are an example those placed in this category. He noted that:"I never socialize with my professional peers—except when they force themselves on me. . . . [No colleagues] are welcome at my home or in my office." The fourth and final category is for those who indicated that they did little or no "off-work" socialization.

Table 5.14 presents the distribution of our respondents across these categories. As shown there, most of our respondents (52 percent) noted that they socialized either almost exclusively with colleagues when off work, or that they socialized with a mixture of colleagues and others, whereas a quarter (26 percent) rarely or never socialized with colleagues when not at work. Twenty-two percent of our respondents said that they did little or no off-the-job socialization. Examining the distribution of responses to the question by gender reveals that female respondents were more likely to socialize with colleagues or with colleagues and others than were males (60 percent versus 47 percent); they were also slightly less likely to report that they rarely or never associated with colleagues when compared with their male counterparts.

Class Backgrounds of Closest Academic Friends

We also inquired about the class background(s) of our respondents' closest academic friends. Our examination of their responses led to the creation of a six-category scheme that included working class, working class/lower middle class, lower middle class/middle class, middle class, upper middle class, and a variety of different class backgrounds. The distribution of our respondents among these categories is presented in Table 5.15. The modal response category in the table for all three samples (i.e., total, male, and female) is the "varied-class-locations" category (this probably reflects the class heterogeneity of most departments). A typical response placed in this category is from a forty-four-year-old female, who said, in response to this question: "I socialize with a

Table 5.14
Respondents' Perceptions about "off-the-Job" Socialization Partners

	N(%)		
		Samples*	
Response Categories	Total	Male	Female
Solely/Mostly with Colleagues	4(15)	1(6)	3(30)
With Colleagues, but also with Others Outside the Academy	10(37)	7(41)	3(30)
Rarely/Never with Colleagues	7(26)	5(29)	2(20)
Little "Off-Work" Socialization	6(22)	4(23)	2(20)
Totals	23(100)	17(99)	10(100)
		[Reliability = 94%]	

*Samples exclude students and six respondents who did not answer the question.

number of academics who come from a variety of different backgrounds, some working class and other[s] upper middle class." However, it is interesting to note that, if we combine the bottom two class categories (i.e., working class and working class/lower middle class) into one, it would contain nearly half (44 percent) of our respondents. This finding suggests that there may be some class-specificity among our respondents in terms of their closest academic friend(s) despite the fact that "varied class locations" was the modal category of the distribution. This more class-specific trend was even stronger when we stratified the sample by gender. Here, class appeared to be more closely linked to the selection of close academic friends for males—one in four males indicated that their closest academic friends are from a working-class background and fully half of their close friends are from either working or lower middle classes, as compared with one in five (and four in ten) of the females. In contrast to males, the remarks of a majority of female respondents on this subject led us to put them into the "varied-class-locations" category of the table and this proportion remains the modal category even when two lowest class categories are combined into a single category for them.

Table 5.15
Respondents' Perceptions of the Class Background(s) of Their Closest Academic Friend(s)

N(%)

Class Background(s) of Closest Academic Friend(s)	Total	*Samples* Males	Females
Working Class	6(22)	3(25)	3(20)
Working Class/Lower Middle Class	6(22)	3(25)	3(20)
Lower Middle Class/Middle Class	1(4)	—	1(7)
Middle Class	2(7)	1(8)	1(7)
Upper Middle Class	1(4)	1(8)	—
Varied Class Locations	11(41)	4(33)	7(47)
Totals	27(100)	12(99)	15(101)
No Answer	3		

[Reliability = 97%]

*Samples exclude nine respondents who did not respond to the question and one respondent who claimed to have no close academic friends.

Relations with Students

Our next subject is the nature of our respondents' interaction(s) with students. Earlier research has noted that academics from working-class backgrounds, particularly those who teach at private universities, often have difficult relations with students (Ryan and Sackrey 1994). Given that the overall focus of our study is on the impacts of class on various features of the lives of our sample of sociologists from working-class backgrounds, we asked our respondents if class had impacted the way they relate to students in any way. Nearly nine in ten of the respondents who answered the question (87 percent) indicated that class definitely impacted their interactions with students (the proportion answering either way was not impacted by gender). We then asked those who answered in the affirmative to specify the way(s) in which they saw class as impacting their interactions with students. Our analysis of these responses yielded three major kinds of impacts. The most frequently mentioned impact of class on interactions with students was respondent identification with, and sympathy for, students from working-class backgrounds. Over one-third of our respondents mentioned this particular impact. We provide a couple of examples of this impact with the following quotes. The first comes from a forty-one-year-old female: "It is clear to me that my class background has impacted the way I relate to students. I find myself willing to go the extra mile for students from a working class background and for those who clearly have to 'work' for a college education." A twenty-eight-year-old female summarized the impacts of class on her relations with students this way: "I've noticed that I have a definite soft spot for the working class kids that do occasionally find their way into my classrooms. I know that they've had to work harder to get there."

The second most frequently mentioned impact of class on relations with students was the impact of our respondents' backgrounds within the working class on their pedagogical approaches. Several mentioned that they often talked about their own class backgrounds in class and even asked their students to do the same. These respondents argued that this strategy usually encouraged working-class students to be more involved in the classroom, to approach instructors more readily, and sometimes even to establish a more close relationship with them. A forty-six-year-old female respondent who teaches at a predominantly working-class university put the matter this way: "Once my undergraduates understand the concept of class background, many things that they have experienced start to 'make sense.' Those who find we share common background often seek me out with problems and issues they feel I will understand." Another forty-four-year-old male respondent mentioned that his sensitivity to his own background in the working class, and the problems he faced as a result, were beneficial to working-class students:

One of my most important goals as a working class academic is to make college a viable route for upward mobility. . . . My ability to do this is enhanced by my understanding of working class worlds and my ability to be a faculty who can understand working class students' problems/situations better than my middle-class colleagues. This ability is also useful in my ability to convey to these [working class] students that,   despite what their parents or peers think of them,   their questions,   thoughts and abilities do have value in larger worlds.

A third way that our respondents mentioned that being a working-class academic has had positive impacts on their students is through serving as role models for them.[20] In the words of a thirty-one-year-old male: "In essence, I serve as a role-model of sorts to show them that people of working class origins do belong in the university. I'm trying to demystify academia for these students. I'm trying to show that you can do well and use your time in college to help understand your situation and the world around you." In sum, a large majority of our respondents reported that their backgrounds within the working class had not only impacted their interactions with students, but also that these impacts were positive in nature.

Feeling Somehow "Different" from Colleagues

Given the findings of previous research that academics from working-class backgrounds often feel themselves to be virtual "strangers" within the academic environment,[21] we next asked our respondents if they felt that they were somehow "different" from their colleagues. As shown in Table 5.16, more than eight in ten of them responded that they did, indeed, feel different, in some ways, from their colleagues. Examining the pattern of response to the question by gender reveals that though male respondents were more likely than females to feel somehow different, fully three-fourths of our female respondents reported that they also felt different. For those who indicated that they did feel somehow different, we asked them to detail just why or how they felt different from their colleagues. Three major reasons were predominant in their responses. Class differences were mentioned by more of our respondents as the reason they felt different from their colleagues than was any other reason. The response of a forty-seven-year-old male participant is a good example of this group of respondents: "I have often said to myself, and to a few friends, how much I love sociology but hate sociologists. I have only recently explored the thought that this is because most sociologists, like most academics, are from middle and upper middle class backgrounds. . . . Their agenda in life, and the way they play their academic roles, is seemingly very different than mine." The second most frequently mentioned reason why some members of our sample of sociologists from working-class backgrounds felt themselves to be different was that they were more radical and more concerned with social justice than were most or all of their colleagues. The remarks of a thirty-seven-year-old female respondent exemplify this reaction:

Yes, I *do* feel different from my "colleagues," because I am. Not only is my background different, but so are my choices. I have no respect for those whose careers are built on writing for other academics, who engage in esoteric academic discussions about methodology, theory, etc., and actually think it's important! I became a sociologist because I believe that a sociological perspective can help liberate people. I think we ought to be concerned with policy, with social change, with liberating teaching, with making our research results accessible to the general public.

The third most important difference that was mentioned deals with cultural capital skills. A forty-three-year-old female respondent put it this way:

I see myself as disadvantaged in terms of social skills. Though not all fit the mold exactly, I think the expectation is that one is articulate, confident, fluent in conversation, knowledgeable about current affairs as well as history, music, art and movies, etc. To the extent that I see myself as not these things, I feel awkward in situations which show off my shortcomings.

As is obvious from these respondents' remarks, there are a number of ways

Table 5.16
Respondents' Perceptions of Feeling Somehow "Different" from Professional Colleagues

N(%)

Samples

Response	Total	Males	Females
Yes, Feel Different	23(82)	14(88)	9(75)
No, Do Not Feel Different	5(18)	2(12)	3(25)
Totals*	28(100)	16(100)	12(100)

[Reliability=97%]

---

*Totals exclude students, two male respondents who did not answer the question, and a male respondent who was not employed in a professional position.

in which they felt themselves to be different from their colleagues, many of whom come from different (and generally higher-) class backgrounds. These findings are consistent with earlier research on the subject.

This section of the chapter has dealt with our respondents' perceptions about a number of different features of the professional academic role. Previous research on the subject suggests that academics from working-class backgrounds have more difficulty adapting to the demands of this role than do other academics (Dews and Law 1995; Ryan and Sackrey 1984; Tokarczyk and Fay 1993). The data reviewed in this section of the chapter support this conclusion in a number of important ways: Our respondents, whether male or female, were not happy with the current balance among the various academic roles they were forced to play and felt that this imbalance negatively affected their abilities to do good sociology; a majority of our respondents, again regardless of gender, were more likely to characterize their relationships with authority at their institutions as negative and inhibitive of their efforts to do competent work; nearly half of our respondents reported that they felt uncomfortable with the academic role, and nearly three-quarters of them felt either uncomfortable with or were ambivalent about the extent to which they fit into it. In terms of their relations with students, over nine in ten of our respondents indicated that class played a role in their interactions and three important impacts of class on their interactions with students were frequently mentioned: increased sympathy for working-class students, employing teaching strategies that encouraged working-class students to make personal contact with the respondent, and serving as role models for working-class students. Finally, eight in ten of our respondents felt themselves to be somewhat different from their colleagues and, in some senses, "outsiders" in academia. Although this was slightly more true for our male than for our female respondents, fully three-fourths of the females also felt this way. Three commonly mentioned reasons for feeling different included perceived class differences in behaviors and attitudes, differences in terms of politics and social activism, and feelings of discomfort because of perceived social skills deficits. These findings are consistent with the notion that sociologists from the working class occupy a *marginal* position within the academy and that this marginality impacts their lives in a number of important ways including the way(s) they play their academic roles; their relations with colleagues, students, friends, and academic administrators; and their perceptions that they are somehow different from many of their colleagues within the academy, most of whom come from different social class backgrounds. The next section of the chapter examines the impacts of the class background of our respondents on their ideological, political, and sociological perspectives as well as their overall satisfaction with the choice of sociology as a career.

RESPONDENTS' IDEOLOGICAL/THEORETICAL/ POLITICAL ORIENTATIONS

In this third section of the chapter, we examine our respondents' political/ideological orientations, their viewpoints about social activism, their theoretical preferences, their general assessments of the nature of life in contemporary American society, and, finally, their overall satisfaction with their choice of sociology as a career. For each of these issues, we are especially interested in our respondents' perceptions concerning the impact(s) of their class background on their viewpoint(s).

Political/Ideological Orientations

The first issue we explored was our respondents' political/ideological orientations. We asked our respondents to address this issue in a multipart question: How would you describe your "politics"? Do you see them as related in any way to your class background? Have these changed over the years? If so, how have they changed? Although not all of our respondents addressed all parts of the question, most did. For the first of these issues, our respondents' politics, our coding resulted in a scheme with four categories that moved from the right to the left on the political spectrum. We coded respondents into our first category, labeled "left of center" if they only mentioned this phrase in their characterization of their politics. A typical response placed in this category is that of a forty-six-year-old female, who wrote: "Left of center . . . has been the same since undergraduate school. Before that my opinions were left of center, but I didn't know that. My ex-husband just told me I was stupid." Our second category is labeled "liberal/democrat" and respondents had to mention one (or both) of these to be classified here. Typical of such responses is that of a fifty-seven-year-old male who simply said "I would describe myself as a liberal

Democrat." Our third category is "socialist." Those placed in this category had to mention the word "socialist" in their response to this part of the question. A typical response of those placed here is that of a fifty-one-year-old male who reported: "I moved from New Deal Democrat to Democratic Socialist over the years." Our final category is "radical/Marxist." To be placed in this category, a respondent had to mention either of the terms in the label or to suggest in some other way that (s)he had a radical approach to politics. A typical response placed here is that of a fifty-one-year-old male who characterized his politics as: I guess I'd call myself a left wing anarchist who has drawn heavily on Marxist analysis"[22]

Table 5.17 displays the distribution of our respondents across these categories. The first thing to notice about the political/ideological orientations of our sample is that each and every one of its members claimed an orientation that was to the left of the political/ideological center. The modal category for our respondents is the "liberal/democratic" category—that category contained nearly four in ten of our respondents. The rubric "left-of-center" contained an additional three in ten. When these two are combined, two-thirds of our respondents were classified as what we would label "moderate leftist" in their political/ideological orientations. When we stratify these data by gender, there are clear differences between our male and female respondents in terms of political/ideological orientation—nearly four in ten of our male respondents were placed into the two more extreme leftist categories as compared to fewer than two in ten of our female respondents. In response to the second part of our question—any possible linkages between a respondent's political/ideological orientation and her/his class of origin— four in ten of our respondents explicitly mentioned such a linkage. A typical affirmative response to this issue is that of a forty-one-year-old female respondent, who noted: "My left politics, communist with a little 'c,' are clearly related to my class background." Finally, we asked our respondents to indicate whether or not their political/ideological orientation had changed during the course of their lives. Of those who responded to this part of the question, eleven (46 percent) indicated that their orientation had not changed; nine (38 percent) said that they have become more radical as they have aged, and four (16 percent) noted that their views have moderated over time. The only gender difference present on this latter issue was that seven of the nine respondents who indicated that their political/ideological viewpoint had become more radical over the years were males.

Perspective(s) on Social Activism

Since earlier research has also noted that academics from working-class backgrounds are more likely to be sympathetic to social activism (Ryan and Sackrey 1984), we next asked our respondents to address the issue of the role that social activism should play in the lives of professional academics. We coded their responses into two categories. The first we labeled "unqualified advocacy,"

Table 5.17
Respondents' Political/Ideological Orientations

N(%)

Samples

Political/Ideological Orientation	Total	Males	Females
Left-of-Center	9(30)	5(26)	4(26)
Liberal/Democrat	11(37)	6(32)	5(45)
Socialist	5(17)	4(21)	1(9)
Radical/Marxist	5(17)	4(21)	1(8)
*Totals**	30(101)	19(100)	11(99)

[Reliability = 97%]

---

*Excludes student respondents and two who failed to respond to the question.

and we placed respondents into this category if their support for social activism was unequivocal. A typical response we placed in this category is that of a forty-four-year-old male who wrote: "My view of activism among professional academics is [that it] is a moral, ethical and professional responsibility. Such activism is necessary not just because of [an] ethical need to engage in praxis, but the need for academics to stay in touch with the issues and people over which they claim expertise." Our second category is labeled "qualified advocacy." Here we placed respondents who supported social activism among professional academics, but who qualified their support in some way such as separating off-campus from on-campus (or in-classroom versus out-of-classroom) activities or by noting that professional associations should not engage in social advocacy. A good example of the former type of response comes from a fifty-seven-year-old male, who responded: "I support social activism on the part of professional academics when it takes place within clearly defined parameters. Professors should take great care to ensure that social activism is not forced upon students in general education courses which are required of all students." An example of the latter type of response placed in this category is from a sixty-four-year-old-female respondent who wrote: "I feel that the ASA should NOT take formal positions on political issues, but that they can provide analyses re pros and cons. In cases such as academic freedom, professional integrity and scientific ethics, I also believe that there is an appropriate role for that professional group." Turning now to the pattern of response of the members of our sample to this issue, Table 5.18 shows that all of our respondents either gave unqualified or qualified support to the notion that professional academics should play an activist role in society. Nearly seven in ten (68 percent) did not qualify their advocacy for social activism, whereas slightly more than three in ten (32 percent) specified some limiting conditions on their support. Examining the impact of gender on these responses reveals that male respondents were slightly more likely to provide unqualified support for social activism than were females (72 percent versus 60 percent).

Class Background and Ideological/Theoretical Perspectives

In response to the vocalizations of many of the essayists in the three books on academics from working-class backgrounds (Dews and Law 1995; Ryan and Sackrey 1984; Tokarczyk and Fay 1993), we next asked our respondents to provide us with their assessments about the impact(s) of their class backgrounds on perspectives that they use in their efforts to understand society. We divided the responses into three categories: "definitely yes," when respondents clearly indicated a link between class background and the perspectives they employ in their research and teaching; "uncertain," when respondents weren't sure that there was a linkage between the two; and "definitely no," when the respondent insisted that there was no linkage between the two. The results of placing our respondents into these categories are presented in Table 5.19. As demonstrated there, more than eight in ten (83 percent) of our respondents saw a definite link between their working-class background and the perspective(s) that they employ in their research; two of our respondents were uncertain that the two were linked, and three denied any linkage between the two. When these results are broken down by gender, female respondents were more likely to link the two than were our male respondents (nine of ten of the females versus three-quarters of the males did so). We asked those of our respondents who linked the two to specify the various ways in which their class backgrounds influenced their work. Inspection of their responses to this question revealed four major types of influence. Of the twenty-four respondents who linked their class backgrounds to their overall perspectives on society, twenty linked their class backgrounds to their choice of theoretical frameworks (typical perspectives identified were conflict, Marxist, feminist, [and even anarchist]), fourteen linked their class backgrounds to their choice of area or topics of research interest (most mentioned various social inequalities as their major focus of research attention); six linked their class backgrounds to their choice of research methods (specific methods noted were qualitative, autobiographical, historical, etc.); and one linked his class background to his choice of sociology as a field of study. A couple of examples from the remarks of our respondents on this issue demonstrate just how strongly they view their sociological perspective(s) as linked to their backgrounds within the working class. The first is by a fifty-one-

Table 5.18
Respondents' Perspectives on Social Activism among Professional Academics

		N(%)	
		Samples	
Perspective on Social Activism	*Total*	*Males*	*Females*
Unqualified Advocacy	19(68)	13(72)	6(60)
Qualified Advocacy	9(32)	5(28)	4(40)
*Totals**	28(100)	18(100)	10(100)

[Reliability = 97%]

---

*Excludes students, three respondents who did not address the question and a fourth who misunderstood the question.

year-old male, who wrote:

I employ a radical conflict approach to understanding social realities and spend my time examining the causes, correlates, and consequences of the social inequalities that pervade contemporary capitalist societies. In my view, both these reflect my class background and the things that I noticed about the world as I matured in post-1950s American society, particularly the lack of correspondence between my perceptions about some of the people I knew and loved and where they fell in the class structure of society.

The second is from a twenty-eight-year-old female who observed: "I look at everything in society from a working class vantage point and I approach everything with this firmly entrenched in my mind. I approach absolutely everything with the understanding that society is not equal and that all people are not equal and do not have equal opportunity and that these inequalities are rooted in productive practices of a capitalist society." These findings and examples offer strong evidence that biographical factors such as class background remain important influences on the "social construction" of perspectives that sociologists employ to help them in their efforts to understand and interpret the world that surrounds them.

Assessments of the Nature of Contemporary Society

We next asked our subjects to provide their own sociological assessments of contemporary American society and any role(s) that factors such as class, race, or gender play in defining its contours. As might be suspected from the previous topic of discussion (and, perhaps, the fact that the question was, in some senses

Table 5.19
Respondents' Perspective on the Impacts of Class Background on Theories, Conceptualizations, Approaches to Research, Etc.

	N(%)		
		Samples	
Does Class Background Influence Your Sociological Perspective?	*Total*	*Males*	*Females*
Definitely Yes	24(83)	12(75)	11(92)
Uncertain	2(7)	1(6)	1(8)
Definitely No	3(10)	3(19)	—
Totals*	29(100)	16(100)	12(100)
		[Reliability=97%]	

*Totals exclude students and three respondents who did not answer the question.

"leading" as well), the assessments provided were generally pessimistic in nature and focused on the negative consequences of life in advanced capitalist society for individuals, particularly those occupying lower-class positions and members of ascriptive minorities. The examples below capture the flavor of these assessments. Some of our respondents gave more narrowly orthodox or neo-Marxist assessments that focused on the centrality of class. A forty-year-old-male respondent is typical of such a perspective: "I still believe that class is the fundamental social relationship organizing life in the contemporary US and other capitalist societies. Gender color-race-ethnicity, while not reducible to class, can only be adequately understood in relationship to class/social relations of production." Others offered what has been labeled a post-Marxist interpretation, which stresses race and gender as equal forms of social oppression.[23] A thirty-six-year-old male put it this way: "I find life in contemporary American society as extremely repressive and fraught with class, race, and gender inequalities. While my theoretical perspective is Marxist in its premises and in its inspiration, I regard class, race, and gender inequalities as autonomous and in no way reducible into one another." Others avoided specific theoretical frameworks and simply described the growing economic inequalities in society and the consequences for its members. In the words of a thirty-nine-year-old female respondent: "I believe the country has become more economically polarized than ever during the past ten to fifteen years. The standard of living has dropped dramatically for large segments of the population and even the middle class cannot expect their [*sic*] children to enjoy the same standard of living that they achieved." Interestingly, none of our respondents provided a positive assessment of life in contemporary American society, and some explicitly stated that a basic "restructuring" was essential if the society were to reach the goals its founding fathers placed in the Declaration of Independence and the Constitution. A forty-seven-year-old male put the matter this way:

What is needed is, of course, a complete reevaluation and probable change of the basic assumptions and practices of [society's] institutions to at least make them more inclusive in their thinking, not just their representativeness. This is important not only for the goal of democracy in our nation (whether one views it as participatory or representative) but also because the ultimate success of these institutions within the context of the broader goals of North American society (freedom, justice and equal opportunity) will require it, for practical as well as moral reasons.

HAPPINESS WITH SOCIOLOGY AS A CAREER CHOICE

The final question we asked our respondents regarding their professional lives was a simple one: "In retrospect, are you happy that you chose a career as a sociologist? If so, why? If not, why not?" Twenty-nine (94 percent) said "yes" and two (6 percent) said "no." Among the reasons offered by those who claimed to be happy with their choice of sociology as a career (in order of frequency of nomination) were: that sociology was an exciting, insightful, and useful perspective (nine nominations); the opportunity to share knowledge with students (six nominations); the opportunity to do research on important social issues (five nominations); income and job security (four nominations); having a position with high autonomy (three nominations); working with students and colleagues, helping others, and the opportunity to do intellectually creative and stimulating work (two nominations each); and personal fulfillment, academic freedom, and a positive work environment (one nomination each). The reasons given by the two respondents who said that they regretted their choice of sociology as a career included unhappiness that sociology is "dead" and has lost its liberating purpose; and being separated from relatives, both socially and geographically.

The results of our review of materials on the impacts of class background on the various perspectives of our sample of sociologist from working-class backgrounds, as well as their general satisfaction with having chosen sociology as a career can be summarized as follows: All of the members of our sample viewed their politics as "leftist," and four in ten explicitly linked their political/ideological perspective to their backgrounds within the working class; male members of our sample were more radical than were females, and two-thirds of our respondents indicated that their political/ideological perspectives had either remained the same or had become more radical over the years (males were more likely than females to claim that their views had become more radical); all the members of our sample were in favor of academics/ sociologists engaging in social activism (males were more likely to give unqualified support for social activism than were females); eight in ten of our respondents felt that their class background had impacted their sociological perspective(s) in various ways; our respondents viewed the nature of contemporary American society using a "conflict" perspective, and some explicitly called for dramatic social changes in order to bring the society more in line with the notions of freedom, justice, and opportunity for all. Finally, despite the complaints raised earlier about such things as the balance among academic roles, relations with academic authority, and perceptions of not "fitting into" the academic role, over nine in ten of our respondents were, nonetheless, happy with their choice of sociology as a career. Justifications offered for their happiness with their choice included the insights offered by sociology, the opportunity to teach others about the field, the chance to do research on important social issues, income, job security, and autonomy. The two respondents who were not happy with their choice of the discipline as a career mentioned that the discipline had lost its original liberating purpose, and being forced to live far away from relatives and friends as reasons.

CONCLUSIONS

This chapter has reviewed data concerning key aspects of the professional careers of our sample of sociologists from working-class backgrounds. The findings indicate that the professional career histories of our respondents are distinct in several significant ways from those of other American sociologists. Our comparisons between the positional and institutional locations of our sample with a sample of the members of the ASA, for example, revealed several important differences: The members of our sample held academic ranks that were lower than those held by the members of the ASA sample; the relative disciplinary rankings of our sample members'institutions were also lower than those of the ASA sample; and the association between the relative prestige of the sources of their Ph.D.s and those of their current institutional affiliations was also less robust for the members of our sample than for those of the ASA sample. Such differences as these are consistent with the fact that many of our respondents expressed dissatisfaction with their current positions within the academy. It is also interesting that a number of our respondents linked their relative lack of success to deficiencies in their class backgrounds and the quality of their educational preparation for graduate study. At any rate, these findings agree those of previous studies of working-class academics. Gardner (1993:53), for example, observes that: "Working-class academics may . . . experience more difficulty reaching academic goals than their middle-class counterparts." Ryan and Sackrey's (1984:99) landmark study offers this assessment: "The evidence suggests that class mobile academics are less likely to be affiliated with the most prestigious institutions. . . . Hence, many can be found clustered toward the middle or the bottom of the academic heap."

With regard to their perceptions concerning life within the academy, our results indicate that our respondents were not happy with the current "balance" among the various roles within the academy; they found their relationships with the academic authority structure both negative and inhibitive of their work; most either felt uncomfortable with or were ambivalent about the academic role; though most were more comfortable with their relations with colleagues, some were not; although most associated both on- and off-campus with colleagues and friends from a variety of different class backgrounds, a large number also noted that they felt more comfortable with persons located either in or near the working class; almost all of our respondents reported that their class background influenced the way(s) they interacted with students; and, finally, eight in ten of our respondents felt themselves to be different from their colleagues, and, in some senses, saw themselves as "outsiders" because of perceived differences in attitudes and behaviors, orientations toward social activism, and perceptions about "social skills" differences between themselves and their colleagues. Several previous researchers have offered support for an alleged "lack of fit" between professors from the working class and the academic environment. Gardner (1993:52) argues that working-class faculty often see themselves as "outsiders" or as "marginal" members of the academy. Langston (1993:67) echoes this sentiment in her statement: "Coming from a working-class background guarantees that you will feel uncomfortable in middle- and upper-class settings. . . . Keeping up a different set of "manners" and pretentious small talk is an exhausting experience." Ryan and Sackrey (1984:119) argue that, because the interests of his or her class of origin and class of destination are so "inimicable" and "antagonistic," a kind of "internalized conflict" is created within the mind of the upwardly mobile academic. Another good example of the lack of fit between the two very different "worlds" of working-class academics comes from Overall (1995:215) who observes: "While working-class culture is not by any means uniform and monolithic, it socializes its participants . . . to see the world with different beliefs, hopes, and expectations from those held by middle-class people." It seems obvious from these examples that the findings we observed concerning the professional careers of our sample of academics from working-class backgrounds are not out of line with those of other research that has previously examined the subject.

Third, our respondents' perceptions of their political orientations was that they were left of center to radical; they all favored some form of social activism for academics; and most felt that their class background had impacted both their choices of theoretical perspectives, research problems, and methodological approaches as well as their overall assessment of the nature of contemporary American society and the role(s) that class and other ascriptive factors in play in influencing its structure. Since most previous research on academics from the working class has not focused specifically on the subject matter of our study—sociologists from working-class backgrounds—it is somewhat more difficult to place these latter findings into the context of previous research. Suffice it to say that many of the findings reported in the final section of this chapter are compatible with what has become known as a conflict perspective on society; to our knowledge, this perspective has not been, prior to our study at least, explicitly linked to the class backgrounds of its numerous contributors.

Finally, we found that gender differences between our respondents played a significant role in "structuring" our findings in all three sections of the chapter. For example, with regard to the professional career histories of our respondents we found that females were more likely than males to select their first positions based on criteria other than characteristics of the university/ department; women were more likely than men to take research appointments following their departure from graduate school; females were more likely than males to currently hold "junior" rather than "senior" positions; males were more likely than females to express dissatisfaction with their current positions; males were more likely than females to explicitly link their class backgrounds with their careers; and females were more likely than males to argue that gender was at least as important as class in influencing their careers. With regard to perceptions of academic/professional life females were more likely than males to say that their initial expectations had been met in their careers; females were more likely than males to express satisfaction with their colleagues; and males were more likely than females to say that their closest academic friends were from working- or lower-middle class backgrounds. Concerning the last set of issues discussed in the chapter (political/ideological and theoretical perspective and overall assessment of the nature of contemporary American society) males were more extremist than females in their political/ ideological viewpoints, and they were also more likely than females to offer unqualified support for social activism. These findings (as well as those noted in earlier chapters) support Barker's (1995:76) conclusion that although male and female academics from working-class backgrounds share many of the same experiences within the academy, there are also important differences between the two that need to be explored more completely. We will return to this task in the final chapter of the book.

NOTES

1. Holmwood and Stewart (1983) have argued that such terms as "contradictory locations" have little theoretical utility and are sometimes employed by theorists who do not have a more sophisticated theoretical explanation for some form of social behavior. Although we agree with their assessment in general, we do not think that Wright (1976) is guilty of this usage of the term or phrase.

2. Wright (1976) shares with Poulantzas (1973) the notion that a major role of these classes is the political and ideological justification of the current distribution of the ownership of productive resources in society.

3. Wright (1985) does link the contradictions of these class locations to both objective interests and to the subjective states of consciousness of their members, but his focus is more clearly on the former (i.e., the linkage between the structural location and the objective interests) than on the latter.

4. Bourdieu (1984) has noted that upwardly mobile members of the working class have to first "unlearn" the ways they were taught to think and act and then "relearn" a very different set of thoughts and actions that are appropriate to their new location in the middle (or upper middle) class.

5. To place these data in context, whenever other data are available, we will compare our sample's distributions to those of a sample of the membership of the national professional association of sociologists, the ASA.

6. We coded all the responses of each respondent to this question, since if a respondent mentioned more than one factor, it was not always possible to rank them in terms of relative importance. The figures in the table, then, total more than the respondents who were both eligible for inclusion (i.e., they were not students) and answered the question.

7. It is difficult to place these research appointments (and the gender differences in the occupancy of same) into a meaningful context. Although there may be general agreement between both faculty and graduate students that a traditional academic appointment that involves both teaching and research (and that may lead to tenure) is more desirable than a straight research appointment (more particularly so if the latter is a "soft" money appointment), some within the academic community would prefer the latter to the former. The question here becomes, do more women prefer to pursue careers in research, or are there constraints operating on their choices that are different from those operating on the choices made by males? An example of some of the constraints that might operate on a female is provided by the response of a thirty-nine-year-old female to this question—she noted that she was a single parent and chose a research position in the same city where she completed her Ph.D. over other academic opportunities so that she wouldn't have to uproot her children from their home and social support system. Unfortunately, our data do not permit an assessment of the typicality of this response.

8. We will use "academic prestige" in this chapter in several different ways. Here, we are simply using the diversity of degrees offered by an institution as a rough measure of its prestige. Later in the chapter we will use the disciplinary prestige of the department as our measure of academic prestige.

9. We suspect that many of these gender differences are the result of the history of discrimination within the academy (and the larger society) against women and the efforts on the parts of both the federal government and universities to expand opportunities for women that have occurred during the past twenty-five or so years. Many sociology departments continue to practice active "affirmative action" programs for women and color minorities, and this could reflect in higher proportions of women in "better" entry-level positions; likewise, the history of discrimination against women also contributes to the higher proportions of men in senior-level positions.

10. We employed the *1990 Biographical Directory of Members* (American Sociological Association 1990) as our source of information about member characteristics, since it is the last directory that publishes biographical information on members of the association. We randomly sampled a total of 60 of the 13,858 members of the association using a skip-interval sampling method.

11. Recall that we entertained the notion of a bias in membership in the ASA among sociologists from working-class backgrounds in Chapter 4 as a potential explanation for the marked differences in the relative prestige of the source of the Ph.D. degree between our sample and the sample of the members of the ASA. We concluded that since over ninety percent of our sample were members of the ASA, this was not a likely explanation for the differences observed.

12. As noted in Chapter 4, the source for the prestige rankings of departments and institutions is the National Research Council's *Research-Doctoral Programs in the United States: Continuities and Change* (1995). Because we suspected (and observed) some volatility in these rankings, we combined the 1992 with the 1982 rankings to derive a more stable ranking for each school (i.e., we simply took the average of the two rankings).

13. We realize that graduating from a department with a strong disciplinary reputation is only one of many factors that influence where a given individual will end up in the institutional prestige hierarchy. We also believe, however, that many of these other factors, such as quality of prior preparation, quality of training, publishing in major media, being active in national and regional professional organizations, receiving outside funding, being recommended/nominated for positions and awards, and so on, are facilitated by the training and social contacts/networks of these more prestigious institutions.

14. We also broke these distributions down by gender of respondent, but since the sizes of the N's in the categories that resulted make interpretations suspect, we chose not to discuss them in the text of the chapter.

15. We also examined two issues that relate to tenure. Recall that in our comparison between the characteristics of our sample and data on the membership of the ASA reviewed in Chapter 2 above (see Table 2.2), exactly half of our sample hold tenured positions, and another 16.7 percent are in tenure-track positions (note as well that slightly higher proportions of our sample are in these two locations when compared with the overall membership of the ASA). We also computed the average length of time between the granting of the Ph.D. and the receipt of tenure for the members of our sample who had tenure and found that it was 5.3 years (males in our sample took 5.1 years, whereas females took 5.8 years). Since we have no comparable data from other sources with which to compare these data, we chose not to discuss them in the text of the paper.

16. In some senses, this finding needs to be placed in context. Since our sample is a volunteer sample who responded to an advertisement in professional newsletters, sampling bias is an obvious problem. Thus, it is likely that the members of our sample were attracted to the study by their heightened sense of interest in the subject of the study and that they should believe that class has influenced their careers should come as no surprise given the means by which they were selected.

17. This difference probably reflects the relative importance of class for the two groups. Given that males are members of the gender majority, in a class-stratified society, it should be expected that class would be more salient for them (and thus be perceived by them as more important). For women, on the other hand, any impacts of class must compete with the impacts of also being in the minority in terms of gender. In contrast to this rationale, however, remember that in Chapter 4 our female respondents generally placed class before gender or weighted them equally in terms of influence on their higher educational careers.

18. Remember that earlier in this section of the chapter, a number of women stressed the role that family ties played in influencing their career choices.

19. It should be noted here that a number of our respondents made the point that they had no idea what to expect from an academic career until they either entered graduate school, or decided, once they were in graduate school, that they might have a chance to get the credentials that would give them access to an academic career. This finding, of course, is consistent with one of the conclusions in Chapter 3 above that children from the working class often do not have adequate information about the working conditions in non working-class occupations, since they have less exposure to the occupants of these occupations while growing up than do their middle-class counterparts.

20. Recall that in Chapter 3 one of the problems mentioned by many academics from the working class was that, when they were growing up, they did not have adequate role models.

21. See Ryan and Sackrey 1984, Tokarczyk and Fay 1993, and Daws and Law 1995, for evidence supporting this linkage.

22. We are aware that the potential for overlap among our categories for this portion of the question is more than minimal. One of our major criteria in selecting these categories was to preserve as much of the integrity of our respondent's remarks as possible; thus, some overlap was unavoidable.

23. The distinction(s) between Marxist and post-Marxist perspectives on late capitalist society are outlined by Wright (1985). Grimes (1989) both summarizes and provides an empirical assessment of the two perspectives.

6

Personal Relationships

This last analysis chapter deals with our respondents' perceptions about their interpersonal relationships with intimate partners, personal friends, members of their families of origin, and childhood friends. The issues we examine here include the educations, occupations, and class backgrounds of our respondents' adult intimate partners; the role that their own class backgrounds and the class backgrounds of their partners have played in their relationships; the class backgrounds of their closest personal friends; the class character of the neighborhoods within which they now reside; the nature of their current relationships with members of their families of origin and childhood friends; and their feelings about their own successes when compared to those of their parents, siblings, friends, and associates who have remained within the working class.

THE PERSONAL LIVES OF SOCIOLOGISTS FROM WORKING-CLASS BACKGROUNDS

Previous research on academics from working-class backgrounds has not adequately dealt with their personal lives, yet we think that this dimension of their lives is an important part of the puzzle that both makes up and, in turn, helps to define their daily realities. If, as earlier research has argued (cf. Barker 1995; Dews and Law 1995; Ryan and Sackrey 1984; Tokarczyk and Fay 1993) academics from working-class backgrounds do indeed feel themselves to be "strangers," or "outsiders," within both the academy and the upper-middle-class environment that surrounds it, then the way(s) in which they cope with this professional marginality is (are) vitally important, not only for them, but also for those around them.[1] If the cultural/social differences between the middle and the working class do, in fact, exist, then the contrast between the two that academics from working-class backgrounds must face daily might encourage them to seek to escape from this environment (and the conflicts within them that it generates) whenever and by whatever means they can. Since they cannot easily do so during the work day without compromising their professional livelihoods, then a second possibility would be to do so during their "off-duty" hours. One way to get away from the academy and its cultural trappings after hours would be to retreat back into a more hospitable cultural/social environment that contains an intimate partner, children, friends, and perhaps other family members, all of whom share a cultural/social perspective that is more similar to the one into which the upwardly mobile academic was socialized as a child and young adult.[2] We explore the ways our sample of sociologists from working-class backgrounds attempt to construct their off-the-job realities in the paragraphs that follow.

Characteristics of Intimate Partners

The first, and perhaps most important, part of a potentially more familiar environment is the respondent's intimate partner. Given the antipathies between middle- and working-class values in general, and values concerning domestic life in particular, which have been demonstrated by Komarovsky (1962), Rubin (1976, 1994), and others (cf. Bourdieu 1984), it seems reasonable to assume that upwardly mobile individuals from working-class backgrounds might feel more comfortable with intimate partners from within the working rather than the middle or the upper middle classes. However, given the tendency toward hypergamy within the larger society, it also seems reasonable that women from working-class backgrounds might prefer to marry men from middle- or upper-middle-class backgrounds.[3] And, since women have, historically at least, tended to place more stress on instrumental qualities in a mate (e.g., a good education, financial resources, etc.), it would also seem reasonable that highly educated women, *even those from working-class backgrounds*, would prefer mates with more education and earning power.

The importance of resources in decisions surrounding marriage and marital power is well established (Blood and Wolfe 1960; Collins and Coltrane 1995; Gillespie 1971).[4] Since mate selection is conducted within the larger context of a patriarchal society, men begin with an advantaged position. Thus, in considering who is an appropriate mate, *ceteris paribus* men are able to maintain a superior bargaining position. The general norm of homogamy, a situation in which people from similar backgrounds, with similar levels of education, similar occupations, and what are considered to be similar amounts of physical attractiveness and social skills select each other as mates, is widespread. Interestingly, however, this case presents no inherent challenge to societal patriarchy because, as stated above, men have higher gender status than women. When partners bring different amounts of other key resources to the union, however, things get more complicated. In the paragraphs below, we will first examine the educations, occupations, and class backgrounds of our respondents' intimate partners separately. We will then combine three of these resources—education, class background, and gender—into a multivariate model and examine the joint effects of these variables on our respondents' choices of intimate partners. By these means, we can, perhaps, resolve some of the differences in perspectives on mate selection that we've just discussed.

Educational Attainments of Intimate Partners. Table 6.1 displays data on the formal educational attainments of our respondents' current intimate partners. As may be seen there, the modal category for the entire sample is the Ph.D. degree, with the Master's degree ranking second. When the cases in these two degree types are combined, fully two-thirds of our respondents' current intimate partners hold either of these two degrees. These data suggest that, for educational attainment at least, our respondents' choices of intimate partners contradict the hypothesis that academics from working-class backgrounds are more likely to choose as their intimate partners persons who are working class. When we stratify these data by gender of respondent, we find that the current intimate partners of over half of our female respondents have attained the Ph.D., whereas only a quarter of our male respondents' partners have done so. Combining those partners who have attained either of the two highest degrees, 73 percent of our female respondents' intimate partners have either the Master's or the Ph.D. degree; in contrast, only 61 percent of our male respondents' partners possess these degrees. Notice as well that, though a few of the intimate partners of the males do not have college degrees, none of the partners of the females has this little formal education. These findings show that though a majority of each gender group selects mates whose educational credentials place them out of the working class, our female respondents are more likely to do so than are our males.

Occupations of Intimate Partners. When we examine the occupations of our respondents' intimate partners, our findings are similar to those reported for education (see Table 6.2). The modal category for the occupations of our respondents' partners is "college professor." When we organize these data by gender of respondent, once again, we find important differences. For example, over half of the intimate partners of our female respondents are college professors, whereas fewer than a third of our male respondents' partners are so employed. Furthermore, two-thirds of our female respondents' partners are either college professors or managers/administrators/technical workers;[5] this contrasts with only about 55 percent of our male respondents' partners who have such occupations. It appears that, for occupation at least, our female respondents are slightly more likely to pair up with their equals in terms of occupation than are our males (80 percent versus 55 percent do so).

Class Backgrounds of Intimate Partners. Realizing that, although it may be the case that our respondents, in part because of their upward mobility, are more likely to choose partners with similar educational/occupational achievements,

Table 6.1
Respondents' Self-Reports of the Formal Educational Attainments of Current/Last
Intimate Partner

Formal Educational Attainment of Current Intimate Partner	N(%) Samples		
	Total	Males	Females
Elementary School	1(2)	1(4)	—
High School Graduate	1(2)	1(4)	—
Some College/Technical	3(7)	3(15)	—
College Graduate	8(19)	4(17)	4(21)
Some Postgraduate	1(2)	—	1(6)
M.A./M.S.	12(29)	8(35)	4(21)
Ph.D.	16(38)	6(26)	10(52)
Totals*	42(99)	23(100)	19(100)

*Totals exclude three respondents who have neither been nor are currently in an intimate
 interpersonal relationship. Data are taken from the questionnaire.

it may also be possible that because of their working-class backgrounds, they
might, nonetheless, pair up with other successfully upwardly mobile partners
who share their working-class backgrounds. For obvious reasons, this option
seems to us a more reasonable choice than the selection of an intimate partner
who has remained within the working class. To examine this possibility, we
asked our respondents about the class backgrounds of their intimate partners.
Our examination of their responses resulted in a coding scheme that included six
categories: working class, working class/lower middle class, lower middle class,
lower middle class/middle class, middle class, and upper middle class.[6] Table
6.3 displays the distribution of the class backgrounds of our respondents' current
intimate partners. As displayed there, 43 percent of our respondents reported
that their current intimate partner came from a working-class background,
whereas a majority indicated that their partners came from higher class
backgrounds. Obviously, the former group is more consistent with the
argument advanced earlier in the paragraph than is the latter.

Table 6.2
Respondents' Self-Reports of Current Occupation of Current/Last Intimate Partner

| | | N(%) | |
| Current Occupation of Intimate Partner | | Samples | |
	Total	Males	Females
College Professor	17(43)	6(30)	11(55)
Managers/Administrative/ Technical	10(25)	5(25)	5(25)
Public School Teacher	5(13)	3(15)	2(10)
Counselors/Social Worker	3(7)	3(15)	—
Sales	1(3)	1(5)	—
Service	1(3)	—	1(5)
Student	3(7)	2(10)	1(5)
Totals*	40(101)	20(100)	20(100)
NA	2		

*Totals exclude four respondents who have neither been nor are currently in an intimate interpersonal relationship. Data are taken from the questionnaire.

Although both class background and various other (ascribed and achieved) characteristics are all considered marketable assets in resource models of mate selection, these findings suggest that achieved assets may be more important than background assets in the mate-selection process, at least for these particular members of the upper middle class.[7]

When we stratified these data by gender, we also found differences. For example, though women were marginally more likely than men to have a current intimate partner from a working-class background, when we looked at the proportion of the members of our sample's intimate partners who come from higher class backgrounds, we find that the women in our sample were no less likely than men to have a current intimate partner from either a middle- or an upper-middle-class background.

Thus, for the entire sample, the majority of intimate partners were neither currently members of the working class nor do they come from working-class

Table 6.3
Respondents' Self-Reports of Class Background of Current Intimate Partner

	N(%)		
Class Background of Current Intimate Partner		Samples	
	Total	Males	Females
Working Class	15(43)	8(40)	7(47)
Working Class/Lower Middle Class	1(3)	—	1(7)
Lower Middle Class	4(11)	3(15)	1(7)
Lower Middle Class/ Middle Class	2(6)	2(10)	—
Middle Class	10(29)	6(30)	4(27)
Upper Middle Class	3(9)	1(5)	2(13)
Totals*	35(101)	20(100)	15(101)
NA	7		

[Reliability = 89%]

---

*Totals exclude four respondents who have neither been in nor are currently in an intimate personal relationship.

backgrounds. Regarding gender, the female members of our sample were even more likely than the males to have intimate partners with the Ph.D. degree and who held upper-level white-collar occupations. Not only this, but they were no less likely than our male respondents to have an intimate partner from a middle- or an upper-middle-class background. In short, these data suggest that academics from the working class, no matter their gender, are slightly more likely to "marry up" in terms of class background rather than to select a mate who is either currently working class or who comes from a working-class background. These findings contradict our thesis that academics from working-class backgrounds might try to compensate for their marginality in their professional lives by selecting an intimate partner who is either working class or who has a working-class background.

The Multivariate "Match" with Intimate Partners. With these facts in mind, we will now crudely quantify the various positive and negative influences on the mate-selection process and then conduct a multivariate examination of the correspondence between our respondents' characteristics and those of their partners. To keep this comparison as simple as possible, we limit our examination to three key factors: class background, level of formal education, and gender.[8] For class background, given what has been said both earlier in the book and in other places as well, we believe that to grow up with a working-class background is a negative asset within the upper-middle-class environment that surrounds the academy. For the education variable, all of our respondents rank high, so we must consider that as a positive asset that they bring to the mate-selection market. For gender, because of patriarchy, being a man in this society is more a positive asset, whereas being a woman is a negative asset.

Under these conditions, the "typical" match that maintains homogamy (or "equity" in resource theories of mate selection) is between individuals who are similar on at least two of these three variables. Thus, the types of matches we would expect are those between either men and women who each have a higher class background and who are highly educated (diagrammatically for HE: + [for class background], + [for education], and + [for gender]; for SHE: + [for class background], + [for education], and - [for gender]; or those men and women who have lower class backgrounds and who have less education (diagrammatically for HE: -, -, +; for SHE -, -, -). Notice that in *both* these cases, HE has the advantage over SHE (counting the pluses and minuses HE has more than SHE in each case). Because patriarchy prescribes that men have more status and privileges than women, partnerships between individuals with other similar resources present no challenge (other than gender) to its hegemony.

Let us now turn to the various varieties of matches between partners with *dissimilar* resources. These are cases in which the partners have different class backgrounds and levels of education, or both. Since the unions we are particularly interested in are those between working-class academics and their partners, exhausting all combinations of the three factors results in four types of unions each for both men and women. Beginning with the men, the unions can be illustrated as follows:

Type One—a union between a man from a working-class background who is highly educated (HE -,+,+) and a woman from a working-class background who is not highly educated (SHE -,-,-).

Type Two—a union between a man from a working-class background who is highly educated (HE -,+,+) and a woman from a working-class background who is highly educated (SHE -,+,-).

Type Three—a union between a man from a working-class background who is highly educated (HE -,+,+) and a woman from a higher class background who has less education (SHE +,-,-).

Type Four—a union between a man from a working-class background who is highly educated (HE -,+,+) and a woman from a higher class background who is highly educated (SHE +,+,-).

Note that only the *last* type of union approaches resource equality. For the first three, the man has more positive factors than does his mate. Thus, these unions do not present a challenge to the patriarchal authority structure of society. For the last type of union, however, there is apparent parity (i.e., both partners bring two positive and one negative factor to the union). Thus, a relationship between a male academic from a working-class background and a female partner who both comes from a higher-class background and who is also highly educated represents the closest thing to a challenge to the patriarchal authority structure than any of the other possible pairings.

Table 6.4,A, presents our data organized in such a way that we can simultaneously examine the operation of all three of these resources. The first thing to notice is that a third of the twelve intimate partners of our male respondents whose class backgrounds are middle class or higher have the Ph.D. degree; if we combine these with those from higher-class backgrounds who have postbaccalaureate training, then 75 percent of the intimate partners of our male respondents are involved in Type Four relationships (recall that such relationships challenge the patriarchal normative structure in society). The second most frequent "match"—that between male academics from working-class backgrounds and intimate partners from working-class backgrounds, who are also highly educated (57 percent of all relationships with intimate partners from working-class backgrounds)—does not challenge these norms.

If we turn to the situation for female academics from working-class backgrounds, we find that there are also four possible combinations of the three variables:

Type One—a union between a woman from a working-class background who is highly educated (SHE -,+,-) and a man from a working-class background who has less education (HE -,-,+).

Type Two—a union between a woman from a working-class background who is highly educated (SHE -,+,-) and a man from a working-class background who is highly educated (HE -,+,+).

Type Three—a union between a woman from a working-class background who is highly educated (SHE -,+,-) and a man from a higher-class background who has less education (HE +,-,+).

Type Four—a union between a woman from a working-class background who is highly educated (SHE -,+,-) and a man who is from a higher-class background and who is highly educated (+,+,+).

Table 6.4
Respondents' Current/Last Partners' Levels of Education by Their Class Backgrounds by Gender of Respondents

N(%)

A. Male Respondents

Current/Last Partner's Class Background

Current/Last Partner's Level of Formal Education	Working Class	Not Working Class	Total	NA
Less Than College Degree	1(14)	1(8)	2(11)	1
B.A./B.S.	2(29)	2(17)	4(21)	2
M.A./M.S.	3(43)	5(42)	8(42)	—
Ph.D.	1(14)	4(33)	5(26)	1
Totals	7(100)	12(100)	19(100)	

B. Female Respondents

Current/Last Partner's Class Background

Current/Last Partner's Level of Formal Education	Working Class	Not Working Class	Total	NA
Less Than College Degree	—	—	—	—
B.A./B.S.	3(33)	—	3(19)	1
M.A./M.S.	3(33)	2(29)	5(31)	—
Ph.D.	3(33)	5(71)	8(50)	2
Totals	9(33)	7(100)	16(100)	3

As these types reveal, the situation for an academic female from a working-class background is somewhat different from that of her male counterpart. In three of the four possible combinations, her partner begins with more positive bargaining factors than she does. Thus, her working-class background with her higher education approaches parity with only one of the four types of matches--and only for that type (when her partner is from a working-class background and has less formal education than she does) does the union present an inherent challenge to the patriarchal authority structure of society. As shown in Table 6.4,B, only about a third of our female respondents' intimate partners come close to satisfying these criteria, and even they are questionable since each of them possesses a college degree. As we previously noted, for the women in our sample, *none* is currently intimately involved with anyone from either type of class background who has less than a college degree. In fact, nearly half of our female respondents are involved with intimate partners who are both highly educated and who are not from working-class backgrounds (note that every single female who is involved with an intimate partner who is *not* from the working class is involved with a partner who has a postbaccalaureate education).

To summarize our argument to this point, we would expect to find that homogamy on the dimension of class background presents a problem (a challenge to the patriarchal structure of marriage) only when the wife/female partner has more education than does her husband/male partner. On the other hand, heterogamy on the class background variable is only a problem when the wife/female partner comes from a higher-class background than does her husband/male partner *and* is also highly educated. Each of these types of union imply a challenge to the normative structure of patriarchal power both within society as a whole and within the family itself. Likewise, for female respondents, the only contradictory category is for intimate partners who are from working-class backgrounds and who have less education than they do.

Relationships with Intimate Partners. We next focus on the effects of class background similarities/differences on the nature of our respondents relationships with their partners. We asked them to characterize any role(s) that their class backgrounds have played in their relationships with their intimate partners. Our inspection of their responses to this question reveal that they tended to answer the question in one of three ways. Some thought that their class background has had virtually no impact on their relations with their intimate partners. A typical response from this group is that of a forty-five-year-old female who wrote: "I can't think of any impact at all. My partner finds it remarkable that I have worked all my life and put myself through high school and college." A second group of respondents noted that they thought that their working-class backgrounds have had a positive impact on their relationships with their intimate partners. The response of a thirty-nine-year-old female is typical of this group: "We understood certain things about what was typical about our cohort in our neighborhood, and how we differ, i.e., we're doing much more in terms of intellectual pursuits. Pursuing advanced education for the labor market rewards is a more logical reason to my husband, rather than the pure pleasure of it, as it is for me." A third group of respondents reported that their class background has had a number of negative consequences in their relationship(s) with partners. The remarks of a forty-four-year-old male respondent are a good example of responses coded into this category:

I feel that working class males are particularly attracted to middle class women because of issues which range from definitions of beauty to a marker of upward mobility. Unfortunately, the gender privileges and orientations along with the general cultural class tend to make such relationships difficult [with regard to his current intimate partner]. . . . Class differences still represent one of the greatest sources of conflict in our relationship. . . . I still feel a sense of cultural inferiority in the relationship.

Each of these responses is consistent with the explanation outlined above. For example, the male academics from working-class backgrounds whose intimate partners are from similar class backgrounds overwhelmingly (71 percent of the total sample) report that the effects of class background are benign (Table 6.5,B). An almost equal proportion (69 percent) of those men whose intimate partners are from higher-class backgrounds report that class background differences have had a negative impact on their relationships.[9]

Most female respondents with class backgrounds similar to their partners report that class background has had no impact on their relationships (see Table 6.5). In contrast to our male respondents, nearly two-thirds (63 percent) of those women have partners from higher class backgrounds than themselves report that class background differences have no impact on their relationships (in contrast to only 23 percent of our male respondents who reported that class background differences had no impact on their relationships with their higher-class background intimate partners).

These results reinforce the notion that academics from working-class backgrounds tend to follow the same normative mate selection patterns as most other members of society (and, thus, for their choices of mates at least, are not consistent with our prediction that they might compensate for their "outsider" status at work by seeking a relationship with a partner who is either working class or whose background is working class). That is, academic women from working-class backgrounds tend to select mates with more net resources than themselves, and their male counterparts tend to select mates who have fewer net resources than themselves. Even in cases wherein the class backgrounds and levels of formal education are similar for both of the intimate partners, challenges to the societal pattern of patriarchy are avoided because the lower social status of women defines the union as unequal (and the women as subordinate to the man). These results are reinforced by the finding that the negative impacts of class background on relationships with intimate partners are found primarily in unions where there are differences between the spouses in terms of class background (although these differences appear to be more of a problem for our male than for our female respondents).

Table 6.5
Respondents' Perceptions of Impact of Class Background on Their Relationships with Intimate Partner(s)

N(%)

Samples

A. Class Background Similarities/Differences Ignored

Responses	Total	Males	Females
Class Background Has No Impact	18(53)	8(40)	10(71)
Class Background Has Positive Impact	2(6)	1(5)	1(7)
Class Background Has Negative Impact	14(42)	11(55)	3(21)
Totals	34(101)	20(100)	14(99)
NA	5		

B. Class Background Similarities/Differences Controlled

	Total		Males		Females	
	Same	*Different*	*Same*	*Different*	*Same*	*Different*
Class Background Has No Impact	10(77)	8(38)	5(71)	3(23)	5(83)	5(63)
Class Background Has Positive Impact	1(8)	1(5)	—	1(8)	1(17)	—
Class Background Has Negative Impact	2(15)	12(57)	2(29)	9(69)	—	3(37)
Totals	13(100)	21(100)	7(100)	13(100)	6(100)	8(100)

[Reliability=91%]

The Class Locations of Closest Friends

Since close friends could also be a part of an "off-duty" environment that could serve as an alternative to the upper-middle-class academic world, we also asked our respondents about the class positions of their closest friends. Our inspection of their responses to this question yielded a four-category scheme that included: upper-middle-class professional, middle class, a mixture of different classes, and lower-middle class. We display these data in Table 6.6. As shown there, the closest friends of our respondents were from variety of different class locations; the modal category was a "mixture of different classes" and the largest of the subcategories under this rubric was the "middle class/working class" subcategory. Notice that though no respondent claimed that his/her closest friends were exclusively from the working class, three in ten of them (the percentage in the bottom two subcategories of the "mixture" category) claimed members of the working class as a part of their close friendship network. There were modest gender effects on the class locations of our respondents' closest friends: Females were slightly more likely than males to claim that their friends came from a mixture of different classes (61 percent as compared with 47 percent), and female respondents' located their close friends in the bottom two of the "mixture of classes" subcategories more frequently than did males (44 percent of the females versus 16 percent of the males claimed that their closest friends were either from the middle class/working class or the lower middle class/working class). These data show that though most of our respondents' close friendship circles did include members of the working class, they by no means confined their choices of close friends exclusively to the working class. Such class-exclusive choices are probably more difficult (whether they are preferable or not) because the work lives of our respondents are spent in the company of others, most of whom are not from working-class backgrounds, and, as the data in Chapter 5 demonstrated, it is not uncommon for at least some of these associations to be carried over into the personal, off-the-job lives of our respondents.

The Class Nature of Respondents' Neighborhoods of Residence

Another potential part of a strategy for coping with an "outsider" status within one's professional life might be to choose to live in a neighborhood in which most or all of the families were working class. To address this issue, we asked our respondents to describe the class character of the neighborhood within which they currently live. Our inspection of their responses to this question led us to construct a five-category scheme: upper middle class, middle class, a mixture of different classes, lower middle class, and working class.[10] The distribution of our respondents across these categories is presented in Table 6.7. The modal category for the class composition of our respondents' neighborhoods of residence is the "mixture of different classes" category; based on their

Table 6.6
Respondents' Self-Reports of Class Location of Closest Friends

N(%)

Samples

Class Location	Total	Males	Females
Upper-Middle-Class Professionals	2(5)	1(5)	1(5)
Middle Class	13(35)	7(37)	6(33)
Mixture of Different Classes	20(54)	9(47)	11(61)
All Classes	[7]*	[5]	[2]
Middle Class/Lower Middle Class	[2]	[1]	[1]
Middle Class/Working Class	[8]	[2]	[6]
Lower Middle Class/Working Class	[3]	[1]	[2]
Lower Middle Class	2(5)	2(11)	—
Totals	37(99)	19(100)	18(100)
NA	3		

[Reliability = 78%]

---

* Numbers in brackets indicate the number of respondents who chose the particular combination(s) of classes noted when they gave the "Mixture of Different Classes" response.

responses to this question, we placed 44 percent of our respondents into this category. There are modest gender differences in response to this question—males were more likely to report living in an upper-middle-class or a middle-class neighborhood (39 percent versus 28 percent), whereas females were more likely to report living in a mixed-class neighborhood (50 percent versus 39 percent). If we add together the frequencies in the various categories that contained at least some working-class families, then four in ten (41 percent) of our respondents reported living in either exclusively working-class neighborhoods or in neighborhoods that contained at least some working-class families (gender of respondent does not impact this proportion).

Since we were curious about any impact that the class background "match" between our respondents and their current intimate partners might have on their

Table 6.7
Respondents' Self-Report of Class Composition of the Neighborhood in which They Currently Live

	N(%)		
		Samples	
Class Composition of Neighborhood	Total	Males	Females
Upper Middle Class	3(9)	2(11)	1(7)
Middle Class	8(25)	5(28)	3(21)
Mixture of Different Classes	14(44)	7(39)	7(50)
Upper Middle Class/Middle Class	[3]*	[2]	[1]
Middle Class/Lower Middle Class	[3]	—	[3]
Middle Class/Working Class	[4]	[2]	[2]
Lower Middle Class/Working Class	[4]	[3]	[1]
Lower Middle Class	2(6)	2(11)	—
Working Class	5(16)	2(11)	3(21)
Totals	32(100)	18(100)	14(99)
Unclear**	6		
NA	2		

[Reliability = 82%]

---

*Numbers in brackets indicate the number of respondents who chose the particular combination(s) of classes noted when they gave the "Mixture of Different Classes response.
**Respondents were assigned to this category if their remarks did not permit us to assign them to one of the other categories.

neighborhoods of residence, we first collapsed the latter into two categories—some/all working class and nonworking class—and we then cross-classified the two. The results are presented in Table 6.8. As presented there, for the total sample, although about three-in ten of our respondents currently live in a neighborhood that contains at least some working-class families, nearly seven in ten of them currently do not. These proportions are similar to (but slightly

Table 6.8
Couples' Class Backgrounds by Neighborhood of Residence

N(%)

Respondent and Current Intimate Partner Both from Working-Class Backgrounds		Samples	
	Total	*Males*	*Females*
Some/All Working-Class Neighborhood	5(33)	3(50)	2(22)
Nonworking-Class Neighborhood	10(67)	3(50)	7(78)
Totals*	15(100)	6(100)	9(100)

Respondents' Current Intimate Partner not from Working-Class Background		Samples	
	Total	*Males*	*Females*
Some/All Working-Class Neighborhood	5(31)	3(27)	2(40)
Nonworking-Class Neighborhood	11(69)	8(73)	3(60)
Totals*	16(100)	11(100)	5(100)

[Reliabililty=82%]

*Totals reflect only those respondents for which we had data for both issues.

lower than) those that were presented in Table 6.7. Since they are nearly identical for both subgroups of our respondents, it appears that, for the total sample at least, the class background compositions of our respondents' households do not seem to impact the kinds of neighborhoods within which they live. When we break these responses down by gender of respondent, however, some interesting differences emerge. For example, among respondents whose intimate partners come from working-class backgrounds, males are more likely than females to report that they live in neighborhoods that contain at least some working-class families (50 percent versus 22 percent). In contrast, among those respondents whose intimate partners come from higher class backgrounds, males are less likely than females to report that they live in neighborhoods that contain at least some working-class families (27 percent versus 40 percent). To put it another way, for males, having an intimate partner who is not from a working-class background *decreases* the likelihood of living in neighborhoods that contain at least some working-class families, whereas for females, it *increases* this likelihood.

Relationships with Members of Family of Origin and Childhood Friends

One last way our respondents might attempt to cope with their outsider status within the academy is by maintaining close relationships with the members of their families of origin and friends from their childhood years. We asked our respondents to characterize their relationships with these groups and to comment on any impact that their upward mobility out of the working class might have on these relationships. Because this question involved a number of different potential referents (i.e., parents, siblings, other relatives, and childhood friends), and our respondents didn't always comment on each (or on each one separately), we first constructed categories that identified the persons/groups to which they referred (i.e., whether parents, siblings, childhood friends, or what we labeled "undifferentiated family/friends"). Next, we characterized their reports of their relationship with each group as "close" or "distant." Finally, we coded their assessment of the impact(s) of class background differences on these relationships into "little impact" or "negative impact." We organize our presentation of the findings below in terms of the referent in question. Of the eleven respondents who explicitly mentioned their current relationships with parents, six (55 percent) characterized their relationships with parents as close, whereas five (45 percent) said that their relationships with their parents were more distant. Only one of the respondents whose remarks led us to place him in the "close relationships" category mentioned that class differences had a negative impact on his relationships with his parents, whereas two of the respondents whose characterizations led us to place them in the "distant" category found class differences to be a major source of difficulty in their relationships with their parents. The comments of a thirty-one-year-old male provide a good example of the difficulties faced by our respondents in their relationships with parents who have remained within the working class: "My relationship with family is a caring but awkward one. They frankly are not quite sure what I do for a living. I've even gone so far as to give them an introductory sociology textbook to give them a sense of the kinds of things I work on/teach about. The incredible gap in life experience is extremely difficult to bridge." Of the twelve respondents who explicitly commented on their relationships with siblings, we coded seven of them (58 percent) as reporting "close" relationships, and five (42 percent) as reporting "distant" relationships. Four of the five respondents whose relationships with siblings were coded as "distant" mentioned that class differences were a major source of difficulty in their relationships with siblings, whereas only one of the respondents whose relationships with siblings were coded as "close" mentioned that class difference mattered in these relationships.

A third group about whose current relationships with our respondents we were interested was their childhood friends. Of the seventeen respondents who explicitly discussed their relationships with childhood friends, over three-quarters (76 percent) said that they had little or no current contact with their friends from childhood, whereas only two (12 percent) characterized the nature of their contacts with childhood friends as "close." The reasons offered for this lack of contact were diverse and included geographic distance as well as class differences. The remarks of a thirty-five-year-old female include reference to both of these reasons: "I expect that working class background has something to do with loss of childhood friends. Because I went to college and then graduate school, I rapidly outdistanced most of my friends and classmates—educationally and then geographically. Many of my classmates are working in grocery stores, factories, on farms, and as waitresses." Finally, some of our respondents chose to lump family, relatives, and childhood friends into a single group. Of these sixteen respondents, nine (56 percent) reported that their relationships with families and friends remained close, whereas seven (44 percent) reported that they had little, or more distant contact with families and friends. Three of this latter group explicitly mentioned that class differences were implicated in their estrangement from families and childhood friends, but none of the members of the former group did.

From these data, it seems clear that there is diversity among our respondents in terms of the nature of their relationships with members of their families of origin and childhood friends. No matter the specific family referent (i.e., parents, siblings, or other relatives), a majority of our respondents in each case reported that their relationships have remained close over time, although the pluralities were not large for any of these groups. In contrast, most of our respondents reported that they had little or no current contact with friends from their childhood years. For both families and friends, both class and geographic factors were frequently cited as rationales for their lack of continued contact and/or closeness. It is also interesting that gender did not impact responses to these questions.[11] The response of one forty-three-year-old female respondent about her frustrations in dealing with the lack of understanding about her achievements among her family and childhood friends, when combined with her feelings of difference between herself and her academic colleagues, provide a good example of the dilemma faced by many academics from working-class backgrounds: "This whole issue bothers me—it makes returning to my origins difficult. And, considering what a stranger I feel in this new land—the one my class mobility has brought me into—this means that I have become a freak—I can't go back to where I came from (they know that I'm not still one of them) and I don't 'belong' where I am (they know I can never really become one of them)." This sense of not belonging to either the old or the new—or, as we phrase it, feeling caught in the middle, is both a constant theme of earlier research on academics from working-class backgrounds and a pervasive finding in this study.

FEELINGS ABOUT RELATIVE SUCCESS

Our final concern about the private/personal lives of our respondents is how they feel about their successes when compared with those of their parents and others from their childhoods. Since a number of the essayists in the edited books on academics from working-class backgrounds have mentioned that they felt, in many ways, guilty because of their successes (Dews and Law 1995; Ryan and Sackrey 1984; Tokarczyk and Fay 1993), we asked our respondents to comment on the extent to which they currently felt (or had ever felt) guilty about their relative successes when compared with those of the members of their families of origin and childhood friends. Our examination of their responses led us to code them either "yes" or "no"; we further divided the "yes" category into "both now and in the past" and "more so earlier than now" to better reflect the ways our respondents answered the question. We present these data in Table 6.9. An examination of the distribution of our respondents across the categories reveals that nearly two-thirds (65 percent) said that they have never felt guilty about their relative successes. The remarks of a sixty-two- year-old female respondent provide a good example of those placed into this category: "Neither my husband nor I have guilty feelings about our social mobility because we were socialized by our parents to achieve beyond their social positions. In fact, our successes were a source of pride for our parents and families." The other third or so of our respondents noted that they either currently felt guilty about their successes or had felt so in the past. A thirty-five-year-old female, whose response led us to place her in the "yes" category, provides a good example of respondents who said that they still feel guilty about their relative successes when compared with family members and childhood friends:

I am aware that my income and university position have given me direct and indirect benefits. I have been able to get apartments and secure loans because I am considered a good risk. . . . I wonder what happened to the gas station attendant's daughter. Or where is the single mother who became a waitress? Only a couple of us made it out of the economic mire that working-class existence can bring. . . . I have come to realize that sociology . . . is both my working-class legacy and my obligation.

Finally, some of our respondents' whose answers led us to place them in the "yes" category also made the point that their feelings of guilt were greater earlier in their lives than they are now. A thirty-nine-year-old female put it this way: "I felt a sense of guilt at first, but when I convinced myself that what I was doing was something that they could do too if they wanted to, that sensation abated."

Table 6.9
Respondents' Perceptions of Feeling Guilty Because of Their Relative Successes When Compared with Their Parents and Others from Their Childhood Years

	N(%)		
		Samples	
Response	Total	Males	Females
Yes	13(35)	6(30)	7(41)
Both now and in the past	[10]*	[4]	[6]
More so earlier than now	[3]	[2]	[1]
No, not now or ever	24(65)	14(70)	10(59)
Totals	37(100)	20(100)	17(100)
NA	3		

[Reliability = 100%]

*Numbers in brackets indicate the period during which respondents who reported feeling guilty felt this way.

There are also modest gender differences in response to this question. Males were more likely to offer responses that indicated that they did not feel (and had not felt) guilty about their successes than were females (70 percent versus 59 percent). Despite these few exceptions, as the overall distribution of our respondents across these categories demonstrates, a majority of our respondents did not report feeling the sense of guilt that other academics from working-class backgrounds have expressed about their relative successes when compared with the members of their families and childhood friends/associates. Obviously, this finding is also at odds with our theoretical expectations (as well as with those of previous research on the subject).

CONCLUSIONS

We began this chapter with the observation that the personal lives of academics from working-class backgrounds have not received adequate attention from previous research. We also made the point that for those who work in occupations/professions whose cultural/social environments contrast sharply with those they experienced during their child- and early adulthoods, a likely reaction to this contrast is to feel like an outsider or stranger. Previous research on academics from working-class backgrounds has shown that individuals facing such contrasts attempt to cope with them in a variety of different ways including efforts to create a more familiar cultural/social environment off the job. We then suggested that such an environment might include an intimate partner, family members, close friends, and a neighborhood setting who/that are more similar to the cultural/social environment of the individual's child- and early adulthood than to that which they encounter in their work setting.

The data we reviewed in this chapter are mixed in terms of these expectations. For example, concerning the intimate partners of our sample of sociologists from working-class backgrounds, we first laid out a model that is based on the norm of hypergamy, or the tendency for women to marry "up" and for men to marry "down." As we explained above, the relative value of an individual's resources in the mate selection process must be examined in order to understand the complexity of the process and its different implications for men and women. Our examination of each of our resource variables individually revealed that contrary to our expectations, the members of our sample of sociologists from working-class backgrounds tended to choose intimate partners who were highly educated, who had high occupational status, and who were not from working-class backgrounds. We then set forth a set of ideal types of the matching process to examine the multivariate patternings of mate selection for our sample. Based on these types, we proposed the explanation that class background becomes a problem in an intimate relationship when resources combine in such a way as to produce relative parity between partners. When resource parity is approached, the norm of patriarchal authority that is usually taken for granted in U.S. society is challenged and problems arise. The data for our respondents and their intimate partners supported this notion. For example, the highest frequency of respondents reporting that class background differences presented problems in their relationships were male respondents whose intimate partners were not from working-class backgrounds.

Concerning friendships, our data showed that though many of our respondents' friendship circles did include members of the working class, a majority of them did not; females were slightly more likely than males to report having members of the working class among their close friends.

Contrary to our expectations, a majority of our respondents did not report living in exclusively or even partially working-class neighborhoods, yet four in ten of them said that they lived in neighborhoods that contained at least some working-class families. When we added controls for the class backgrounds of our couples, we found that *more* of our male respondents who were in class (background) homogeneous relationships lived in neighborhoods that were at least partially working class than did those who were in class (background) heterogeneous relationships; for our female respondents, it was just the opposite—those paired with intimate partners who were from working-class backgrounds were *less* likely to live in neighborhoods that contained at least some working-class families than were female respondents who were paired with their families. However, in contrast to those expectations, most of our respondents claimed to have little or no contact with their childhood friends. Gender did not impact either of these findings. Both geographic and cultural/ social differences were mentioned by respondents as factors that complicated their continued relations with families and childhood friends.

Finally, contrary to our expectations (and those of earlier research on the subject), most of our respondents did not express feelings of guilt about their professional successes when compared with members of their families of origin and childhood friends who remained working class—females were more likely to report feeling guilty than were males, even though a majority of each reported that they did not feel guilty.

What we have shown in this chapter is that, in many ways, academics from working-class background are not too different from the members of the larger society in terms of their personal lives. They tend to select their intimate partners and to deal with them in ways similar to the remainder of society,[12] they tend to make and maintain friendships with people from a variety of class backgrounds, they tend to live in mixed-class neighborhoods, and they remain in touch with their families of origin. Finally, despite the hardships that many of them have suffered during their child- and early adulthoods, and in their professional lives, most of our respondents do not feel a sense of guilt about their successes relative to others who have remained within the working class. In the final chapter, these findings will be integrated with those of the earlier chapters.

NOTES

1. Ryan and Sackrey (1984) have isolated four different forms of adaptation that academics from working-class backgrounds employ in their efforts to cope with the academy: acceptance, separate pathways, balancing class locations, and outsiders. Although we feel certain that our respondents have employed, at one time or another, each of these strategies,we also believe that the data reviewed thus far in the study point toward the "balancing class locations" alternative as the one most frequently employed by the members of our sample. They characterize this form of adaptation as, in many ways, the "most difficult" because of the "inner conflict[s]" it generates for academics from working-class backgrounds (Ryan and Sackrey 1984:205). Our belief that this particular coping strategy is the one most often used by our respondents motivated us to include in our book's title the phrase "caught in the middle".

2. We are also aware, from the findings of previous research on academics from working-class backgrounds, that even this alternative is not without its difficulties, since it is compromised by the growing cultural and social distances between upwardly mobile academics and their families and childhood friends.

3. Barker (1995) reaches the opposite conclusion for women. She argues that male academics from working-class backgrounds are more likely to "marry up" in terms of class background than are women from such backgrounds.

4. See Sabatelli and Shehan (1993) for an overview of the use of exchange theory in family sociology.

5. The "technical" part of this label was added to accommodate a chemist with an M.S. degree.

6. These categories may seem a bit messy since a number of them contain multiple class locations, but, in their defense, they reflect the actual labels our respondents used instead of our own.

7. We add this qualifier because class background remains a significant variable in upper-class courtship and family life (cf. Collins and Coltrane 1995).

8. In doing this, we realize that we are ignoring other important resources that individuals bring to the marriage market such as occupation, personal attractiveness, and social skills. We believe, however, that the attributes chosen are the most important ones in mate selection in North American societies.

9. When we controlled for the education of the intimate partner in these relationships, we did not find any large differences between those who reported benign or negative impacts in terms of their intimate partners' level of formal educational attainment.

10. Once again, these categories are a bit messy, but we wanted to reflect the labels our respondents chose to employ rather than to force them into a cleaner set of categories that we might have chosen.

11. We mention this because research cited earlier in the book has argued that there is greater pressure on females to stay in contact with and otherwise tend to family relationships (cf. Barker 1993, 1995). This led us to suspect that female respondents would report feeling closer to their families of origin and childhood friends than was the case. In fact, the one gender difference that we did observe was that, of those respondents who reported no contact with childhood friends, all were female. This is contrary to our expectations.

12. Barker's (1995) research on pairings among academics from the working class found that men were more likely than women to "marry-up." Our findings contradict her claim.

7

Summary and Conclusions

In Chapter 1 we presented the conceptual model that has guided our study. In this chapter we organize, summarize, and interpret our findings in light of the points in that model. We then identify and discuss some of the study's limitations. We also make some suggestions for future research. Finally, we end the study with a discussion of some of its broader implications.

THE CONCEPTUAL MODEL AND THE FINDINGS

1. *Class remains a major variable influencing the life chances of the citizens of late capitalist society.* This study began with a simple premise—that class still matters in advanced capitalist societies. In Chapter 1 we outlined the historical development of two major theoretical perspectives on class within American sociology—evolutionary liberalism and structural realism. As we pointed out there, evolutionary liberalism, based on beliefs associated with the dominant ideology of the United States in the early twentieth century, avoids discussion of social class per se, preferring instead to view the social structure of society as comprising numerous locations called "statuses" that are loosely arranged in a hierarchy with fluid boundaries. The relationships between these locations are viewed as cooperative at best and competitive at worst and generally positive sum in outcome. The other perspective, structural realism, presents a very different picture of the nature of classes and their interrelationships. This perspective uses the term "classes" to describe societal locations that are differentiated based on their control of different amounts of valued societal resources. It views their interrelationships as antagonistic and conflictual and, generally negative sum in outcome. Although both perspectives

have their relative strengths and weaknesses, we believe that the structural realist
perspective offers greater insights into the nature of the class structures of late
capitalist societies, and we chose it as a framework to guide our research. In
particular, we employed Erik Wright's (1985) exploitation-based model of the
class structure of advanced capitalist societies to conceptualize and measure
class. Wright defines the working class in terms of three criteria: (1) its
members do not own the means of production; (2) its members do not possess
organizational assets; and (3) its members have few skills/credential assets. The
parents of our study's participants met these criteria during their (our
participants') childhoods and early adulthoods.

2. *The life experiences of the middle and the working classes are not
converging as some earlier theorists have suggested but, instead, remain
divergent in many crucial respects—particularly in the relative material,
cultural, and social resources that each class has available for expropriation by
its members.* More conservative scholars, taking the perspective of evolutionary
liberalism, suggest a "weakening" of class stratification and point to such factors
as the growth of the middle class, the diminution of life style differences
between the middle and the working class, and the increased role that education
and acquired skills, rather than such factors as family background and other
ascribed characteristics, play in determining the location of individuals in a
putatively equal opportunity society. As pointed out in Chapter 1, we disagree
with this viewpoint and offer as supporting evidence for our position the findings
of a number of scholars who have studied the working class in post–World War
II American society. For example, scholars such as Rubin (1976, 1994), Sennett
and Cobb (1972), and Shostak (1969), maintain that the relative position of the
working class within postwar American society was never as solid materially and
as secure as some scholars during the late 1950s proclaimed (c.f. Bell 1960;
Galbraith 1958; Nisbet 1959). Furthermore, others claim that the relative
material circumstances and security of the working class have declined even
more as a result of the growing competition among advanced capitalist
economies that has intensified since the late 1960s. These researchers cite such
trends as the decline in manufacturing jobs, an increase in the automation of
production, a diminution in union memberships, eroding wages, the increased
demand for formal training and credentials, and the virtual disappearance of job
security among blue-collar workers to support their claims (Bluestone and
Harrison 1982, 1986; Danziger and Gottschalk 1993, 1995). The consensus
among these scholars is that the relative material affluence of the working class
remains one of America's most enduring myths.

3. *The opportunities for success afforded children in late capitalist society
(still) depend heavily on the relative resources that their families make available
for their appropriation [and]*

4. *The relative resource advantage of middle-class families (not to mention
those of families located even higher in the class structure), all other things
being equal, means that more of their children will acquire greater human*

capital skills than will children from the working class—this difference serves to "reproduce" the class structure of American society intergenerationally. In Chapter 1 we began our overview of the process through which individuals are located within the class structure of advanced capitalist society with a consideration of the perspectives of neoclassical economists such as Gary Becker (1964) and functionalist sociologists such as Talcott Parsons (1940, 1953). These scholars have claimed that when contrasted with earlier societies, in advanced capitalist societies the role that family background plays in the "human capital" acquisition or the "status attainment" process has declined and that individual abilities, efforts, and motivation are now the most significant influences on this process. We disagreed with their claims and presented a review of the findings of more contemporary research that supports the conclusion that class background remains a significant influence on the eventual success of an individual (Bourdieu 1984, 1986; Coleman 1988; Lareau 1987; Robinson 1984). This later research shows that the material, cultural, and social resources that a family possesses and makes available for its childrens' use remain crucial in either facilitating or inhibiting their efforts to compete for and acquire the skills, knowledge, and training necessary for better occupations (and, thus, higher class positions) in advanced capitalist societies. Furthermore, we argued that the impacts of family differences in resources are also reflected in the class-biased nature of American education (Bowles 1972; Kozol 1991).

5. *Despite the relative resource disadvantages that working-class children face, some (few?) do, nonetheless, acquire the "institutionalized" human capital skills necessary to move upward in the class structure, some even to upper-middle-class status.* When we scrutinized the childhoods and early educational experiences of our sample of sociologists from working-class backgrounds, we found that in addition to their self-identification with the working class, the members of our sample met the objective criteria we had specified: All were reared in working-class households, a large majority of which were multigenerational. Their parents worked in blue-collar jobs that were not particularly rewarding for them, and although they believed in the value of hard work, most did not see their jobs as having any larger importance for society as a whole. Our respondents' parents had little formal education beyond high school and a number of them did not even have a high school diploma. Their parents were aware that a class structure exists, of their family's location within it, and most of them agreed that class had/has important negative consequences for both themselves and their families. The cultural environments of their homes and neighborhoods were also working class—so much so that a number of our respondents reported being ashamed of their families, their homes, and/or their neighborhoods at some point in their lives.

Our data also showed that, during their early educations, our respondents attended schools whose student bodies were either exclusively working class or a mixture of working and lower middle class and that many of them reported that their early educational experiences were more negative than positive, with the nature of their assessments depending largely on the class composition of the schools they attended (i.e., students from exclusively working-class schools were more likely to report a negative experience than were students who attended mixed- or higher-class schools). Most of our respondents reported being aware of class differences between themselves and their classmates during these early years, and they also commented on some of the negative consequences of this realization. We contend that these early experiences place our respondents clearly within the working class with all the negative material, cultural, and social "baggage" that that location in the class structure entails.

In our efforts to explain *why* our respondents were successful despite the fact that the (class) deck was stacked against them, we isolated three important positive influences on their efforts to do well in school and then to go on to college and graduate school. First, most of our respondents reported that they were either above average or exceptional students during this stage of their educational careers. Second, almost all of our respondents reported that their parents and their teachers provided important support and encouragement for their educational efforts. Third, being socialized in a working-class environment taught our respondents both the necessity for and the value of hard work. We contend that it is these influences that enabled them to overcome the numerous barriers to higher education and upward social mobility that resulted from their working-class backgrounds.

Although much of the evidence we summarized above concerning the childhood and early educational experiences of our respondents supports the claim that our respondents' backgrounds within the working class were inhibitive of their efforts to succeed, there is even stronger support for this claim when we turn to the undergraduate and graduate educations of our respondents. As reported in Chapter 4, we found that both the undergraduate and graduate school experiences of our respondents were heavily influenced by the levels of material, cultural, and social resources that their working-class backgrounds provided. Beginning with their first steps toward higher education—the selection of an institution—our respondents were at a disadvantage. Given their parents' lack of direct experience with and limited knowledge about higher education, many of our respondents complained that a lack of adequate information often limited their aspirations and often sidetracked or delayed their careers. For most of those in the study, the selections of both undergraduate and graduate institutions were made without the benefit of adequate information; thus, their selection was often made for more practical than for academic reasons—each of these examples demonstrates how class background played an important *inhibiting* role in their higher educational experiences. Furthermore, since more geographically proximate colleges and universities had high name recognition for our respondents and were also more affordable, they were often selected by our respondents despite the quality of their programs in sociology. We also found that, since most of our respondents received little material support from their families, they were forced to work and to depend on loans and grants for support during their undergraduate careers. Among the themes that emerged from our analysis of their remarks about their undergraduate careers were such things as: recurrent financial difficulties, feeling less well prepared than their classmates, choosing more "applied" majors, being forced to interrupt their educational careers, taking longer to finish their degrees, and feeling different from their classmates. These themes are obviously more inhibitive than facilitative of their eventual educational successes.

When we turned to their graduate school experiences, we found that the members of our sample continued to be plagued by many of the same problems that were inhibitive during their undergraduate careers: recurrent financial difficulties, feelings about being less well prepared than their classmates, feeling that their cultural skills were inadequate, taking a long time to finish their graduate training, and feeling somehow "different" from their classmates. We also found that our respondents felt that their class backgrounds had inhibited their pursuit of higher education. For example, when we compared the institutions from which they received their graduate degrees, we found that they were graduated from programs that ranked lower in the disciplinary prestige hierarchy than those of a sample drawn from the membership of the ASA. Despite these factors, however, our data revealed three important positive influences on their educational successes. First, many of them entered higher education during the postwar period of great expansion and the benefitted from the high demand for college/university professors that accompanied this expansion. Second, the work ethic that our respondents had acquired during their childhoods within the working class boosted their perseverance despite the numerous fiscal, cultural, temporal, and psychological obstacles they faced in pursuing their higher educational credentials. Third, many of our respondents mentioned the important role that mentors played in encouraging them during their educational careers.

6. *Such upward mobility from the working to the middle and upper middle classes is never complete, however, because it is impossible to completely escape the influence(s) of one's class background.*

7. *As a result, upward mobility carries with it a number of significant structural, social, interpersonal, and psychological consequences for those members of the working class who do manage to move upward in the class structure because of their acquisition of human capital skills.* The sociologists who participated in this study have achieved significant upward social mobility when compared with their parents, but as our findings have shown, their accomplishments have often been achieved at considerable personal and professional costs to them. Some of these costs are psychological, like the perception of many of our respondents that they are somehow "different" from their colleagues and even that they are impostors who will, eventually, be found out and cast out of the academy. Others are more tangible, such as delayed entry into the field because working one's way through school takes longer than not or the burden of large student loans whose repayment extends well into one's

academic career.

In addition to these costs, some of the most poignant findings of our study concerned the long-term effects of class background on the professional careers of our respondents. For example, when we examined our respondents' perceptions about their professional careers, a number of key findings emerged. First, geographic proximity and economic necessity rather than academic prestige or working conditions were often cited as the important factors influencing our samples' choices of first positions. Second, most of our respondents' first jobs were positions in departments *without* graduate programs in sociology. Third, when we examined their current academic ranks and compared them with those of a sample drawn from the membership of the ASA, we found that the positions held by our respondents were lower in the academic hierarchy of their universities; the association between the relative prestige of the sources of their Ph.D. degrees and the prestige of their current employers was also lower; and, for those who were currently employed in a department that offered the Ph.D. degree, the association between the prestige of the source of their Ph.D. and that of their current institution of employment was also lower than for those of a sample of the members of the ASA.

In addition, many of our respondents expressed dissatisfaction with their current positions and a number of them linked their relative lack of success to deficiencies in their (class) backgrounds. And, when asked about their perceptions about life within the academy, two important findings emerged: our respondents were not happy with the current balance among teaching, research, and service; and many of them also claimed that their relationships with academic authority were negative and, in many ways, inhibitive of their work.

A number of our respondents also expressed a preference for associating with working-class friends, and, importantly, most of our respondents felt themselves to be "outsiders" within the academy because of perceived differences between themselves and their colleagues in terms of attitudes, behaviors, orientations toward social activism, and feelings of inadequacy concerning cultural/social skills.

For most of our respondents, then, it was difficult to overcome the disadvantages of having grown up within the working class and then moving to an upper-middle-class environment. They reported a number of negative consequences associated with the mismatch between their class background and their new class location. They also described numerous difficulties in "feeling at home" in this new (and, in many ways, alien) class location. So, although it was possible for some to complete the "objective" requirements for upward mobility into an upper-middle-class professional class location, life in this "alien" cultural location remains difficult for many of our respondents, even years after the move was made. Bourdieu (1986:244) explains this disjuncture in terms of the relationship(s) between the various forms of capital. He states that the "economic and social yield of the educational qualification" is dependent on types of capital that can only be acquired through experience. He defines "embodied" cultural capital as: "the set of distinctive features, bearing, posture, presence, diction and pronunciation, manners and usages, without which . . . all scholastic knowledge is worth little or nothing" (Bourdieu 1984:91). His position is that the "embodied" form of cultural capital is *also necessary* for successful adaptation to life in the upper-middle class and that a deficit in this form of cultural capital cannot always be offset by other resources (such as formal educational credentials) that an upwardly mobile individual possesses.

We also examined the personal lives of our respondents to see if, in some ways, their "off-the-job" lives might have been structured in such ways as to meliorate some of the marginality they suffered in the upper-middle class world of the academy. In this context, we hypothesized that some potential strategies for "coping" with this marginality were to have an intimate partner who either was working class or who came from a working-class background, to seek out friends who were working class, to live in a neighborhood that contained working-class families, or to retain close ties with their families of origin and childhood friends. Our results showed that only in the case of keeping close ties with parents and siblings were our respondents able to maintain any linkages to their working-class backgrounds. And, as a number of our respondents reported, even these ties were often strained by the "cultural gap" between our respondents and their families that resulted from their educational and professional successes.

The class mobility of this group of sociologists, then, remains incomplete. Our data clearly show that though it is possible to move from the working class to the upper middle class in terms of location within the class structure of society, a move such as this does not automatically *make* one a member of the upper middle class, at least not completely, and the long-term impacts of this fact are clearly evidenced in various aspects of the lives of our respondents.

8. *Since gender has also been shown to be an important structural variable affecting the life chances of individuals in late capitalist society, its interaction with class means that the nature of the various consequences of upward social mobility will be different for men and women from working-class backgrounds.* Since we were also convinced that the consequences of class are mediated by gender, we examined how gender affected our participants' responses to the questions we posed. We found differences in all areas. For example, during their childhood years, our female respondents were more likely than our males to report that they were ashamed of their families and their class backgrounds. They were also more likely to report that they received less encouragement and help in their early educational efforts than did our male respondents. On the plus side, they were also more likely than our males to rate themselves as high achievers in school.

Gender differences were also present during the undergraduate and graduate careers of our respondents. Females were more likely to have to depend on grants and loans than were males. Females were also more likely to have suffered career interruptions between high school and college than were males. Our female respondents' dependence on grants and loans rather than on scholarships and/or assistantships continued in graduate school. Finally, females were more likely than males to stress the importance of mentoring in influencing their success in graduate school.

Gender also played an important role in structuring responses to questions concerning our respondents' professional careers: Women were more likely than men to initially take and to remain in research appointments; they were also more likely to hold junior- rather than senior-level positions. On the other hand, men were more likely than women to be dissatisfied with their current position; they were also more likely to link their current professional position to deficiencies in their class background than were women. Females were more likely to see a closer correspondence between their initial expectations and the realities of academic life than were males, and they were also more likely to express general satisfaction with their colleagues. In contrast, males were more likely than females to say that their closest academic friend was from the working class, and that their political viewpoints were more radical.

The most obvious gender differences emerged when we explored the interpersonal relationships of our sample of sociologists from working-class backgrounds. Although most of our respondents reported being in intimate relationships with other upper-middle-class professionals, there were some interesting differences between men and women. Men were more likely than women to be involved with an intimate partner who had less education; they were also more likely to be involved with a partner from a higher class background. Yet, in contrast to women, men who were involved with partners from higher class backgrounds were more likely to report that class background differences negatively impacted their intimate relationships.

Women were slightly more likely than men to mention that their friendship circle included members of the working class; they were also more likely than men to report living in neighborhoods that contained at least some working-class families. Finally, women differed from men on the issue of feeling guilty when comparing their relative success with that of the members of their families of origin and childhood friends. Although two-thirds of our respondents denied that this was a problem for them, women were more likely to report occasionally feeling guilt about these differences in outcome than were men.

SOME CONSEQUENCES OF BEING CAUGHT IN THE MIDDLE

Our data have shown that our group of sociologists from working-class backgrounds are, in many ways, caught in the middle between their childhoods as members of the working class and their new class location as members of the upper-middle class academy. We have provided explanations, often using our respondents' own words as examples, of what that phrase means and how it feels to be located there. Our implied use of "place" is metaphorical. "Place," in this context, relates to social mobility and conjures up social versions of concepts like "journey" and "path" and "climbing." Our intent has been to portray this process as both active and intentional and accompanied by both pride and trepidation. We wanted to capture the irony that seems so clearly a part of the results of these individuals' successes. On the one hand, they have reached their goals and, for many, they have achieved far more than they ever thought possible from their initial vantage points as daughters and sons of working-class families. But their arrival at their new class destination, for many, if not most, of them remains a source of frequent anguish. The class-cultural standards that they internalized during their child- and early adulthoods, and which they took (and may still take) for granted, are not compatible with the foreign terrain of the upper middle class, the destination of their social mobility. Yet, they have little choice but to adapt—at least in appearance, if not in reality. To the extent to which they adapt, they no longer "fit" into their old structural and cultural niches in the social structure. Furthermore, adaptations to this new cultural landscape, even if for expedience only, must be cast off if, whether by necessity or desire, they should even temporarily return to the working-class world from which they came. The threat of exposure for behaving "out of place" exists in both places. The lingering of working-class speech patterns, manners, and appearance impedes full self-acceptance, as well as acceptance by one's peers in the academic world. Yet the precision of articulation and presentation of self that are a part of life in the upper-middle-class academy and that they have learned after years of self-conscious attention often are objects of reproach if not effectively concealed in the presence of family and childhood friends. There seems to be a common theme (and thus a common dilemma) present in both class cultures. In the working-class culture, to "pretend" to be something other than the product of your origins, as evidenced in speech, dress, and manners, is offensive to those who remain in the working class. In the middle or upper middle class of destination, that same speech, dress, or manners, unless *flawlessly* portrayed, can also be interpreted as "pretending" to be something other than the product of your origins and, thus, are also viewed with contempt.

In short, as the evidence reviewed in this study suggests, it is clear that these individuals fit into neither the working-class world nor the upper-middle class world. In many ways, then, the phrase "caught in the middle" seems to us to capture the situation within which the members of our sample and other academics from working-class backgrounds find themselves. In the words of one academic from a working-class background: "We [see] ourselves as living on the margins of two cultural worlds, but as members of neither (Gardner 1993:50). Such is the plight of our sample of sociologists from working-class backgrounds and, we suspect, many others who have journeyed upward from the working class into the middle and upper middle classes.

GENDER AND SOCIAL/CULTURAL MARGINALITY

Our data also show that these feelings of marginality are, in a number of ways, worse for female than for male academics from working-class backgrounds since these women must break *both* class and gender barriers in order to succeed. Thus, once they arrive in the upper-middle-class world of the academy, their status is *doubly* marginalized by the effects of both class and gender.

Some of the differences we noted above are the result of the additive effects of both class background and gender. For example, the impacts on professional careers show that coming from a working-class background has a negative effect on one's career, but the effect is amplified for women. It is not possible, with our data, to specify the origins of these negative effects. Are they the result of gender bias in the environment of the academy, or are they result of socialization that instilled different attitudes and coping strategies, thus inhibiting women from competing more effectively in the academic world?

On the other hand, some of the gender differences we found appear to originate in the early socialization of women from working-class backgrounds. Other researchers (Barker 1995), for example, have pointed out that women's attitudes toward their families of origin are typically different from their male counterparts. Women are more likely to remain more closely connected, to feel an obligation to make themselves available to their families, and so on. Again, we cannot verify the origins of some of the patterns of behavior we found. For example, our female respondents were more likely to report that they felt self-conscious about their working-class status in their early lives. This may mean that their early gender-role socialization made them more sensitive to the reactions of others (a trait that is a widely accepted difference between the gender socialization of girls and boys). If so, they may have interpreted many of their school and college experiences in light of an early determination that their combination of class background and gender placed them at a special disadvantage and presented an additional obstacle for them to overcome. This interpretation would also help to explain why our females respondents were more likely than our males to feel guilty about the class differences between themselves and relatives and friends from their childhoods. Likewise, women were less surprised at their experiences in the academy than were men and they were also less likely to view their class backgrounds as impediments to their careers. Unlike men, these women have long experience with the combination of class and gender that contributes to the devaluation of their contributions. To have survived the struggles to acquire the "institutionalized" cultural capital necessary to be qualified to enter the academy, and then to deal with the heavily gendered environment of the academy, it is no wonder that these women see many issues differently from their male counterparts. The white male academic from a working-class background can, after all, "pass" as a member of the white male elite that holds most of the power in the academic world (an option that is not open to women and nonwhites). Should he choose to "pass" in this way, the obstacles he must overcome are purely class cultural in nature. But, as our data suggest, even these class cultural characteristics are, in themselves, deeply ingrained and become obstacles to be overcome for both genders. Often they are large enough to be insurmountable, even for males. These various elements of class culture are, after all, the very things that help to assure the reproduction of the class structure of society.

LIMITATIONS

When interpreting our findings, the reader should be aware of number of limitations, some of which are unavoidable given the nature of our subject matter, others that resulted from choices that we made among various alternatives. Among these are our approach to data gathering, the type and size of the sample we employed, and the variety and content of the questions we asked.

The major studies of academics from working-class backgrounds that have appeared in print thus far share a common approach to data gathering (Dews and Law 1995; Ryan and Sackrey 1984; Tokarczyk and Fay 1993)—they asked their participants to write autobiographical essays about their experiences, giving them few if any guidelines to structure their responses. Such an approach to data gathering is common in exploratory research when little knowledge is available to assist the researcher in providing greater structure (Babbie 1995:84). The author of one of these studies defends this strategy as follows: "Only autobiography is a sensitive enough instrument to register the subtle activity of social class in a milieu in which class is supposedly a nonfactor" (Law 1995:5). Although she may be right, as we noted in Chapter 2, we chose to modify the approach(es) taken by earlier researchers for two reasons. First, the availability of previous research on the subject, particularly *Strangers in Paradise* by Ryan and Sackrey (1984), provided us with a great deal of useful information about the subject that was not available when they conducted their study. It seemed to us that to ignore the insights provided by these authors and their respondents would have been scientifically irresponsible. Second, an advantage of posing a specific set of questions and asking respondents to reply to each of them offers the researcher the opportunity to systematically compare their responses in a way that is far more difficult with unstructured, autobiographical essays. Of course, it could be argued that there are several potential limitations to this approach as well, including "putting words into respondents' mouths" and omitting questions about key issues that might have emerged from a less-structured format that would allow each respondent to define his or her own unique reality. Since research decisions usually involve choices among less-than-perfect alternatives, we decided that the advantages derived from providing our respondents with a specific set of questions outweighed the liabilities, particularly since we took great pains to ensure that the range of questions we asked was as exhaustive as possible, given the knowledge we had at our disposal. Some may disagree with our judgment in this matter, and among our regrets is the fact that we did not ask some questions that we wish we had, and we also wish we had posed some questions differently from the way we did. Despite these regrets, however, we remain convinced that the approach we took is superior to those employed by earlier research on the subject.

A second major limitation is our sample. Since there is no existing list of sociologists from working-class backgrounds from which to draw a probability sample, we were forced to rely on a sample of volunteers. As noted in Chapter 2, we advertised our interest in contacting sociologists from working-class backgrounds in the newsletters of the national and all ten regional sociology association newsletters and asked interested parties to contact us (we also asked them to nominate others from similar backgrounds). We then mailed materials to those who responded and encouraged their participation in the study. We eventually received materials from forty-five participants. There are three things about this sample that have potential impacts on the findings of the study. First, and most obvious, this sample is not a random sample of sociologists from working-class backgrounds. This problem was unavoidable given the inherent difficulties in sampling unknown or hidden populations and our limited resources. As we reported in Chapter 2, a comparison between our sample and the one sociological universe about which we did have information—the membership of the ASA—revealed that the two were similar, but not identical, on a number of important attributes. However, since we have no data on the parameters of the universe of sociologists from working-class backgrounds, and we suspect that this group is different from both the membership of the ASA and the larger universe of North American sociologists, the representativeness of our sample remains an open question. Second, we would have preferred to have had a larger sample than the one we ended up with. This also raises questions about representativeness (and, thus, generalizability). Although our hunch is that the results would not have been greatly different had the sample been larger, we can't know this for sure. We also made an explicit effort to increase the number of minority (especially African American) sociologists from working-class backgrounds in the sample by advertising the study in the newsletter of the Association of Black Sociologists. This effort did not prove to be successful. As a result, although about half of our sample comprised women, members of the African and Hispanic American minorities are not adequately represented in the sample. Generalizing of our findings to these two latter groups is thus especially risky. A third potential limitation is that we did not include the members of other social science disciplines in our sample. Although this limits the generalizability of our findings to sociologists (if even to them), this choice was a purposive one. Our interest was in sociologists from working-class backgrounds and not in (some or all) social scientists from such backgrounds. Because of this decision, we make no claim that the results can be generalized beyond sociologists, and, as noted above, even generalizing to this group is not without its risks.

The third limitation of our study concerns the questions we asked our respondents to address. As we noted in Chapter 2 and earlier in this chapter, previous research on the subject of academics from working-class backgrounds simply asked respondents to write autobiographical essays and provided little or no additional guidance. Based on the findings of this earlier research, particularly the work of Ryan and Sackrey (1984), we decided to provide greater structure for our respondents. Toward this end, we formulated fifty-nine open-ended questions, organized them according to the life cycles of our respondents, and presented them as an essay guide; we also supplemented this instrument with a lengthy questionnaire. We asked our participants to address each question contained in our instruments so that we could more easily compare their responses. There are several dangers when providing specific questions to respondents: (1) some important issues may be omitted from the list of questions provided; (2) some questions may be loaded and lead to predetermined responses; and (3) some questions may be misunderstood by the respondents. We are sure that a careful review of our instruments will lead some to conclude that we made all three of these mistakes. Our own assessment is that the methodology we employed in assembling the list of questions, when combined with the fact that we asked our respondents to add any additional information they wished after they had responded to our instruments, minimized (but certainly did not eliminate) the first of the three potential dangers. We are also sure that some of the questions we asked were leading, because given our interest in the impact of class background on their lives, it is difficult to ask questions that do not draw attention to the subject. We tried to qualify these questions with phrases like "what impact, if any . . ." but that strategy may not have been sufficient. We also asked a number of complicated questions that contained several parts and sometimes our participants did not respond to all of them. At other times, they misinterpreted the question and/or only responded to some of its parts. These omissions and errors in interpretation also created occasional coding and analysis problems that were noted in the findings chapters. Our own assessment is that we were probably most guilty of this third danger. Given these various limitations, appropriate caution should be exercised when interpreting the study's results.

SUGGESTIONS FOR FUTURE RESEARCH

Given the findings of our study, it seems obvious that additional research is needed on the various impact(s) of class background on the professional and interpersonal lives of sociologists (not to mention other academics and the general population as well) from working-class backgrounds. Our own study profited from earlier researchers such as Dews and Law (1995), Ryan and Sackrey (1984), and Tokarczyk and Fay (1993). Using their perspectives and findings as a starting point, we were able to organize what we labeled a "second-generation" exploratory study whose major data-gathering instrument consisted of a set of fifty-nine open-ended questions that provided a more structured approach than its predecessors. From a more positivistic viewpoint, it seems to us that a logical next step would be to make use of our perspective and results to further refine the issues and questions and then to conduct a more ambitious study that would focus its attention on the impacts of class background on the professional and interpersonal lives of the members of the sociological community as a whole. This study should employ probability sampling techniques so that representativeness and generalizability would be maximized; it should also have a sample that is large enough to permit the use of multivariate data analysis techniques. From our viewpoint, findings derived from such an approach would inspire greater confidence than those of its predecessors, including our study. From a less positivistic viewpoint, there also seems to be plenty of room for additional studies like ours (and those of our predecessors) that explore the impacts of class background on the lives of sociologists, academics in general, or the population as a whole, using less structured approaches. We believe that there is need for both types of studies, since the data provided by each approach are different and each type of data offers unique insights into the subject matter. We personally plan to proceed along both these paths in our future efforts to learn more about the way(s) class and class background impact the lives of the citizens of advanced capitalist societies.

SOME LARGER IMPLICATIONS

As sociologists, we find ourselves, at the end of this study, seeking linkages between our findings and the larger issue of class inequality in American society. As a part of this process, we ask ourselves in what ways, if any, do our insights about class and social mobility among sociologists from working-class backgrounds enhance our understanding of these subjects for the members of the larger society? In response to this question we find that, though much of what we have learned serves to validate and reinforce our own personal experiences and those who took part in earlier research on the subject, there is also a larger lesson here about life in late capitalist society. The insights of our respondents have helped us to further refine the sociological "lens" through which we, ourselves, view society and its institutions. After all, who can better understand and apply the concept "class" than sociologists? In this respect, our respondents, because of their academic training and experience, offer a unique viewpoint on society—sort of from the inside out, so to speak—and this viewpoint is based on more than the formalistic, abstract models of class that are a part of sociological literature. It is also influenced by years of reflection and interpretion since many of our respondents chose sociology as a career *because* they were concerned about the issues their own personal experiences have raised.

The message that comes through to us most clearly from our respondents is a sense of disillusionment with the American dream. These individuals recounted over and over again how they had abided by all the rules, worked hard, and achieved a degree of upward mobility that many of them could not even have imagined when they were kids. Yet, what many of them experienced when they arrived at their new location within the class structure was a sense of estrangement, not just from this new class location but from their working-class origins as well.

The implicit lure of the American ideal of individual achievement and competition is that one will find fulfillment in achieving success—that the prize at the end of the journey will make the sacrifices made along the way worthwhile. Our impression is that our respondents are not sure that this end has justified its means. The message they seem to be sending us is that the "dream" may be just that—ephemeral and imaginary. Thus, the achievement of occupational mobility and a certain level of material success does not automatically guarantee a sense of well-being in a class- (and gender-) stratified society. Social mobility, as our data have shown, is far more complex and incomplete than conservative political rhetoric suggests. In fact, for many Americans, the utility of this "dream" may be more contingent on a view of "success" that shines most brightly when seen from a distance rather than from being experienced firsthand. This inconsistency is just one of the many contradictions that confront the citizens of class-structured societies.

Appendices

APPENDIX A: AUTOBIOGRAPHICAL ESSAY GUIDE

The major focus of our study of sociologists from working-class backgrounds is the autobiographical essay that we are requesting from each participant. For purposes of organization, we request that you divide your essay into four parts: childhood and early educational experiences; later educational experiences, including undergraduate and graduate work; professional and career experiences; and personal relationships with adult intimate partners and members of your family of procreation. We list below each of these areas and a set of issues that both our personal experiences and our review of research on the subject suggest may be relevant for each. For purposes of comparison, we request that you comment on each of these; we also encourage you to identify and discuss any other issue(s) that you feel is (are) important as well.

A. <u>Childhood and Early Educational Experiences</u>
1. What kind of work (including housework) did your parents do when you were growing up? If possible, describe the work of their parents as well.
2. How aware of class, their own location(s) within the class structure, and the consequences of this (these) location(s) were your parents when you were growing up?
3. How much formal education did each of your parents complete?
4. How did your parents talk or feel about their work and its relative importance in society?
5. When you were growing up, were your parents members of unions? What were your parents' attitudes toward unions?
6. What were your parents' perceptions of the nature of the class structure of American society? What evaluations (if any) of this system did they make?
7. Provide a brief overview of the employment patterns of both of your parents when you were growing up.
8. What was the nature of the gender division of labor in your household when you were growing up?
9. Describe the cultural environment of your home when you were growing up.
10. As a child, did you ever feel a sense of material deprivation?
11. Have you ever felt ashamed of your parents, siblings, home, neighborhood, etc.?
12. What role(s) did your parents play in encouraging (or discouraging) your early education?
13. Describe the educational attainment(s) of your siblings; if they were older than you, did their experiences influence your own goals and plans? If so, how?
14. To what extent were you aware of class differences between yourself (and your family) and others when you were young; when did you become aware of these differences?
15. Have you ever been, or are you currently, ashamed of your class background? Elaborate.
16. Describe the class background of the neighborhood in which you grew up.
17. How would you describe the class composition of the school(s) in your early education? Speculate about any impact(s) that this may have had on your educational experiences.
18. How would you describe yourself as a student between K and 12th grade?

19. If there were major turning points in your early educational career, describe these and note when they occurred.
20. Were any of your teachers particularly important in directing your path toward higher education? If so, describe the nature of their influence. Do you have any information about their class origins?
21. In general, how would you rank the relative influence of class on your early life when compared with other influences such as gender, color, religion, etc.?

B. Later Educational Experiences Including Undergraduate and Graduate Work
1. Did (or do) you feel that your class background has been an impediment to your pursuit of higher education? If so, summarize its impact(s).
2. Did you feel that you were somehow "different" from other students at any time during your educational career? If so, how?
3. Did you go straight from high school into college and then on to graduate school? If not, describe the unique path(s) you took and the reasons why you took the path(s) you did.
4. How did you support yourself during your post–high school education?
5. Where did you receive your undergraduate degree and how did you select this institution?
6. Did you ever feel that you had to work harder that the other students because of your class background?
7. Describe your undergraduate career.
8. When in your life history did you make the decision to become a college professor and sociologist? Why did you make this choice?
9. How did you select the institution(s) from which you received your graduate education? Have you ever felt that your selection of this (these) institution(s) was influenced by your class background in some way?
10. Describe your graduate educational career.
11. What role did mentor(s) play in your success? What do you know about the class background(s) of your mentor(s)?
12. Assess the relative role that class background played in your post–high school experiences when compared with other influences such as gender, color, religion, etc.

C. Professional and Career Experiences
1. What factors were important in your choice of your first professional position? Why did you choose the particular position you did?
2. What are your feelings about the location of your current college or university within the academic hierarchy?
3. Do you see any relationship between the professional positions that you've occupied during your career and your origins within the working class? If so, elaborate on this relationship.
4. Do you feel that your current position (and the path to it that you took) reflects in any way your class (gender, or color) background?
5. Characterize your social and interpersonal relationship(s) with your professional peers in your current position.
6. Do you socialize mostly with your professional colleagues after hours or with others?

7. Do you see yourself as somehow "different" from your professional colleagues? If so, how do you see yourself as different?
8. What is the class background of your closest academic friends?
9. In general, do you feel that your class background has impacted your career as a professional sociologist? If so, how?
10. What is your perception of the current "balance" among the various roles of academic life (teaching, research, and public service). What changes (if any) in this balance would you make if you could make such changes?
11. Does your class background impact the perspective(s) you employ in your professional efforts to understand social reality? (i.e., choice of theories, conceptualizations, approaches to research, etc.). If yes, how does it influence these perspectives?
12. How would you describe your "politics"? Do you see them as related in any way to your class background? Have these changed over the years? If so, how have they changed?
13. What is your viewpoint on the issue of social activism among professional academics?
14. Provide your own personal (sociological) assessment of live in contemporary American society. In your view how (if at all) do factors such as class, gender, color, etc. impact life in America today?
15. Does your class background impact the way you relate to your students? If so, how does it influence these interrelationships?
16. How well do you see yourself as "fitting into" the academic role of a sociologist? Have you ever felt that you were an "outsider" in your career as a professional sociologist?
17. To what extent do the realities of everyday life in the academy correspond to your early perceptions of what they should/would be? Describe your major disappointments (if any).
18. Describe your general orientation toward authority within the academic enterprise.
19. In retrospect, are you happy that you chose a career as a sociologist? If so, why? If not, why not?

D. Social Relationship(s) with Adult Intimate Partner(s) and Family of Procreation
1. Describe the class background(s) of your intimate partner(s).
2. What role(s) (if any) has your class background played in your relationship(s) with your partner(s)?
3. Describe the age, education, and career/employment status(es) of your intimate partner(s).
4. Describe the class background of the neighborhood in which you now live.
5. Describe the class background(s) of your closest friends (both "single" and "couple").
6. Describe your current relationship(s) with parents, siblings, and friends from your childhood years. If any of them has remained in the working class, has this fact impacted your relationship with them? If so, describe these impacts.
7. Do you now, or have you ever felt "guilty" because of your relative success when compared with that of your parents and/or significant others from your childhood years?

Please feel free to add to the information we've requested above anything else that you feel is important in understanding the impact(s) of your class background on your life and career. Thanks for the time and effort you've spent constructing this essay. Finally, please provide us with an estimate of the total time you spent providing the information requested via the two instruments.

APPENDIX B: WORKING-CLASS STUDY QUESTIONNAIRE

I.D. Number:_____

1. Degrees obtained:

Degree	Year
a. Bachelor's	_____
b. Master's	_____
c. Ph.D.	_____

2. Nonacademic work history:

    a. Work during high school?

Occupation	How long?
(1) _____	_____
(2) _____	_____
(3) _____	_____
(4) _____	_____

    b. Work between high school and undergraduate studies? If you did not go to undergraduate school immediately after high school, please fill in your history (including unemployment) during that period.

Occupation, etc.	How long?
(1) _____	_____
(2) _____	_____
(3) _____	_____
(4) _____	_____

    c. Work during undergraduate school?

Occupation	How long?
(1) _____	_____
(2) _____	_____
(3) _____	_____
(4) _____	_____

    d. Work between undergraduate degree and beginning graduate school? If you did not go to graduate school immediately after getting your undergraduate degree, please fill in your history (including unemployment) during that period.

Occupation, etc.	How long?
(1) _____	_____
(2) _____	_____
(3) _____	_____
(4) _____	_____

    e. Work during graduate school (other than assistantship, work for stipend, etc.)?

Occupation	How long?
(1) _____	_____
(2) _____	_____
(3) _____	_____

f. Work after graduate school, before taking an academic position? If you did not take an academic position immediately after getting your graduate degree, please fill in your history (including unemployment) during that period.

<u>Occupation, etc.</u> <u>How long?</u>

(1) _____ _____
(2) _____ _____
(3) _____ _____
(4) _____ _____

3. Please list all positions since receiving your highest degree.

Position (title)	Tenure track?	Year started?	Year tenured?
a. _____	_____	_____	_____
b. _____	_____	_____	_____
c. _____	_____	_____	_____

4. Overall, how important do you think professional ties and networking are in obtaining academic jobs?
    1. Not important at all
    2. Only marginally important
    3. Yes, pretty important relative to other factors
    4. Probably the most important factor

5. Do you feel that professional ties or networks have played an important part in <u>your</u> obtaining academic jobs?
    1. No, not at all
    2. Only marginally important
    3. Yes, pretty important relative to other factors
    4. Probably the most important factor

6. What is your current marital status?
    1. Married
    2. Widowed
    3. Divorced
    4. Separated
    5. Never married, but sharing household with a significant other
    6. Never married (skip to question 9)

7. Current spouse's/significant other's (or most recent spouse's/significant other's) years of formal education: _____(if you've had more than one spouse/significant other, please detail this information below for each)
    Spouse/Significant other # 2 _____
    Spouse/Significant other # 3 _____

8. Spouse's/Significant other's (or former spouse's or significant other's) occupation?

    _____
    (if you've had more than one spouse, please provide the same information for each of them below)
    Spouse/Significant other # 2 _____

Spouse/Significant other # 3 _____

9. Please answer the following questions about adults living in your household while you were growing up (through age 16). If you lived in more than one household while growing up, focus on the one in which you spent the largest amount of time. Try to answer questions according to the situation at the time (e.g., if a parent has changed jobs since you left home, focus on the job (s)he had before). Note: If there were more than two adults living in your household, please xerox copies of one of these sheets and complete for each additional adult.

Household member # 1
a. Relationship to you: _____
b. Years of formal education: ____
c. Approximate number of years employed while you were living at home: ____
d. Main occupation: _____
   While working in the above occupation:
   Y or N (1) Ever self-employed?
   Y or N   If so, did they employ others?
              How many? _____
   Y or N (2) Set his/her own work schedule?
   Y or N (3) Make decisions about how to do his/her own work?
   Y or N (4) How would you categorize their level of autonomy?
              4=high autonomy (design/plan significant aspects of work, problem solving a central aspect of the work)
              3=intermediate autonomy (design/plan most of the procedures of one's work but influence limited, problem solving a regular aspect but routinized)
              2=low autonomy (design/planning very limited, problem solving an occasional aspect of the work)
              1=no autonomy (Very marginal involvement in designing procedures, most work activities highly routinized with rare problem solving)
   Y or N (5) Ever supervise other workers?
              If so, how many? _____
   Y or N (6) Make/participate in making personnel decisions?
              If so, what type of decision making?
   Y or N   (a) hire/fire a subordinate?
   Y or N   (b) issuing official warnings to a subordinate?
   Y or N   (c) granting/preventing a pay raise to a subordinate?
   Y or N (7) Make/participate in making organizational decisions?
              If so, what type of decision-making?
   Y or N   (a) to increase/decrease the total number of employees?
   Y or N   (b) policy decisions about products?
   Y or N   (c) policy decisions about pace of work/amount of work performed, etc.?
   Y or N   (d) policy decisions about work procedures/methods?
   Y or N   (e) budget decisions?

10. Household member # 2
a. Relationship to you: _____
b. Years of formal education: ____
c. Approximate number of years employed while you were living at
   home: ____
d. Main occupation: _____
   While working in the above occupation:
   Y or N (1) Ever self-employed?
   Y or N   If so, did they employ others?
              How many? _____
   Y or N (2) Set his/her own work schedule?
   Y or N (3) Make decisions about how to do his/her own work?
   Y or N (4) How would you categorize their level of autonomy?
              4=high autonomy (design/plan significant aspects of work, problem
              solving a central aspect of the work)
              3=intermediate autonomy (design/plan most of the procedures of one's
              work but influence limited, problem solving a regular aspect but
              routinized)
              2=low autonomy (design/planning very limited, problem solving an
              occasional aspect of the work)
              1=no autonomy (Very marginal involvement in designing procedures,
              most work activities highly routinized with rare problem solving)
   Y or N (5) Ever supervise other workers?
              If so, how many? _____
   Y or N (6) Make/participate in making personnel decisions?
              If so, what type of decision making?
   Y or N   (a) hire/fire a subordinate?
   Y or N   (b) issuing official warnings to a subordinate?
   Y or N   (c) granting/preventing a pay raise to a
              subordinate?
   Y or N (7) Make/participate in making organizational decisions?
              If so, what type of decision making?
   Y or N   (a) to increase/decrease the total number of employees?
   Y or N   (b) policy decisions about products?
   Y or N   (c) policy decisions about pace of work/amount of work
              performed, etc.?
   Y or N   (d) policy decisions about work procedures/methods?
   Y or N   (e) budget decisions?

11. Please complete the following information about your siblings.
    Gender   Age Relationship Education   Occupation

a. I have no siblings.
b. Brother or Sister Older or Younger _____   _____
c. Brother or Sister Older or Younger _____   _____
d. Brother or Sister Older or Younger _____   _____
e. Brother or Sister Older or Younger _____   _____

12. What position do you occupy in the birth order of the children of your biological parents?
    1. first-born
    2. second-born
    3. third-born
    4. fourth-born
    5. fifth-born or higher
    6. other (explain: _____)

13. What is your racial/ethnic origin?
    1. European American
    2. African American
    3. Hispanic American
    4. Asian American
    5. Other (please specify) _____

14. Sex
    1. Male
    2. Female

15. What is your age? _____

Thanks!

APPENDIX C: CALL FOR PARTICIPANTS

We invite inquiries from potential participants for a study of sociologists from working-class backgrounds. Volunteers will be asked to write a biographical essay focusing on details about class background, educational experiences, and subsequent career as a professional sociologist. These narratives will be used in two different ways. First, they will provide unique insights into the issues and problems that confront sociologists from working-class backgrounds in their professional lives. This information will be used to construct a framework which outlines these problems and details the various adaptive strategies used to confront them. Second, the narratives will provide inputs into a larger, empirical, comparative study of the impacts of class background on the careers of professional sociologists. If you are interested in participating in this study (or know someone who might be interested) or wish to obtain additional information prior to deciding whether or not to participate, please contact either Mike Grimes (Sociology, LSU, Baton Rouge, LA 70803 [504 388-5319]) or Joan Morris (Sociology and Anthropology, University of Central Florida, Orlando FL 32816 [407 275-2227]). Thanks in advance for considering our request.

APPENDIX D: DETAILED CODING OF QUESTIONNAIRE DATA

The detailed coding of data from the questionnaire is described in the paragraphs that follow. Question 1 (a, b, c) asked respondents to indicate the year of the award of each of their degrees (bachelor's, master's, and Ph.D). The last two digits of the year indicated were coded for each degree, with 99 reserved for missing or not applicable responses.

Question 2 (a, b, c, d, e, f) requested information on respondents' non academic work history. Here respondents were asked to list both the nature and the duration of the employment at several points in their work history. The occupations themselves were coded using a twelve-item scheme that included the following categories: (1) manager, (2) health professional, (3) other professional, (4) sales, (5) clerical, (6) service, (7) farm, (8) crafts, (9) operators, (10) laborers, (11) housewife, and (99) missing or not applicable. Duration of employment (in months) was coded into a three-digit field, with 999 reserved for missing or not applicable responses.

Question 3 (a, b, c, d) asked respondents to list all positions since the receipt of highest degree, whether they were tenure track or not, the year started, and the year tenured. These positions were coded using a nine-item scheme that included the following categories: (1) postdoctorate, (2) research assistant, (3) instructor, (4) assistant professor, (5) associate professor, (6) full professor, (7) other, (8) unemployed, and (9) for missing or not applicable responses. The tenure status of the position was coded using a single-digit field as follows: (1) if tenure track, (2) if not tenure-track; (9) if missing or not applicable.

Questions 4 and 5 asked respondents to rank professional ties and networking in terms of influence in obtaining academic jobs, both in general and for their jobs in particular. The closed-ended response categories to these questions were coded in a single-digit field as follows: (1) not important at all; (2) only marginally important; (3) yes, pretty important relative to other factors; (4) probably the most important factor; (9) missing.

Question 6 asked respondents to note their current marital status. The closed-ended responses provided (and their values) are: (1) married; (2) widowed; (3) divorced; (4) separated; (5) never married, but sharing household with a significant other; (6) never married; (9) for missing data.

Question 7 asked respondents to provide the educational attainment of spouse(s) and/or significant other(s). The actual years of formal education were coded into a two-digit field, with 99 reserved for missing or not applicable data.

Question 8 asked respondents to list their spouse's and/or significant other's occupation. These data were coded using the occupational scheme described above for question 2.

Questions 9, 10, and 11 asked respondents for information about adults living in their household when they were growing up. The first of these (9a, 10a, 11a) asked the respondent to identify the person's relationship to them. These responses were coded into a single-digit field as follows: (1) father, (2) mother, (3) older sibling, (4) grandparent, (5) other relative, (6) non-relative, (9) missing or not applicable. The second question (9b, 10b, 11b) asked the respondent to provide the years of formal education of the person. These responses were coded in a two-digit field with 99 reserved for missing data. The third question (9c, 10c, 11c) asked the respondent to provide the number of years this person was employed while the respondent was living at home. These responses were coded in a two-digit field with 99 reserved for missing data. The fourth question (9d, 10d, 11d) asked the respondent to list the main occupation of the person in question. These responses were coded according to the scheme described for question 2 above.

The next set of questions asked respondents to describe characteristics of the occupation in question (these characteristics are derived from Wright's [1985] class scheme described in Chapter 1). Included here is whether the person was ever self-employed (coded as: [1] yes, [2] no, [9] missing or not applicable); if so, the number of employees (actual number coded in a three-column field, 999 missing or not applicable). Other items dealing with attributes of the adult householder's occupation include setting one's own work schedule (coded as: [1] yes, [2] no, [9] missing or not applicable); making decisions about work (coded as: [1] yes; [2] no; [9] missing or not applicable); the level of autonomy (coded as: [4] high, [3] intermediate, [4] low, [5] no autonomy, [9] missing or not applicable); whether the adult householder supervised others (coded as [1] yes, [2] no, [9] missing or not applicable) and, if so, how many (coded in a two-column field with [99] reserved for missing or not applicable data). Other job attributes include making personnel decisions (coded as: [1] yes, [2] no, [9] missing or not applicable). If the answer to this question was "yes," then the respondent was asked more detailed questions such as the adult household member's role in: hiring/firing of subordinates, issuing warnings to subordinates, and granting/preventing pay raises to subordinates (coded as: [1] yes, [2] no, [9] missing or not applicable).

Finally, respondents were asked whether or not the adult householder makes/participates in organizational decisions (coded: [1] yes; [2] no; [9] missing or not applicable). If the answer to this question was "yes", then respondents were asked to respond to more detailed questions about that participation including participation in decisions about the number of employees, decisions about products, decisions about the pace and amount of work, decisions about work procedures/method, and decisions about budgets (coded as: [1] yes, [2] no, [9] missing or not applicable).

Question 12 asks a number of questions about respondent's siblings, including whether or not the respondent has siblings (coded as: [1] yes, [2] no, [9] missing or not applicable). If the answer to this question was yes, respondents were asked to characterize the sibling's gender (coded as: [1] brother, [2] sister [9] missing or inapplicable) and whether (s)he is older or younger (coded as: [1] older, [2] younger, [9] missing or not applicable). The respondent was also asked the level of education of the sibling (actual years coded with [99] for missing or not applicable data), and their occupation (coded the same as question 2 above).

Question 13 asked respondents to identify their position in the birth order of their biological parents' children (actual position coded through 5 or more, with an "other" category [6] and [9] reserved for missing or not applicable).

Question 14 asked the respondent's racial/ethnic origin (coded as: [1] European American, [2] African American, [3] Hispanic American, [4] Asian American, [5] other, [9] missing.

Question 15 asked the respondent's sex (coded as: [1] male, [2] female, [9] missing). Finally, question 16 asks the respondent's age (actual age coded; [99] for missing).

References

American Sociological Association. "August Biennial Report on the Participation of Women and Minorities in ASA for 1990 and 1991. [mimeograph] Washington, DC: American Sociological Association, 1992.

———. *1990 Biographical Directory of Members*. Washington, DC: American Sociological Association, 1990.

———. *Directory of Members, 1995*. Washington, DC: American Sociological Association, 1995.

Analytica, Oxford. *America in Perspective*. New York: Houghton Mifflin, 1986.

Aronowitz, Stanley, and William DiFazio. *The Jobless Future: Science-Technology and the Dogma of Work*. Minneapolis: University of Minnesota Press, 1994.

Aronowitz, Stanley, and Henry Giroux. *Postmodern Education: Politics, Culture and Social Criticism*. Minneapolis: University of Minnesota Press, 1991.

Babbie, Earl. *The Practice of Social Research*, 7th ed. Belmont, CA: Wadsworth Publishing Company, 1995.

Barker, Judith. "Outsiders on the Inside: White Working-Class Women in Academia," pp. 275-287 in J. Gonzalez-Calvo (ed.), *Gender: Multicultural Perspectives*. Dubuque, Iowa: Kendall/Hall, 1993.

———. "White Working-Class Men and Women in Academia," *Race, Gender & Class* 3 (Fall, 1995): 65-77.

Bartlett, Donald, and James Steele. *America: What Went Wrong?* Kansas City, MO: Andrews and McMeel, 1992.

Becker, Gary. *Human Capital*. New York: National Bureau of Economics Research, 1964.

Bell, Daniel. *The End of Ideology*. New York: The Free Press, 1960.

Belle, Deborah. "Gender Differences in the Social Moderators of Stress," pp. 257-277 in Rosalind Barnett et al. (eds.), *Gender and Stress*. New York: The Free Press, 1987.

Blood, Robert, and Donald Wolfe. *Husbands and Wives*. New York: The Free Press, 1960.

Bluestone, Barry, and Bennett Harrison. *The Deindustrialization of America*. New York: Basic Books, 1992.

———. "The Great American Job Machine: The Proliferation of Low Wage Employment in the U.S. Economy," A study prepared for the Joint Economic Committee of Congress, 1986.

Bourdieu, Pierre. *Distinction: A Social Critique of the Judgement of Taste*. Cambridge, MA: Harvard University Press, 1984.

———. "Forms of Capital," pp. 241–256 in John Richardson (ed.), *Handbook of Theory and Research for the Sociology of Education*. Westport, CT: Greenwood Press, 1986.

Bowles, Samuel. "Unequal Education and the Reproduction of the Hierarchical Division of Labor," pp. 218–229 in Richard Edwards, Michael Reich, and Thomas Weisskopf, (eds.), *The American Capitalist System*. Englewood Cliffs, NJ: Prentice-Hall, 1972.

Bowles, Samuel, and Richard Edwards. *Understanding Capitalism*, 2nd ed. New York: HarperCollins, 1993.

Bowles, Samuel, and Herbert Gintis. *Schooling in Capitalist America*. New York: Basic Books, 1976.

Brandt, Dick. "Autobiographical Essay," pp. 71–74 in Jake Ryan and Charles Sackrey (eds.), *Strangers in Paradise*. Boston: South End Press, 1984.

Brown, Robert. "Autobiographical Essay," pp. 133–141 in Jake Ryan and Charles Sackrey (eds.), *Strangers in Paradise*. Boston: South End Press, 1984.

Callello, Mary. "Useful Knowledge," pp. 127-136 in C. L. B. Dews and C. Law (eds.), *This Fine Place So Far from Home*. Philadelphia: Temple University Press, 1995.

Charlip, Julie. "A Real Class Act: Searching for Identity in the 'Classless' Society," pp. 26–40 in C.L.B. Dews and C. Law (eds.), *This Fine Place So Far from Home*. Philadelphia: Temple University Press, 1995.

Clark, Terry, and Seymour Lipset. "Are Social Classes Dying?" *International Sociology* 6 (December, 1991): 397–409.

Clark, Terry, Seymour Lipset, and Michael Rempel. "The Declining Political Significance of Social Class," *International Sociology* 8 (September, 1993): 293–316.

Coleman, James. "Social Capital in the Creation of Human Capital," *American Journal of Sociology*. 94S (1988): 95–120.

Collins, Randal, and Scott Coltrane. *Sociology of Marriage and the Family*, 4th ed. Chicago, IL: Nelson-Hall Publishers, 1995.

Converse, Jean, and Stanley Presser. *Survey Questions*. Newbury Park, CA: Sage Publications, 1986.

Danziger, Sheldon, and Peter Gottschalk. *America Unequal*. Cambridge, MA: Harvard University Press, 1995.

———. *Uneven Tides: Rising Inequality in America*. New York: Russell Sage Foundation, 1993.

Davis, Kingsley and Wilbert Moore. "Some Principles of Stratification," *American Sociological Review* 10 (1945): 242–249.

Denzin, Norman. *The Research Act*, 3rd. ed. Englewood Cliffs, NJ: Prentice-Hall, 1989.

Dews, C. L. B., and Carolyn Law. *This Fine Place So Far from Home*. Philadelphia: Temple University Press, 1995.

Dillman, Don A. "Mail and Self-Administered Questionnaires," pp. 359–377 in P. Rossi, J. Wright, and A. Anderson (eds.), *Handbook of Survey Research*. New York: Academic Press, 1983.

Drucker, Peter F. *Post-Capitalist Society*. New York: HarperBusiness, 1993.

Edgell, Stephen. *Class*. New York: Routledge, 1993.

Edwards, Richard. *Contested Terrain*. New York: Basic Books, 1979.

Ehrenreich, Barbara. *Fear of Falling: The Inner Life of the Middle Class*. New York: HarperCollins, 1990.

Eitzen, D. Stanley, and Maxine B. Zinn. *The Reshaping of America*. Englewood Cliffs, NJ: Prentice-Hall, 1989.

Frost, Norman. "Autobiographical Essay," pp. 251–257 in Jake Ryan and Charles Sackrey (eds.), *Strangers in Paradise: Academics from the Working Class*. Boston: South End Press, 1984.

Galbraith, John. *The Affluent Society*. New York: The New American Library, 1958.

Gardner, Sandra. "What's a Nice Working-Class Girl Like You Doing in a Place Like This?" pp. 49–59 in M. Tokarczyk and E. Fay (eds), *Working-Class Women in the Academy*. Amherst: University of Massachusetts Press, 1993.

Gecas, Victor. "The Influence of Social Class on Socialization," pp. 365–404 in W. Burr et al. (eds.), *Contemporary Theories about the Family*. New York: The Free Press, 1979.

Gilbert, Dennis, and Joseph Kahl. *The American Class Structure: A New Synthesis*. Belmont, CA: Wadsworth Publishing Company, 1993.

Gillespie, Dair. "Who Has the Power? The Marriage Struggle," *Journal of Marriage and the Family* 33 (1971): 445–458.

Gordon, David. *Theories of Poverty and Underemployment*. Lexington, MA: D. C. Heath and Company, 1972.

Gouldner, Alvin. *The Future of Intellectuals and the Rise of the New Class*. New York: Seabury Press, 1979.

Granovetter, Mark. "Economic Action and Social Structure: The Problem of Embeddedness," *American Journal of Sociology* 91 (1985): 481–510.

Grimes, Michael. "Class and Attitudes toward Structural Inequalities: An Empirical Comparison of Key Variables in Neo- and Post-Marxist Scholarship." *The Sociological Quarterly* 30 (1989): 441–463.

———. *Class in Twentieth-Century American Sociology*. Westport, CT: Praeger Publishers, 1991.

Gwartney, James. *Economics: Private and Public Choices*. New York: Academic Press, 1976.

Halle, David. *America's Working Men*. Chicago: University of Chicago Press, 1984.

Harrison, Bennett, and Barry Bluestone. *The Great U-Turn: Corporate Restructuring and the Polarizing of America*. New York: Basic Books, 1988.

Haveman, Robert, and Barbara Wolfe. *Succeeding Generations: On the Effects of Investments in Children*. New York: Russell Sage Foundation, 1995.

Heilbroner, Robert, and Aaron Singer. *The Economic Transformation of America: 1600 to the Present*, 3rd ed., Fort Worth, TX: Harcourt Brace College Publishers, 1994.

Higginbotham, Elizabeth, and Lynn Cannon. "Rethinking Mobility: Towards a Race and Gender Inclusive Theory," [Research Paper 8]. Memphis, TN: Center for Research on Women, 1988.

Hofstadter, Richard. *Anti-Intellectualism in Americal Life*. New York: Alfred Knopf, 1963.

Hollingshead, August. *Elmtown's Youth*. New York: John Wiley, 1949.

Holmwood, John, and Andrew Stewart. "The Role of Contradictions in Modern Theories of Social Stratification," *Sociology* 17 (1983): 234–254.

hooks, bell. "Keeping Close to Home: Class and Education," pp. 99–111 in M. Tokarczyk and E. Fay (eds.), *Working-Class Women in the Academy*. Amherst: University of Massachusetts Press, 1993.

Hout, Mike, Clem Brooks, and Jeff Manza. "The Persistence of Classes in Post-Industrial Societies." *International Sociology* 8 (September, 1993): 259–277.

Karoly, Lynn A. "The Trend in Inequality Among Families, Individuals, and Workers in the United States," pp. 19–97 in S. Danziger and P. Gottschalk (eds.), *Uneven Tides: Rising Inequality in America*. New York: Russell Sage Foundation, 1993.

Kennedy, Paul. *The Rise and the Fall of the Great Powers*. New York: Vintage Books, 1987.

Kirk, Jerome, and Marc Miller. *Reliability and Validity in Qualitative Research*. Newbury Park, CA: Sage Publications, 1986.

Kohn, Melvin. *Class and Conformity*. Homewood, IL: Dorsey Press, 1969.

Kohn, Melvin, and C. Schooler. *Work and Personality*. Norwood, NJ: Ablex Publishing Corp, 1983.

Komarovsky, Mirra. *Blue-Collar Marriage*. New York: Vintage Books, 1962.

Kozol, Jonathan. *Savage Inequalities: Children in America's Schools*. New York: Crown Publishers, 1991.

Langston, Donna. "Who Am I Now? The Politics of Class Identity," pp. 60–72 in M. Tokarczyk and E. Fay (eds.), *Working-Class Women in the Academy*. Amherst: University of Massachusetts Press, 1993.

Lareau, Annette. *Home Advantage: Social Class and Parental Intervention in Elementary Education*. London: Falmer Press, 1989.

———. "Social Class Differences in Family-School Relationships: The Importance of Cultural Capital," *Sociology of Education* 60 (1987): 73–85.

Law, Carolyn. "Introduction" pp. 1–7. in C. L. B. Dews and Carolyn Law (eds)., *This Fine Place So Far from Home*. Philadelphia: Temple University Press, 1995.

Levy, Frank, and Robert Michel. *The Economic Future of American Families*. Washington, DC: The Urban Institute Press, 1991.

Lindblom, Charles E., and David K. Cohen. *Usable Knowledge: Social Science and Problem Solving* New Haven, CT: Yale University Press, 1979.

Morgan, David L. *Focus Groups as Qualitative Research*. Newbury Park, CA: Sage Publications, 1988.

National Research Council. *Research-Doctoral Programs in the United States: Continuities and Change* (edited by Marvin Goldberger, Brendan Maher, and Pamela Flattau). Washington, DC: National Academy Press, 1995.

Nisbet, Robert. "The Decline and Fall of Social Class," *Pacific Sociological Review* 1 (1959): 11–17.

O'Malley, Hugh. "Autobiographical Essay," pp. 275–282 in J. Ryan and C. Sackrey (eds.), *Strangers in Paradise*. Boston: South End Press, 1984.

Orlans, Kathryn and Ruth Wallace. *Gender and the Academic Experience*. Lincoln: University of Nebraska Press, 1994.

Overall, Christine. "Nowhere at Home: Toward a Phenomenology of Working-Class Consciousness," pp. 209–220 in C. L. B. Dews and C. Law (eds.), *This Fine Place So Far from Home*. Philadelphia: Temple University Press, 1995.

Pakulski, Jan, and Malcolm Waters. *The Death of Class*. Thousand Oaks CA: Sage Publications, 1996.

Parcel, Toby, and Elizabeth Menaghan. *Parents' Jobs and Childrens' Lives*. New York: Aldine de Gruyter, 1994.

Parsons, Talcott. "An Analytical Approach to the Theory of Social Stratification," *American Journal of Sociology* 45 (1940): 841–862.

———. "A Revised Analytical Approach to the Theory of Social Stratification," pp. 386–439 in Reinhard Bendix and Seymour Lipset (eds.), *Class, Status, and Power: Social Stratification in Comparative Perspective*, 2nd ed. New York: The Free Press, 1953.

Pease, John, William Form, and Joan Rytina. "Ideological Currents in American Stratification Literature," *The American Sociologist* 5 (May, 1970): 127–137.

Pelitz, William. "Is There a Working-Class History?" pp. 277–85 in C. L. B. Dews and C. Law (eds.), *This Fine Place So Far from Home*. Philadelphia: Temple University Press, 1995.

Podhoretz, Norman. *Making It*. New York: Random House, 1967.

Poulantzas, Nicos. *Political Power and Social Classes*. London: New Left Books, 1973.

Puck, George. "Autobiographical Essay," pp. 189–194 in J. Ryan and C. Sackrey (eds.), *Strangers in Paradise*. Boston: South End Press, 1984.

Robinson, Robert. "Reproducing Class Relations in Industrial Capitalism," *American Sociological Review* 49 (1984): 182–196.

Rubin, Lillian. *Families on the Fault Line*. New York: HarperCollins, 1994.

———. *Worlds of Pain*. New York: Basic Books, 1976.

Ryan, Jake and Charles Sackrey (eds.). *Strangers in Paradise: Academics from the Working Class*. Boston: South End Press, 1984.

Sabatelli, Ronald, and Constance Shehan. "Exchange and Resource Theories," pp. 385–411 in Pauline Boss, William Doherty, Ralph LaRossa, Walter Shumm, and Suzanne Steinmetz (eds.), *Sourcebook of Family Theories and Methods: A Conceptual Approach*. New York: Plenum Press, 1993.

Sennett, Richard, and Jonathan Cobb. *The Hidden Injuries of Class*. New York: Vintage Books, 1972.

Shostak, Arthur. *Blue-Collar Life*. New York: Random House, 1969.

Sidel, Ruth. *Urban Survival: The World of Working-Class Women*. Lincoln: University of Nebraska Press, 1978.

Spenner, Kenneth. "Social Stratification, Work, and Personality," *Annual Review of Sociology* 14 (1988): 69–97.

Strauss, Anselm. *Qualitative Analysis for Social Scientists*. New York: Cambridge University Press, 1987.

Swidler, Ann. "Culture in Action: Symbols and Strategies," *American Sociological Review* 51 (1986): 273–286.

Thurow, Lester. *The Future of Capitalism*. New York: W. Morrow, 1996.

———. *Investment in Human Capital*. Belmont, CA: Wadsworth Publishing Company, 1970.

Tokarczyk, Michelle. "By the Rivers of Babylon," pp. 311–322 in M. Tokarczyk and E. Fay (eds.), *Working-Class Women in the Academy*. Amherst: University of Massachusetts Press, 1993.

Tokarczyk, Michelle, and Elizabeth Fay (eds.). *Working-Class Women in the Academy*. Amherst: University of Massachusetts Press, 1993.

Trow, Martin. "The Second Transformation of American Secondary Education," pp. 108–118 in Jerome Karabel and A. Halsey (eds.), *Power and Ideology in Education*. New York: Oxford University Press, 1977.

U.S. Bureau of the Census. *Trends in Relative Income: 1964–1989* [Current Population Series P-60, Number 177]. Washington DC: U.S. Department of Commerce, 1990.

Willis, Paul. *Learning to Labour*. London: Saxon House, 1977.

Wright, Erik. "Class Boundaries in Advanced Capitalist Societies." *New Left Review* (July–August, 1976): 3–41.

———. *Classes*. London: Verso Press, 1985.

———. *Class Counts*. New York: Cambridge University Press, 1997.

———. *Interrogating Inequality*. London: Verso Press, 1994.

Zandy, Janet. *Liberating Memory: Our Work and Our Working-Class Consciousness*. New Brunswick, NJ: Rutgers University Press, 1995.

Index

About the Authors

MICHAEL D. GRIMES is Professor of Sociology at Louisiana State University. He is author of *Class in Twentieth-Century American Sociology* (Praeger, 1991). He has also published articles on class, race, and gender.

JOAN M. MORRIS is Assistant Professor of Sociology at the University of Central Florida. She obtained her Ph.D. from Louisiana State University and has taught at Kent State University.

ISBN 0-275-95711-X

90000>

EAN

9 780275 957117

HARDCOVER BAR CODE